Struggling for Life

My Story

Clarita Sierra   Alex Sierra

Author's Note: This is a real-life story. In order to protect the privacy and anonymity of some institutions, people and places and some names have been changed in this book.

Copyright © 2017 Clara Sierra
Cover Design: Mauricio Sierra
Editing Coordination for the Spanish Version: Ana Paula Rivas
Editor (English version): Jodie Greenberg
All rights reserved.

No part of this book may be reproduced in any manner without the written consent of the publisher except for brief excerpts in critical reviews or articles.

ISBN: 978-1-61244-521-2
Library of Congress Control Number: 2016901243

Printed in the United States of America

Halo Publishing International
www.halopublishing.com

Published by Halo Publishing International
1100 NW Loop 410
Suite 700 - 176
San Antonio, Texas 78213
Toll Free 1-877-705-9647
Website: www.halopublishing.com
E-mail: contact@halopublishing.com

*To my son, Eduardo—thank you for your wisdom,
your kindness, your sensitivity, and your strength.*

***To my son, Alejandro—thank you for teaching me the
meaning of unconditional love, for your great heart, your smile,
for your joy of life, and your great capacity for love.***

*To my son, Mauricio—thank you for your tenderness,
your creativity, your compassion, and your honesty.*

*Thanks to you all for coming into my life and illuminating it
with your light, your love, and the grace of your being.*

*To Gerardo—my love, my friend, and travel companion—
thank you for your infinite patience, for always motivating me
to be a better person, for being my guide and my strength,
and for your eternal generosity.*

*To all parents who have lost a child
to this horrible disease.*

Table of Contents

Foreword   7

Prologue   11

INTRODUCTION
I Am Not My Addiction   15

CHAPTER I
Everything a Mother Should Know: My Version of the Facts   19

CHAPTER II
Putting Together the Complicated Puzzle of My Life   25

CHAPTER III
Drugs: My Best Friend   46

CHAPTER IV
Crack: A Different Kind of Drug   61

CHAPTER V
The Magical World of Rehab Centers   85

CHAPTER VI
Back to Mexico   115

CHAPTER VII
The Darker Places   139

CHAPTER VIII
The Happiest Moment of My Life: Marimar   175

CHAPTER IX
Struggling for Life   207

CHAPTER X
The Strength of a Family   242

CHAPTER XI
A Small Journey into the World of Addiction   249

APPENDIX A
Farewell Letters to Alex   271

APPENDIX B
Letters Between Alex, His Parents, and Marimar's Parents   288

APPENDIX C
Talk Given by Alejandro Sierra
June 2011 for the Foundation "Convivencia sin Violencia"   298

APPENDIX D
"Those Things Are So Far Removed from My Family"   303

REFERENCES   307

Acknowledgments   313

About the Authors   315

Foreword

How do I run away from myself?

Clarita and Gerardo are today two great friends of mine, though our friendship was not formed so long ago. There are people with whom you need only spend a couple of hours before becoming enveloped in gratifying warmth, usually those who walk with us on our journey during most of our existence.

The terrible suffering that they have endured from the loss of their beloved child, Alejandro, is no doubt the worst sorrow a human being can face. However, this same suffering made them exceptionally understanding individuals when it comes to the pain of others. In fact, they grew from their experience. They emerged as two huge, leafy trees, possessing a gratifying shade under which we can seek safety, protection, direction, companionship, or a kind, simple word that brings peace and relief.

Clarita's voice is equivalent to a soft caress on the cheek; her concerned gaze betrays her intense search for the necessary, comforting words. It is as if she was born to help, as if helping is the only action she knows: *I help!* I do not think that any other person approaches this concept with such passion and commitment.

And Gerardo? Gerardo is always there. Even if you look for him in the dark, invariably he will be there, of course next to Clarita and his loved ones, but also at the center of his friends' hearts. No matter how far away you are or how complex your problems might be, Gerardo will be there for you through thick and thin, standing up like a powerful lighthouse, a beacon guiding sailors home from dark and stormy seas.

It is rare that you get to see such an alliance of strength in a couple, a strength that was put to the test in an unexpected and damaging way in their lives when the powerful steel hands of addiction, incapable of feeling even the tiniest bit of pity, strongly grabbed Alejandro by the throat, determined to deprive him of his life.

When they discovered the evil, deadly disease—the fatal addiction—they poured the best of themselves and their family into relentless efforts to help, sparing no expense and stopping at nothing to arm themselves with the most modern tools to remove those cursed fingers from defenseless Alejandro's throat. They knocked on all the doors. They used the best of the best. They hired local and international specialists and medical doctors, and they researched the most famous clinics dedicated to combating addictions. They personally studied in order to master the subject. The economic and emotional efforts and dedication of the Sierra-Roffe family never detracted from their exemplary and contagious vigor, nor did it detract from their spirit in order to rescue their son from the clutches of the deaf, mute, blind, and unmovable giant that asphyxiated him day after day.

A merciless cascade of feelings daily bombarded the family from all angles. Sometimes anger would sit at the table, catalyzing an exchange of accusations and complaints. At other times, forgiveness, benevolence, and kindness descended upon the Sierras. Who was to blame? Why? Who was responsible for these events? How much injustice!

Sadness, accompanied by a deep depression, the result of powerlessness, dominated the endless conversation in relation to one subject and one subject only: Alex. Out of hope for a new scientific discovery and the emergence of a leading addictions specialist, they would grow disappointed at continual, thwarted attempts at recovery. Helplessness, fear, desperation, rage, insomnia, lack of attention to daily life, and the lack of desire for everyday, satisfactory things essential to justifying existence were thronging in the family's anguished minds.

In the same way that Alejandro lost control of his days, which seemed to precipitate a frightening escapade of decline, the Sierras—his family—were obliged to keep calm and collected in their frantic search to rescue their loved one, someone who was pawning personal objects, stealing family belongings, and borrowing money from loan sharks to get what he needed in order to get high before he'd go crazy. Of course, Alejandro and other addicts do not care about acting like strangers and losing their minds in front of their loved ones. They will use whatever they can as long as they are able to get some of the damned powder.

There was no remedy. When the drugs destroyed the center of his brain where an individual's willpower is located, Alejandro became like a leaf from a tree, subject to the whims of the wind. The Sierras lost Alejandro. The powerful hands that had held Alejandro's throat for so many years suddenly disappeared when he died. His last breath was barely perceptible. Finally, he had conquered the peace for which he had always fought. We all lost Alejandro. Not only the Sierras and their relatives and friends, but Mexico also lost a valuable young man.

Was his ephemeral pass through life in vain? No! Alejandro fought like a giant to get loose from those sinister hands. His struggle is recounted here, in the pages written by his mother. His never-ending courage to run away from himself and get back his health and joy for living constitutes a clear example of personal effort before the irrevocable repentance, an extemporaneous remorse, a palpable demonstration for today's youth of what can happen when one falls into the temptation of trying narcotics by submitting themselves to the diabolical voice of a "best friend" who affirms that "nothing will ever happen," the invitation of one who perversely wishes to share the guilt of having succumbed to the arms of death by inhaling cocaine for the first time.

For that reason alone, Clarita Sierra's book should be mandatory reading material in all of our country's schools in order to shed light on the fact that the sick person who becomes a narcotics addict not only turns his existence into a tragedy but also drags along his family, parents, siblings, girlfriends or boyfriends, and loved ones into a hell from which he himself cannot escape. How difficult it is to witness the slow death of a loved one who has destroyed his nervous system with drugs, the system on which his willpower depends, without which any effort aimed at regaining health is useless. The emotional wreckage of the family under such conditions implies a pharaonic effort whose resulting wounds do not heal easily. On the contrary, picking the scabs repeatedly seems to be an indolent and destructive routine that is almost impossible to eradicate.

I am not the one who should be trying to explain why Alejandro and perhaps millions of people fall prey and die, victims of cocaine use or injections of highly toxic and deadly substances. I am not an expert on the subject, nor do I pretend to be, but it is my duty to denounce here an authority incapable of stopping the physical poisoning of the best part of Mexico: our children! Politicians and government officials should read Clarita's *Struggling for Life* in order to see the horrors that a family goes through when they are rendered helpless as one of their members falls prey to drugs that are distributed in the streets or bars or restaurants with absolute impunity. Is there an absolute guilt?

In Alejandro's case, authorities failed in the same way that his family, school, religion, rehab clinics, specialists, love of any kind, teachers, and true friends failed, except for the disgusting criminals willing to kill and murder as long as they can make money, no matter where it comes from. What do we do as a society? Little or nothing, except of course Clarita, who has written these painful passages of her life, her hand guided by her heart and with the true desire to help—her favorite word—so that other families do not succumb to the same hell, buried by helplessness. Clarita gives voice to the warning. Clarita shouts, Clarita explains, Clarita cries out to the heavens, a heaven that is deaf, but she will not stop denouncing in the slightest so that her case is heard and read, and if possible, that this never happens again, at least in Mexican homes.

Students in any Mexican school should read *Struggling for Life*, as should our teachers, PTA members, education authorities, lawmakers, government officials concerned with safety, judges, magistrates, ministers—in short, all citizens who are aware of the dangers facing our youth.

In this Mexico, a Mexico that right now is being threatened, prostituted, and cheated on, we should all call ourselves "Clarita" if we really wish to change it. Clarita fought with all her might because Alejandro was a fanatic addicted to life. She is not to blame; it is the rest of us who are at fault. With our pathetic laziness, we ran away from ourselves instead of joining forces in a dignified, civic front to combat the poisoners of our nation.

Francisco Martín Moreno
Award-winning author and Novelist
February 2016

Prologue

"We all love this guy. He just needs a little help."

These words introduced me to Alejandro Sierra, spoken by a friend who met him in treatment. While the friend had done well after treatment, he was worried about Alex and recommended him to our new sober living home in Utah. Alex was our first resident.

When I met Alex at the airport, I would not have guessed at his relapse after treatment. It must have been brief, because Alex was, to all appearances, a perfectly healthy young man. He was handsome—dashing, even—unfailingly polite, and instantly likeable. Right away, I could tell he was an extraordinary person.

Within a few weeks, our house housed six men, and Alex recreated the same camaraderie he shared in treatment. If we were a family, Alex was our favorite son. He was genuinely supportive of his fellow housemates, well liked by the staff, and did everything we asked of him to strengthen his sobriety. Alex liked to have a good time, and wherever we went, if Alex was there, we always did. I can still remember the night we went bowling. I can still see the smile he flashed after throwing a strike.

We all loved Alex, and he had all the ingredients to build a sober life: the best treatment, a great attitude, and a loving, supportive, committed family. His whole life stretched out in front of him, and it held endless promise. It wasn't long before he had a month sober, then two, and then three.

But Alex possessed the dangerously deep sensitivity that I see so often in people struggling with addiction. He also had what turned out to be the most severe cocaine addiction I have ever seen. And cruelly, cocaine is a drug that cycles between periods of calm and stability, and terrible craving and chaos.

Alex did well in Utah. He moved to San Diego to be with his girlfriend—not my first choice for a person in early sobriety, but I could hardly argue that he wasn't strong again and doing everything right. Everything looked good as he headed south.

But, in time, the relationship collapsed. Alex was crushed. And the dark cycle of his addiction began again.

Over this first year that I knew Alex, I became close with his mother. I have a special place in my heart for mothers of sons with addiction. I can still remember what I put my own mother through as I battled my addiction to cocaine. And so, to make amends, I give all the time I can to mothers struggling to help their sons. But my relationship with Alex's mother, Clarita, was stronger than usual. We talked for hours about Alex. We agreed completely on his many wonderful qualities and strengths, traded hopeful plans for his future, and both recognized this one fragile part of his personality regarding relationships.

Alex would descend into furious drug use. But then, just as quickly, it looked like he might pull out of it. He would gain another foothold in sobriety. A plan was devised. Alex would agree to it. It looked like things were back on track. Then he crashed back down.

His parents went to help Alex in San Diego. They called me, and I flew down immediately. The hope was that he would return to Utah, where he had never used drugs, and try to replicate the period of stability he had previously achieved.

When I got there, I was shocked at how horrible he looked. Although he still had the same charismatic smile, he also displayed the unreasonable, unrelenting demand to use drugs that cocaine commands. No pleas, no promises, no tears, no bargains would cut through it. It took all night to get him into the car, and once he did, I drove as fast as I could straight for Salt Lake City. We talked all night on that drive, laughing at times. Alex was his old self again. He remembered fond times in Utah, and the future looked bright.

Before noon the next day, I dropped him off at detox where he would spend seventy-two hours, a mere formality before he came back to our sober house. We hugged and were both hopeful for the future. I didn't even get home before I got a call from the detox nurse: Alex had left the hospital and was on the run.

After a couple days of trading worried phone calls with Clarita and Gerardo, I managed to find Alex. I returned him to the hospital. I told him to stay put. He promised. We hugged. I drove home, and pulling into my driveway, the nurse called again: Alex left the hospital. This is cocaine.

Finally, Gerardo came to Salt Lake City and took Alex home to Mexico to be with his parents. He would do well for a while and then relapse. Clarita and Gerardo tried everything. They did everything he asked of them, and they did everything right. If there was a treatment center that was right for him, Alex went there. If there was a therapy to be tried, Alex got it. If there was anything, they provided Alex with it, both the unnecessarily comfortable and severely strict. Whatever the addiction treatment world could come up with, Alex got it. And when I think of the huge amounts of money that was drained from this desperate family, I feel ashamed that this is the business in which I work.

We say all the time, "Most people who stick with recovery eventually get it." The studies show it. The numbers tell me that it's true. But that is not the way mental illness works. Addiction is under no obligation to play by the rules.

Everything Alex got, everything that was done, everything *he* did, it should have worked.

Sadly, it didn't.

Our last conversation, Alex called me from Mexico City. He had done well for a long time and was getting married. I wished him the very best because I knew he would give the woman he loved and married his very best. But just prior to the marriage, Alex had a relapse.

He wanted to know, his voice choking: Was it true? Was it true that addicts can never get better?

I know in my heart that it is not true, that people do get better. I reminded Alex of how well he had done in the past, how good he felt when he was sober. I told him I believed in him. I did.

But Alex felt the judgment of the world closing in. Maybe he thought that judgment was worse than it really was, but addicts are full of shame. Only a few can move past it for good. And I think when that shame and judgment threatened the loss of a relationship to which he had given his whole heart, it was too much for him. That says something about addiction more than it does Alex, but I never spoke to him again.

When I got the call from Clarita that Alex had died in a state of cocaine-induced paranoia, my mind went back to my own addiction. I remembered what that terror was like. I am so sad my patient, my friend, Alex, was alone when he died. There were so many people who loved Alex and tried to give him the help he needed. He suffered. And he deserved better.

There are addiction cycles in individuals and in whole countries. It seems that, in the United States at least, we are entering a dark period of addiction again after a period of relative calm and stability. I think of Alex often, and as I speak with parents who have lost a child to addiction, as I fumble in trying to find the words that will give some meaning to their grief, I point them to other parents who have endured and survived. I think when parents such as Clarita and Gerardo are brave enough to tell their stories it guides other families through this darkness. I know that their words in this book will help other parents, and I hope that will give them solace.

There is light in that kind of bravery, and it burns just as Alex's life did—brighter, if shorter—than anything else around it.

Kevin McCauley, M.D.

March 2016

INTRODUCTION

I Am Not My Addiction

Once again, I am sitting on an airplane on my way to rescue Alejandro. They called us to tell us that he relapsed again and is in very bad shape. It is so hard to understand what is happening to him.
Every time we leave him someplace, he seems to be doing well, so filled with dreams, cheerful, and with a great smile he tells us, "This time it is different. It will be the last one. I will not use ever again."
And just a few hours or a few days later, he is using again. Every time I see him I want to hug him. I want to protect him like when he was a child and he belonged only in my arms. Sadly, sometimes I do not recognize him anymore.

Clarita Sierra

This book is a tribute to the life of my son, Alejandro, a tribute to life itself, and an account of the experience of a young man in the world of addictions. In the comings and goings he faced in this dark world, and at a time of an intense and painful recovery, he decided to write the story of his fight against addiction and left, though unfinished, an intimate, powerful, and profound statement about this stigmatized, complex, and destructive disease.

In the end, I think that Alejandro also left us within these pages a history of the valuable and constant struggle within himself, a struggle for self-knowledge during which he always persevered in seeking his true spirit and learning his weaknesses and strengths. He embarked on a long journey, trying to define himself beyond his addiction. Therefore, this is a book that is also about finding ourselves. As I write these words, Alex seems to whisper in my ear, "I refuse. I refuse categorically to be defined by my addiction."

Alex enjoyed life intensely and to the fullest, with all the meaning that life has in and of itself. He was a cheerful and generous guy with a wide smile and deep eyes and a light that radiated out to all who knew him.

For what seems like ages, I remained dedicated in body and soul to trying to understand addiction. Even today, many doubts assail me. At the time, I would read everything on the subject, and nothing would make me feel right. The more I read, the more helpless I felt. I desperately read everything that I found, listened to anybody who offered me a solution to the problem, and spent hours on the computer looking for clinics that would have the best and newest programs to combat this horrible disease.

In my case, I believe that—having been informed about what effects the drugs were having on Alex's brain and how the brain was making these changes in terms of his perception and decision-making processes—the only important thing for him at the moment was to get drugs. This made me feel so powerless, and I had a million feelings. On one hand, I felt a great compassion for him, and on the other, a brutal anger. Unfortunately, this caused me to get involved in his madness, even though I knew that the worst thing I could do at that time was to become part of his crisis.

Little by little, we understood that addiction is a process of many falls and false starts. Pain is inevitable and so are mistakes, but so are growth and wisdom and serenity if families approach addiction with an open mind, a willingness to learn, and the acceptance that recovery, like addiction itself, is a long and complex process.[1]

Unfortunately, it took us a long time to learn that the only thing we could do to help in the recovery process—both ours and Alex's—was to utilize all of our resources to face this illness and be able to support him so he did not destroy himself even more. Alex had a very hard time maintaining his sobriety. He was clean for long periods during which we had with us this wonderful and beautiful soul! Sure…until the next devastating relapse. This, no doubt, caused great sadness for all of our family members, but in the process we became stronger. We learned to not create expectations, and we definitely never lost hope.

In our desire to find answers, we read a lot of literature. Among my readings was the book *Addict in the Family* by Beverly Conyers. Her words made sense to me. She was a mother just like me, trapped in the unknown world of addiction: "Recovery is a long journey of personal growth, a journey that cannot be forced and that takes time. The person has to be ready to make changes in his life."[2]

As Dr. Kevin McCauley advised us, we—as the addict's parents or partners—can only accompany them during this process, making our own changes, listening with love, and respecting their decisions, even when we believe that they are not the right ones. This helps promote growth and self-esteem, gives them a sense of empowerment, and fosters responsibility.

This is our story, with all the mistakes and successes we have had. Maybe for us as a couple and as a family, discovering Alex's drug use came too late, and that is precisely why we want to share our experience. In this testimonial that narrates Alex's stormy voyage in this world, we try to recount his life.

I hope this book achieves its goal of clarifying the stigma that exists around the illness of addiction. I want it to be understood, to be approached correctly, and prevent misinterpretation and judgment. I do not pretend to give a sum total of advice. I only hope that through our experience, addicts and their families might find some answers and feel less alone during the difficult journey of addiction.

CHAPTER I

Everything a Mother Should Know: My Version of the Facts

> Once upon a time, I was just a regular mom, stumbling through parenthood like everyone else. But then I had to figure out how to be the mom of an addict. I had to figure out how to love my child without helping to hurt him... how to trade shame and blame for strength.
>
> It's a very complicated place where love and addiction meet; especially when the addict is your child, lines become blurred. We want to love the child without helping the addict, but they share the same body.
>
> —*Sandra Swenson*

I am in the medical family therapy unit. It is my workspace, which has also become a therapeutic space for my teammates and me. We meet every Tuesday to supervise all the cases we see at our support group for cancer patients. For over ten years, they have heard about and witnessed our story.

For me, this has been my safe place where I have always found a sympathetic ear and a lot of advice. There is a box of Kleenex, and just seeing it makes me sad. I've cried a lot. I'm very sensitive, but at the same time, when the situation demands it, I'm very strong. I am a survivor.

Seated on the sofa, my group awaits. My boss sees in my eyes my need to talk. On other occasions, I have spoken of confusion, guilt, frustration, sadness, anxiety, and helplessness. Today, I am on an endless roller coaster of emotions. They all give me their support; they share different strategies that perhaps can help me. The coffee is now cold, but I still drink it with the feeling of being supported in this place.

I pause during my story, and I say desperately, "How can I talk about all of this without feeling judged by the outside world?" They respond with a smile, a caring silence, and a look of understanding. Somehow, at some point, we have all been in a situation of deep sadness, and at least here, we have the comfort of not being judged. We are not alone, and we feel a deep sense of empathy.

And it is the notion of not feeling judged, at least from this group, that has allowed me to talk over time. From my mouth come words that even I can't understand. I can perfectly perceive what I say, yet I cannot collect my thoughts, so I just let them flow: "As much as you want to do as a family…everything depends only on the addict, doesn't it? It hurts to know that you cannot do anything to make them feel better. They lie, manipulate, abuse, and do not cooperate."

Today I only have to share doubts and fears. Several heads nod, trying to show me their support. Why do all of our attempts to help fail? Is it our fault? What is an addiction? Is it really a disease? Would it help to follow a spiritual path? What else can we do other than what we are already doing?

I never thought I could feel so much pain for not being able to do anything for that being that I love so much and that I do not recognize at all anymore. I never thought I could endure such uncertainty. Alex's encounter with drugs has given me experiences that I do not wish on anyone: powerlessness, a profound helplessness, uncertainty, pain, despair, moments of low tolerance, and a terrible anger with the disease. Throughout the whole addictive process of my son, I have always had doubts. How can I help Alex rebuild himself when inside I'm crumbling apart?

Sometimes I think my voice is very strong. Being a therapist is enough to be heard, to have credibility on this issue, right? Don't all mothers have it? I feel that my husband's voice and mine resonate over and over in Alex's head. Does this have anything to do with his many relapses? There have been many times when I think that Alex and I are so much alike. We both have a very sensitive personality, we care so much about what other people say, and we are always trying to do the right thing. Neither my son nor I really know how to set limits. I have been working my whole life on this, and he really struggles with this issue. I have often thought that not knowing how to say no and set strong limits is a big red flag for addiction. Isn't that true?

I sigh and continue my story. The truth is that the memory of Alex—loving, generous, in awe of life, and surprised by it—is what motivated me today to talk. Almost without asking, I open a small book by Dr. Kevin McCauley. Lately, what he says makes a lot of sense to me, so I start to read:

> It is very clear that there is something much deeper into addiction than a bad behavior. Few experiences in life are compared to situations of horror and despair, feelings of fear, helplessness, and grief that a partner or family lives when a loved one is addicted to alcohol or drugs. They watch with great sadness how from this dark place, this person that they love so much will little by little change into someone we don't recognize and gradually disappears. However, even with this anger and frustration, we still have the memory of our loved one, when he did not act like this. I am sure we all remember a very different person...affectionate, responsible, generous, and decent.[3]

"You know," I say to the group, "sometimes I think I've lost it all, and I wonder where my tender, talkative, sensitive, creative, and loving child is, that being that has brought us so much joy. Alex is impulsive, yes, but sensible and intelligent. He has a wonderful light. He leaves a mark on people who know him. He is spontaneous, generous, and deeply empathetic. That's when I wonder, what changed? Where is the beautiful human being that I remember so clearly and loved so much?"

I remember what perhaps should have been the first warning signs, but at the time, we were so naive! Alex once asked me, "Mom, I have a friend who uses cocaine. What can happen?" I answered him according to the information I was given in a certification course on addictions that I had taken. I should have asked him more, but at the time I did not realize he was the one flirting with the idea of using it.

On another occasion, during the 2006 FIFA World Cup, we invited some friends to watch the game with us. Our sons, family, and friends brought more friends, so we hosted a party for about 200 people. Alex invited some friends that neither my husband nor I knew. They looked like nice boys and girls, but we did not ask who they were. We should have asked Alex to introduce us to his friends. Many years later, we learned that that day they had been drinking heavily and using cocaine—in our house. None of us went to see what they were doing. Perhaps this was a big red flag that we failed to pay attention to.

I have such a clear image in my mind of Alex as a child. How can I not? I brought him into this world. I wanted him so much. I still remember his little face of freedom, of joy and emotion when we took him to Disneyland for the first time. He was tender, sweet, and affectionate; he was always glued to my husband and me. At the same time, since he was little, he never seemed to consider the consequences of his actions. He liked to live life to the fullest. I would have never imagined he would like drugs; he was very healthy, and he loved sports.

Why do I say he was impulsive? Well, he always was. He was totally fearless. He was invincible like Superman, his favorite superhero, and he was constantly challenging the universe. I remember as a child he would tell me, "Mama, if I have to live life in fear, I would rather not live it." And one day, without considering the danger, he got into something he could never control.

If they had offered me a drug, would I have tried it? Alex's personality decided to take the risk. Is addiction genetic, or did he cause it with his use? (We, with our lifestyles, can turn on and off our inherited genes.) My child with an addiction? Until you live it, they are just empty and meaningless words in your head, and even when you live with it, it's so hard to understand! I turn to look at my group, and I find empathetic looks that encourage me to continue.

Alex is going farther and farther down a road of no return. He went from one substance to another and then another, almost without realizing it. One day, he shared this with me: *I tried alcohol at sixteen, and a few years later a friend put coke in front of me. I was so drunk that trying it was like trying a new flavor of Doritos. There was no consciousness. It was simply a new adventure. And then what happened had to happen...I liked it! I had found a new tool for partying.*

Of course! One day it came into my son's life through the front door—the dreaded "crack"—and Alex welcomed it with opened arms.

I had finally found what would become my drug of choice.

Today, I'm sure Alex wishes he had never tried it. Today, I feel like it has been an eternity since he tried it. Countless times I've wondered what went through his mind, what happened to his brain, what happened to my dear son who cannot escape this horrible drug. I guess there is something stronger than addiction itself.

I don't want to use anymore. I want to stop.

But crack is so powerful. Alex is now standing at a crossroads in his life.

What happens to the brain of a person so addicted to crack that he cannot get out? I do not understand.

Today, I wanted to talk because I feel so sad and helpless. Alex has relapsed. We were doing so well, but he is using again. And then I think that maybe Alex just goes back to the way he knows best. It can be a terrible, rocky, slippery road, but he finds it comforting because it's a familiar place that gives him security. Crack gives him the adrenaline he now lacks after his many years of using, and it makes him feel energetic. That's what crack does. Alex has told me many times:

> *Mom, when I'm clean, you start telling me things like, "Alex you have to go to meetings, this is their schedule, and I found three new therapists for you to try," and you start wanting to fix my life. My head starts to get so stressed and I think, "No, Alex, we will not be able to do all of these." Then what do I do? I use again because that is what comforts me; that's what I can do and control.*

In my quest to rescue Alex and in my lack of understanding, I tried fixing his life. I feel in these moments that he is so fragile, vulnerable, and broken that he will not be able to do it alone. How difficult this is! Maybe this is exactly what causes his distress. All this, coupled with his personality—always trying to please everyone at every moment.

Everything is surreal right now. I can't make sense of it. I really do not know if we can save him one more time. I'm scared.

I finish my story. I do not turn to look at anyone, but I feel all eyes on me. It starts raining outside. My body collapses. The sofa envelops me. I feel I have not slept in years, but I cannot falter—not now, not ever. Alex may need us. Somehow, I feel strong. It's in my nature.

CHAPTER II

Putting Together the Complicated Puzzle of My Life

> Unconditional love is one of the deepest longings,
> not only of a child but of all human beings.
>
> —*Erich Fromm*

> The reason stories are so powerful is because they do not (at least the good ones) try to make their point through the lecture of logic. They appeal to our emotions, and they touch our heart.
>
> —*Jake D. Parent*

Alex Sierra...Where did it all begin? Will I have to go to my earliest memories, to find in them somewhere to hold myself? Where do I begin, and where does my addiction end? How can I recover my true spirit when there is so much chaos in my head? Can I take back my life? Can I ever trust myself again? What does it mean to grow and become an adult? I really mean it. I've always felt good when I'm sheltered by someone—for example, some pretty girl—and I refuse to abandon this space so known and comfortable, the only place where I do not feel empty, where I feel safe, where I'm home. Why is it so hard for me to grow, to feel good? I need to hold on to the task of finding in my past the meaning of my existence.

This is the story of my life I started writing a while ago. I was in this place called an *anexo*. I cannot remember the year, maybe 2010. An indescribable place. There, I was alone with my thoughts, trying to understand all the noise in my head…

I'm in Tijuana, Baja California, at a reintegration center, an *anexo* called CRREAD. Places where they take care of very low-income people with alcohol and drug problems. There are two ways to get into one of these places: voluntarily, which is when a person walks in on his own two feet and asks for help—in this case, the minimum stay is six months—or what is called "family request." That's when the addict's family asks for the center's help committing their family member. In the latter case, there is no minimum or maximum stay. The inmate may be here as much time as the family wants. There are people who have been here for more than four years, completely forgotten by their families. I am here at the request of my family. I received a letter from them with a chronological history of all that has happened and all that has been experienced during the course of my addiction, as if I did not remember perfectly:

> Today, you are in this place. You were in a rehabilitation clinic in Tijuana, and by your own decision, you accepted the clinic owner's proposal to get you into the *anexo* if you left the clinic again. Therefore, we believe it is important for you to know the decisions we've made. You may not understand these decisions now, and you will probably not believe us, but they have caused us a lot of pain. But at the same time, we know you have left us no more alternatives. Please realize we have tried everything. We know that time is a decisive factor in your illness, even though you see it as your worst enemy. Therefore, we have decided to hand you over the keys to your recovery. You will decide what you do with this experience, how you live it.
>
> You will be here for some time, not less than six months. You need to get back all you have lost to your disease. You need to restructure your life, change your destructive habits, and build new paradigms. On the other hand, we all need to regain our health. You have to repair the damage you have done to yourself and take responsibility and own your mistakes, and likewise, we have to take responsibility for ourselves and take ownership of our recovery. Yes, Alex, on our part there have also been a lot of mistakes, mistakes made because of the

great love that we have for you and for all the tenderness and compassion you have inspired in us.

We believe we need time to let go of each other, you from us and vice versa. We will only achieve this by putting some distance between us. You will have all you need through our friends, Angel and Becky, or the clinic's therapists. I hope this time gives you the opportunity to raise some awareness in your consciousness, to find your true emotions that have been anesthetized for such a long time, and we also hope that during this process you will be able to connect with what is real and true. It is a great life experience and opportunity to rescue your healthy parts and your values.

In austerity, humility, and especially in pain and suffering, we human beings touch our divine essence. We manage to transform our dark side, and we learn to own it. We grow up from our mistakes, and we are able to be responsible for our lives. All of this helps us to be born again into the light.

We hope you realize that recovery is within you and not outside. The resources are there inside and not in psychologists, luxury clinics, money, girlfriends, or comforts, but only inside you. I hope during this time you get to value all that life has given you, though that may be lost for the moment.

Alex, we really trust with all the love, compassion, and tenderness in our hearts that you will get to recover and find your inner self.

We want you to know and to be sure that when you leave this difficult chapter in your life that only you can close, that you will always be able to count on us, on our love and unconditional support.

We love you so much,

Mom and Dad

Clarita Sierra...Today has been a very difficult day. They agreed to take the letter we wrote to Alex a few days back. These have been very complicated moments, but today especially I have felt a heavy oppression in my heart and a knot in the pit of my stomach. This feeling is not for my pain; it is for the great pain that Alex is going to feel today.

The clinic's owner called to tell us that they read the letter to Alex. They say he felt totally defeated and cried a lot. I do not know what to do with my emotions. I feel very bad. I cannot hug my son, and I cannot dry his tears.

Alex...The time of my stay: INDEFINITE.

A long time ago, I wanted to write a little about the experiences I have lived over time. For some reason or another, I always interrupt this task and put it aside. Hopefully, this time I can complete it and help my readers to not make the same mistakes that have led me to a life of misery and darkness. I intend to remember as best as I can a little of my childhood, my upbringing, the life I had with my family—a family that has always been there for me through thick and thin—and most importantly, how I entered into the dark world of addiction. This is an important task for me, because over the years, I have lost the ability to remember all the good times that I've had. I lost my grounding, and gradually, the ability to interact with the world. I lost my essence, and I hope that writing this story will bring back all those memories and all those feelings that I truly need.

The disease of addiction affects us physically, mentally, and spiritually. With each of my relapses, I feel I break into pieces, each time smaller and smaller, and gradually I have to put them back together to start feeling whole again.

I have become codependent. Codependent on my family, on my partners. I've lost the ability to address the challenges life presents to me, and because of that, I have hidden behind drugs with the intent to fill the void that I have created in my life. In these memories, I find so much suffering; moments of terror that still cause my body to shudder just thinking about them. They say that looking back is not good, that you have to live just for today, because the past is no longer here and the future is still uncertain. I look at my past just to find answers, answers to the many questions that daily go through my head: Where did I get lost? In what moment did I stop being myself? What happened during my childhood that brought me to where I am today? And above all, what do I have to change within me to go back again and have a normal life?

True, the disease of addiction is incurable, and therefore, to return to a "normal" life is perhaps no longer possible; however, from now on, I will have to watch every one of my thoughts, each and every one of my reactions, because if they are not properly analyzed and resolved, they can take me back to the obsession of using drugs again. And if this happens, I will be back in the terrible depths of the abyss, away from reality and sinking more and more into the darkness.

Clarita...To survive, an addict has to have a route with strength and discipline. Alex did not have this because he was never a disciplined person, so he had to watch everything he did. It was essential for him to have a plan of action, a well-planned strategy, so that when the cravings or obsession would come, he would know how to react to every dark thought. We were always stressed because we felt that he had no such plan. If he did not do the necessary things to change his lifestyle, he could fall very easily.

Alex...They say that there is nothing like the strength of one addict helping another. If you are feeling lonely and lost, if you feel you have done things you can never forgive yourself for, if you think life has no meaning, I hope you read my story and in it find a little hope and know that you are not alone, that there are millions of people suffering from this horrible disease, and there is a solution. I think that from all the lessons I have learned during this process, one of the ones that has helped me the most is to be in touch with myself, to take time daily to reflect about who I am, because as the saying goes, the one who does not know his past is condemned to repeat it.

At times, I can be in touch with myself after reading a self-help book, meditating, or after writing in my journal. Other times, I do this before going to a support group, and other times, I do not need any of what I mentioned above. Without a doubt, it has been essential to take this time for myself and acknowledge how I am, how I feel.

Sometimes I write my reflections, and other times I only perceive them in silence, without the influences of anyone.

***

Alex carried himself with all his strengths and disabilities, with all the courage and fear, with all the uncertainty and irregularities that surround the world of addiction. Clearly at the time, he knew he had many tools to cope with life, yet he sometimes felt unable to use them. He had a deep desire to make it and to get out at any cost.

Alex...My Childhood As I Remember It

I was born in Mexico City on July 11, 1983, at the American British Cowdray Hospital (ABC). I am the son of Gerardo Sierra and Clarita Roffe de Sierra. I have a big brother almost six years older than me, Eduardo, and a baby brother named Mauricio. After having Eduardo, my mom had several problems having another child. In fact, she lost a baby when she was four months pregnant. Five years passed before she was pregnant again with me, and I think for that reason my parents always told me that I was a much-desired baby. And since I can remember, they always treated me that way. I always felt loved and protected by my parents.

Gerardo Sierra...Our relationship was very nice, lots of love. We shared many moments together—soccer, tennis, golf, lots of beautiful trips. Each of those moments, always as a family, Alex filled them with his enthusiasm, always with kind gestures, and he was very spontaneous. He had a great spark and zest for life. He was very observant and quick with answers and solutions; no matter the task, he would always find a way, and he was like that until the end. He trusted me, and I trusted him. I always knew, and I am convinced that, Alex tried to stop using every step of the way. He knew we valued his efforts, but we never understood their magnitude.

Alex...I had a beautiful childhood with lots of love and affection. Thanks to the efforts of my father, my family was well taken care of economically, and therefore we could enjoy a life full of love and material belongings. We had the opportunity to travel a lot during our life to very nice places, and we had everything we needed. We went to Disney World in Orlando many times. I was the happiest person on those trips. I still get excited by the mere memory and the happiness I felt when we were there, maybe because it was a "magic" place where everything was designed to make you have a good time, or perhaps because I remember the togetherness of our family. We were inseparable.

Gerardo**...**When he was little, he was like all children—very playful and mischievous. He was very shy and introverted, but when he felt safe he was very outgoing. Always looking for something more, he was hyperactive and very restless. He spent all his time looking for different things to do and searching for new adventures; he was not afraid to take risks. I loved his creativity and imagination, the dynamism of his thoughts. He was quick, proactive, and adventurous. On our trips to Disneyland, it was very funny to watch him. There is a scene I remember very well with Chip and Dale. He must have been four years old. Alex was watching them, and he wanted to touch them, but he would not dare to. He would approach them, trying to poke them with his little finger, and he would back off until finally he did it. It was quite an achievement for him. He never lost this capacity.

***

What happens when you have everything and it is not enough? Alex knew very well that he was wanted, always protected by the loving embrace of a family without any economic concerns, which refutes the widespread cliché that the adult addict is an abandoned child, unhappy and traumatized.

Alex**...**I have always been very attached to my parents. As a child, it was my mother with whom I wanted to be close and spend all my time. I remember when I was in kindergarten, The Little Prince, which was very close to my house. When school was over, I would run to be with her. She would always wait outside for me with open arms. I also remember that a lot of times I would say that I did not feel well just to stay in bed all morning with her watching TV.

Clarita**...**Alex is the middle child. Eduardo was his idol, but he was five and a half years older, and obviously he did not want Alex to be with him or his friends. Alex, being so sensitive, was affected by this. When Mauricio was born, he felt dethroned very quickly, even though

Alex had been so desired. Mau was very friendly and outgoing, and Alex at that time was very shy. Mau would also tell him, "Go play with your friends. Why do you want to be with mine?"

Alex enjoyed activities that involved an adrenaline rush. Some may feel that the thought of bungee jumping is agonizing, but Alex, at age ten, had jumped several times. He had a lot of imagination. He was very inventive, sweet, shy, and insecure about some things. I remember the thing he enjoyed most was being with us. Disneyland was magic for him. We were all together, enjoying it as a family, and that gave him great confidence.

Mauricio Sierra...When we were kids, Alex and I shared the same room. We walked together to school and back home each day. We played together all the time. We grew up in a gated community where there were eight families with children our age. We played soccer, hide-and-seek in the house, and did many mischievous things. Alex was very active and adventurous. Together we behaved foolishly. He would say "jump," and I would say "how high." I followed him; he was my big brother.

Eduardo Sierra...I remember that Alex, as a child, was very cheerful, very hyperactive. He would always be one step ahead of everybody else. He was always trying to discover new things. I was older, but I remember playing a lot with them around the house—in the hallways and in our bedrooms. Sometimes we even played soccer inside the house. Since the time Alex was nine, my dad started taking us to play golf. I had hit puberty, so I was very competitive in all sports, especially golf, but my brothers were still very young and playful. It was a great experience, being all together with my dad. We even made special trips to go play, and I have fond memories of our trips to Hawaii and Palm Springs.

Alex...With my dad, I think the relationship grew over time. He is a wonderful person. When we were small, he spent as much time as he could with us. Later, because of his work, it was harder for him to spend a lot of time with us because he spent a lot of time at the office.

Eduardo...I think for Alex it was complicated to be the middle child. Being sandwiched in the middle, you might think he never had "his moment." He was a year and a half when our brother, Mau, was born, and perhaps Alex felt he no longer had the same attention. I think his personality was always the same. The same Alex I remember at age three was the same Alex who died. He always loved adrenaline. He loved things that would take him to the limit: roller coasters, cars... and women.

***

Alex constantly challenged life. He always believed he was invincible. He found it easier to bungee jump than face responsibilities and the consequences of his actions.

This is how his family describes him: Alex was still a child, with all the positives and negatives that come with childhood. A person with an addiction, much like a child, does not comprehend gray areas; everything is black and white, terrible or grandiose. Addiction makes it difficult to assume a realistic perspective on life. Alex was always looking for perfection, wanting to create the perfect image of himself. Seeing himself caught up in his horrible disease, his self-image continued to deteriorate. If the world is divided into good and bad, Alex would ask himself, "Where do I belong?"

Alex...At five years old, I started going to Colegio Vista Hermosa, a private school that was ranked very high academically. I was always a good student and had a good relationship with my teachers and friends. I remember in elementary school I was not one of the popular students, although I had good friends. I also had bad times when the bullies would tease me. In first grade, I was afraid to go school. There was a boy who would sit on the bench behind me. He would kick me so that I would give him my lunch money. Years later, he would become one of my best friends.

In 1996, when I started junior high school, things were good for the first two years. I really enjoyed playing soccer and was on the school's soccer team. I had a healthy lifestyle and good friends. Of course, at this age I began to be a little more interested in the opposite sex. I was a good-looking guy, but I was not the most handsome. My facial features were still not well developed, my hair was a mess. I remember they nicknamed me "the micro" because my hair looked like a microphone, a look that did not make me very popular among the girls. But the truth is that this was not really an issue. I had my insecurities, but I was still a happy child full of dreams and imagination.

In 1998, during my senior year of junior high, things began to get a little bit more interesting. I started going to parties, and there I met what later became a very good friend: alcohol. I remember clearly how this substance helped me forget my insecurities and made me feel more handsome, charismatic. I could even talk to girls more easily. This was something that I became quite the expert at. I think that from the time I was fifteen, I felt women were especially important. Back then, they were not as important as they became later in life, but they would occupy a good deal of my thoughts every day.

Clarita...The first thing that gave him security in life was girls. Gradually, he learned to relate to them, and little by little, having girlfriends became more important than having friends. Alejandro got along with "nerds" because he saw himself as one; he had braces and glasses. He was a good kid, always on his best behavior. He got good grades.

I started noticing at that time that Alex was having difficulty relating to his friends at school and developing a sense of belonging. Because of his insecurity, he wanted to be friends with the "cool" guys, and during that transition, he lost his group identity, trying to tag along with the girls and the most popular boys. I think he had a constant feeling of inadequacy. Just that process of wanting to belong and have confidence to speak to girls helped him fall prey to alcohol. It is not that everything was about drinking alcohol, but it was the tool he discovered that allowed him to relate to others more easily.

Alex...I managed to finish junior high, even though school was not my priority anymore. I can happily say that I am an intelligent person, and I never had any problem passing my classes. My parents constantly told me that just passing my classes with minimal effort was really not the best that I could do, and they were right. But having good grades and being the best at school was something that did not concern me at the time.

***

Any young man, when he consumes alcohol and drugs, thinks, "I can envision the worst that could happen, but it will never happen to me." Unfortunately, that is the risk. It can happen. The dice can go against anyone, and with drugs, not only can you lose money if the dice fall on the wrong number. It is life itself that you can lose.[4]

Alex...Little by little, as I got older, my life began to revolve around parties, going out with friends and girls, and of course, alcohol. Around sixteen or seventeen years old, it began to matter a lot to me what clothes I was wearing. I wanted to look well dressed. The car my parents drove to take me to parties was also important, along with having a good table at a restaurant and always being invited to the best places. Even with that, the life I wanted to lead was not easy for me. I did not have the most popular friends, and my parents did not give me a lot of money, just an allowance. I remember that part of me wanted to remain the good and innocent child I had been until then, but gradually, the glamour of alcohol attracted me more and more, and I became someone that was not really me.

***

Alex admits that his encounters with alcohol and its disinhibiting effects redirected his life toward other objectives and goals. Life presents you with constant tests, and the way you confront them depends on the tools you have. Apparently, Alex had a number of resources, yet opted for a path that led him to addiction.

Alex...It was during my first year of high school when things were not the same anymore. I lost all interest in my education. Now it was just alcohol, parties, and women that had all my attention. For the first time in my life, I failed a school year, not because of my grades, but because of the number of absences I had. It was more fun to skip classes than to attend, and that's when the school principal told me that I had to leave Colegio Vista Hermosa, where I had grown up and managed to forge friendships.

Around this time, I had my first sexual experience, something that I am not very proud of. I remember it was the peer pressure that made me do it. We went and paid for it. The first time was not a nice experience, and since then it has taken me a lot of work to have a beautiful relationship that was not premature. I was used to having crappy relationships where my sexual performance was never good.

I was very young when I did it for the first time, and I was not even sure of what I was doing. I remember it was in the dirty room of a brothel with an older woman. I felt uncomfortable, and I was scared, but I was also excited for what was about to happen. It was fast and uncomfortable, and it left me with an emotional void. I felt dirty. Having sex, something that people talked about as being wonderful, was not a big deal for me. My first sexual experience was not pleasant. It was only over time and many relationships later that I started enjoying sex and was able to have that wonderful and beautiful connection between man and woman.

During that school year, I met a girl named Andrea, who became one of the most important people in my life. The year was 1998, and she was really special to me. At first, I even thought she was totally out of my league, so I started trying to win her over little by little. It was not an easy task. I often skipped school with some friends and visited her at her school. We were always talking on the phone, and I would visit her at home.

Despite all my efforts, I could not convince her to just go out with me. One day, after spending the afternoon together in a place called El Suspiro, when it was time to say good-bye, I approached her to give her a good-bye kiss on the cheek. I remember vividly how she moved her face so that our lips would touch. I still remember how my legs were shaking with excitement. It was the first of many kisses that would follow over the next few years of our lives.

In 1999, my family bought a beach house in Ixtapa, Zihuatanejo. We have spent countless holidays there, full of adventures and good times. I remember a few months after we started dating, Andrea and I ran into each other on vacation (her parents had a house in the same place as ours). It was something very special. We spent all our time together; we were at the pool the whole time having a great time together. I have incredible memories of this time in my life. It was with her that I felt the sweetness of first love.

Andrea...I met Alex when I was about fourteen. I remember him as a super-kind boy with glasses, always polite and proper, a person with deep eyes and a special look, a profound expression that he always had, and sixteen years later, I still recognized it when I saw him. At that time, we were so young and inexperienced. We were very nervous when we were together. From the moment we met, a beautiful love story began for us.

Alex...My life continued, the parties continued, alcohol remained my friend. I remember I would come home intoxicated a lot, and each time, I was confronted by my parents. I was told to be careful because of the way I was drinking, but at the time it wasn't really seen as a problem, just a teenager experiencing the pleasures of life.

Clarita...I remember that the way my sons sometimes drank alcohol worried me. It really worried me. I did not understand the whole experience of teenagers around alcohol; I never drank when I was that age. However, my husband had attended an all-boys school and told me that it was a part of growing up.

Alex...By this time, I started having problems socially with different groups. I remember that there was a group of guys from a private, all-boys school that constantly tried to fight with me. To this day, I do not really know why. I only remember that I lived in fear.

A week earlier, the same guys had left a boy with a concussion after having slammed his head on the sidewalk outside a dance club. I began to hide from them everywhere I went. I made sure not to cross paths with any of them. I was really scared!

I was invited to a girl's sweet sixteen party at a place called Hacienda de los Morales, where I found myself in front of that entire group. I was in the bathroom. There were about ten or fifteen guys. They started pushing and shoving me, yelling threats at me. They were holding me so that one of them would hit me and break my face. When a security guard came in, he made everyone leave except me. After closing the door, the guard told me that he was not going to let anyone hit me but that I should call someone to come and get me.

I called my brother, Eduardo, and he told me not to worry, that he was going to pick me up. Shortly thereafter, a driver entered the bathroom, a really big man who asked me if I was Alejandro Sierra. He then told me my brother had sent him to get me out of the bathroom and out of the party. Once outside, I found my brother with his friends, ready to defend me. To this day, I am grateful to him for coming to my rescue and taking care of me.

Clarita**...**I think this experience was a watershed moment in my son's life. He began to define himself by women, even more so after this experience. The guys didn't like him, and the girls fell madly in love with him. He says that to this day he does not know why those guys wanted to beat him up, but the reality is that one of the guy's girlfriends kissed Alex.

By this time, he had become very insecure, with no friends. He was all alone, and that's when he asked if he could attend another school. I remember we talked a lot with him and asked him what school he wanted to go to. Then he switched to a school called Colegio Albatros, where he was not happy, either. That is where he completed the school year he had failed. By this time, he was not comfortable anywhere and wanted to study abroad. We chose a very good school in Canada. The truth is that he wanted to leave the country because he was afraid that someone would break his face. That was when he left the country to continue his studies.

The reality is that no one is born a perfect parent; knowing what to do in any situation is hard. Today, almost fifteen years later, I can see clearly. We were solving his problems, but at the time, we obviously thought we were doing what was best for him. And this was probably another red flag that we failed to see. As parents, we try to help our children by resolving all of their problems. In the same way we helped Alex, we also helped my other sons when they needed us; we rescued them from different situations.

This time, my husband and I agreed to do what Alex wanted instead of saying, "There is only one choice here. You stay in your current school, you take the chance they are giving you to repeat your freshman year, and then you finish high school. You can also go get a job because we are not paying another school."

My regret is that at the time, I did not set the proper limits, nor did we understand the significance involved in graduating with your class. Although my other two children later made friends in college, their lifelong friends are the ones they made during their time at Vista Hermosa. Maybe we did not have the insight to guide him in repairing all of his strained relationships and in helping him with his conflicts with other boys instead of helping him escape from his actions and responsibilities.

***

Alex's fear was very real, and it lasted for several years. The threat from this group of guys had not disappeared. Whenever he ran into them, they would say, "We will kill you next time." After returning from a trip when Alex was seventeen, he went to a club, and some guy broke his nose.

Clarita...I remember that day very well. It was a Friday afternoon. We had just come back from summer vacation. My husband did not go with us; he was working, and that day he was not home. He was on a business trip and was returning next day. We got home around six or seven p.m. Then Alex and Mauricio asked me if they could go out dancing. "Of course not," I said. "We just got back from our trip."

"Okay, Mom," they answered, and a few hours later, we all went to sleep.

Suddenly, at four a.m., Mauricio woke me up and said, "Mom, call Ortiz Oscoy [a friend and plastic surgeon] because someone broke Alex's nose." I did not understand what was going on. How could someone have broken Alex's nose when we were all in bed?

I went downstairs, and then I saw Alex with a broken nose, bleeding all over his shirt. My first reaction was to get mad at him. They lied to me and went out. Then they started telling me the whole story. Alex was passing through the tables of a nightclub and accidentally pushed a drunk guy, and this guy says, "Come outside. I'm going to break your face."

Alex started yelling at the guy. "Why do you want to fight with me? I didn't do anything." The security guards took Alex out of the place and told him to go home. At the same time, a close friend of Alex's came out and said, "This guy wants to talk to you and make things right." Alex wanted to do that because he always cared deeply about what others thought of him. So, he waited. The drunk guy came out and said, "Can I give you a hug?" He approached Alex and with his forehead broke his nose.

After this, his insecurities intensified.

Alex...Because of my constant fear of being beaten, I asked my parents for the opportunity to go study abroad. They agreed, and we looked for a school in Canada.

***

When you are frightened by a threatening situation, flight is a natural survival response. Although he had not yet made contact with drugs, this latent defense mechanism lay inside Alex, and it eventually became a way of protecting himself. The constant desire to flee is a way of life for an addicted patient; their substance is not only an escape, but it is the shelter itself.

> *We know that severe stress changes the brain. Chronic severe stress breaks the brain. One kind of stress that can change the brain and create vulnerability for addiction is called Social Defeat Stress. This stress can be observed in monkeys as they form a social hierarchy. There are dominant monkeys at the top of the scale, middle monkeys and the submissive monkeys at the bottom. The dominant monkeys subject the submissive monkeys to a great deal of aggression and intrusion into their territory. Research has shown that if offered cocaine, the dominant monkeys will try it but reject it. Submissive monkeys, on the other hand, quickly become addicted when exposed to cocaine. Additionally, if exposed to a single episode of social defeat after a period of cocaine abstinence, they quickly relapse. The strength of Koob and LeMoal's theory of stress-induced change in the brain's hedonic system is that it provides a model for how environmental stress might set the stage in the brain for drug addiction.*[5]

Alex...I went to Trinity College in Port Hope, Ontario. Here I studied during my second year of high school. I was between sixteen and seventeen years old, and it was really a fun year. I was on the soccer team, where I stood out as one of their best players. I was also the number-one varsity tennis player, a great honor within the school. My grades were good. My teachers gave positive comments about my grades, and although I missed my family a lot, surprisingly it was a good year, full of peace and serenity where nobody wanted to hit me.

I took advantage of my free time to go to the gym where I spent a lot of hours. I became aware of my body, and I liked to see the results after a good workout. The girls were beginning to notice me more, and I had several nice relationships throughout the year.

It was in Canada where I tried marijuana for the first time. I have little memory of the moment. I just remember that I laughed a lot, I had a good time, I felt a sense of well-being throughout my body, and that all food tasted delicious. The feeling is commonly known as "the munchies." My parents gave me my first debit card for any extra things that I might need. I did not misuse it, but sometimes I would use it to buy alcohol for several of my friends.

One of the funniest memories I have was a trip I took to Montreal with three Mexican guys that were at school with me. It was a long weekend, and they gave us permission to spend it in the city. It was my first trip alone. When we arrived at our hotel, we asked the concierge which was the best club to go to that night. We were told it was a place called 737, a private club, and you had to be on the guest list to get in. I came up with a plan. I called the club and told the manager that the son of the Mexican president was with our group of friends—which was not true—and that we wanted to know if we could get into the club and get a good table. The manager was very excited and said it would be a pleasure to take care of us personally.

We arrived at the club at ten that evening. There was a long line. About 200 people were waiting, so we thought we'd never make it in. As we approached the chains, we told the security guard that I was the son of the Mexican president and that the manager was waiting for us. Five minutes later, the manager came down to the door and took us in. The crowd was amazed when we got in; they had been in line for several hours.

***

Over the years, and in a spiritual quest, Alex began to disqualify lifestyles that were shallow and empty, lifestyles that he had sought at the time.

Clarita...Throughout his addiction, Alex tried to fill the void of his existence with material things that dazzled him and gave him security. When Alex returned from that trip, he was told he could no longer get into any high school program to finish his last year before going to college. The program in Canada was different from the Mexican program, so he had to attend a program called open high school, where you study your subjects on your own and take a test to pass them. We were not very happy with this situation. Alex would have a lot of time on his own, but we agreed. We just wanted him to finish school so he could go to college. I remember he told me at the time, "Mom, I promise that I will study hard, and I will be in college by the time the rest of my classmates are." And he did.

Alex...At the end of the year, it was time to return to Mexico. I didn't know exactly which school I wanted to attend for my senior year. In the end, I did not have much of a choice. The program in Canada was very different from Mexico, so I finished high school in an open program. That's how I ended up at that stage of my life—without graduating, without my friends, without a school. I simply presented myself, I passed the exams, and six months later, I was given a diploma that later allowed me to go to college.

I remember at the time that my family traveled a lot to Ixtapa, where there was a club called La Valentina. At night, my parents would let my brothers and me go to the nightclub. It was a very popular place, and gradually, my brothers and I became good customers. Our table was always empty, waiting for us to arrive. That always made me feel important. When the table was not available, I remember feeling insecure and uncomfortable and did everything possible to move people to other tables so I could sit there with my people.

***

Alex's testimony is that his self-affirmation depended on an image of status and prestige that he wanted to project to others. If anything, this image spiraled out of his control, and he got very anxious. Alex acknowledged that he required accessories (e.g., women, the best tables) that gave him the confidence that he could not find within himself. The superficiality of his relationships with the opposite sex and his fun-loving character are evident.

Alex...At La Valentina, I became friends with a guy who always sat with us. Together we felt really popular, and we always had a lot of alcohol and had girls who wanted to be with us. Andrea always remained very important in my life, and every time we were in Ixtapa, our love was constantly reborn. We did not have a stable relationship because of my infidelity and my lack of commitment, but every time we met we just had to be together. We had a very special connection. Today, when I remember those times, I truly regret not being more responsible with what we had. It could have turned into something wonderful. But I never gave the relationship the importance I should have. I always pushed her aside and played with her emotions. I thought at the time that I would never lose her.

Andrea...I remember when Alex returned from Canada. He was not the same sweet kid, and I was not a part of his priorities. He just wanted to go out with the "cool" people. I felt really bad because I would have given everything for him. I was the typical girl in love with a boy that ignored her.

First Time

Alex...The person I considered my best friend introduced me to a dangerous and unfamiliar world. One day, we were very drunk outside the nightclub, and he approached me with a bag of white powder. He said it was cocaine, and he offered me some. I asked him what I was going to feel. He said not to worry, that it was an incredible feeling, and that I would not feel drunk anymore. In fact, I was going to be very energetic and euphoric.

I did not think twice. He showed me how to inhale by making a straw from a dollar bill. I put the straw into the bag, and I snorted cocaine for the first time in my life. I have to be honest and accept that I do not remember that moment now. I do not remember being euphoric, either. I do not remember anything from that night. I only know that that's how I tried it for the first time. But I'm sure I must have felt something good since for so many years this substance has taken over my life.

It was not immediately that I became addicted to it. We are told that addiction is a disease that is progressive and chronic, and when it is not treated, it is fatal. My life can be a good example of this progression. I started using only in Ixtapa, maybe once a month. Then I started using weekly, and soon I was using every day. I could not live without it. I would wake up and I would do a line, another line when I got out of the shower, driving to college, during classes, at any possible moment. Now I've added a new activity to the important things in my life: alcohol, women, parties…and cocaine.

The relationship with my family became very distant, something that has always caused me so much pain. As I mentioned earlier, my family and I were inseparable. We did everything together. But over time, things changed. Without realizing it, I was getting further and further away from them. I felt that the magic was lost, or that maybe my brothers and I had grown in different directions. Sadly, when I look back, partying and women were more important than spending some time with my parents or my brothers. Many times I found myself asking God to turn back time so I could do things differently.

Clarita…For me, there is no doubt that addiction is a disease, and unfortunately, it is treated as a criminal act. We have the famous stereotypes that addicts are bad people, morally weak, that they come from dysfunctional families, or that they were mistreated and abused when they were young. We cannot grasp that an addict may be the most kind, loving, decent, and generous person in the world but lives with feelings of emptiness and inadequacy. It is very sad to realize, as parents, how peer pressure influences and leads our children to abuse drugs, smoke, and drink. This pressure is intensified by the search for a sense of belonging to some social group. Unfortunately, when our children are insecure, they are much more vulnerable to using.

When a person has a genetic predisposition for addiction and tries any drug for the first time, his or her chances of becoming an addict are higher. It is not the bad behavior but genetic disposition that makes them more prone to continue using. Dr. Kevin McCauley says that a vulnerability to addiction that is genetically determined is how an individual responds to drugs, how they make you feel.

There is a very fine line between abuse of drugs and addiction. A person who consumes drugs regularly and in excess may become an addict because his continuous use of drugs or alcohol can change his brain chemistry. However, a person with a genetic predisposition in a stressful environment can easily become an addict. Drugs become their survival coping mechanism. Here, as parents, we find ourselves in an uncertain place, not knowing whether our children have this genetic predisposition and the vulnerabilities they are facing as teenagers. It is scary to know that just by experimenting with alcohol or drugs, they can become addicts. It is like playing Russian roulette.

I keep thinking that besides all the risk factors that there are in the world of addiction, there is an additional element: luck. More than luck—destiny; I mean, what we are meant to live. Perhaps if we had not bought a house in Ixtapa, Alex would have never tried drugs or would have done it at another moment of less vulnerability. Maybe someone can mock me when I say that his soul came to work in this lifetime in specific situations for him to grow and for us to learn. And no matter what Gerardo and I would have done, the end would have been the same. I can only add that, at the end of the day, Alex and we as a family had to learn, had to live all these experiences to grow as human beings. For me, understanding this was very important.

***

Would Alex have tried cocaine if he had not been drunk? Unfortunately, alcohol is a gateway to the world of drugs. Many alcoholics never try another drug, but that doesn't make their fall any less painful. But many others continue experimenting with increasingly harmful substances (e.g., designer drugs, crack, heroine, meth, marijuana), trapped in such a manner that the way back seems—in many cases—impossible to regain.

CHAPTER III

Drugs: My Best Friend

Temptation is that dynamic through which the soul is graciously offered the opportunity to learn without creating karma, to evolve directly through conscious choice.

—*Gary Zukav*

God leaves us free to choose, even if He knows the danger this represents. Sometimes we use this liberty in a wrong way. We use it to hurt ourselves. And when this happens, I have to believe that God cries, even though we are the ones who are responsible.

—*Rabbi Harold S. Kushner*

Alex mentions in his story that at this point in his life, he felt totally at the mercy of drugs: **"I found myself often asking God to let me go back in time to do things differently."** *However, the road became more and more complicated. Slowly, Alejandro was walking a fine line until there was no possibility of return.*

Alex...By the year 2000, I was at Anahuac University where my dad and my brother, Eduardo, had finished their degrees. I was studying business administration. I remember attending classes high all the time, and each day it was harder for me to pay attention. However, I was still a relatively good student and continued my studies, even though my addiction kept growing.

Juanita Monroy...Alex would hide around the house, and he would tell me, "Juanita, when my parents leave, let me know." To me that was strange, but I did as I was told. He did everything not to attend school and only use drugs.

I remember telling him, "You have already missed school for a week. I'll tell your parents," but he would not answer me at all, unlike when he was younger. He already had a different personality. When someone called him, he used to get mad at me for interrupting him, a sign that meant he was using. Other times, he used to tell me, "Today I didn't feel like going to school, but don't tell my parents because I'll get mad at you." When they realized he was not going, they got really mad at him, his mother more so, but he always got what he wanted. He never accepted "no" for an answer. "They won't make me do it," he used to say.

When his father used to talk to the boys, they were more respectful. I told Alex, "Do not be rude to your mom. Do as the others do." But he replied, "I won't give in if I think they're being unreasonable."

Mauricio...I lived with Alex during what I thought was a fun stage. I did not realize it was already an addiction problem, where dependence was a theme for him. To me, that part was very hidden because I did not see it. I used to go out with him, and I used to think, "A time will come when he calms down. It is only a stage, and all my friends party like him." I never saw him getting into real trouble.

***

Mauricio, as an eighteen-year-old teen, did not have the tools to support his brother, and it was not a matter of age. Often, not even parents have the right tools to support their children in this process. If you have never lived the experience, it is quite natural that common sense and emotion intermingle so much that they cannot be controlled.

Alex...I started having problems with math. I was slowly falling behind until I had to leave school. But during those three years, many things happened. I changed friends constantly. I do not remember how my friendship with Raul began. He invited me to his summer house on the weekends. We went to nightclubs, and we drank a lot. I used to snort cocaine, but I noticed that he could keep on going all through the night. It was six a.m., and he and his friends were still jumping and dancing. I could not keep up with them.

One night, I asked one of his friends what made them look so happy and energized. He showed me a red pill branded with two fish. He told me it was ecstasy, a designer drug that should not be mixed with alcohol. He gave me one and told me it would help me have a good time. I fell in love immediately with this drug. The feeling of pleasure and euphoria I felt when taking it was unforgettable. I danced and jumped all night. All my senses were sharpened; the overall feeling of my body was very special. I felt I could see better, hear better, feel better. I was the king of the world, and as with cocaine, I felt there was no problem in the world that could affect how good I felt inside.

Clarita...Today, I feel that the big difference between Alex and this friend was that his friend took ecstasy to have some fun, like a lot of youth who experiment with drugs. Alex did it to forget his problems and fill his emptiness. Many years later, talking with this friend, he told me that he was worried to see Alex's compulsion when it came to drugs. He was not content with just one pill but would take one after another in one night.

Alex...By this time, I met a beautiful girl that I really liked. I liked her a lot. But I was using too much, and I was always high. It was very difficult for me to maintain a stable relationship. I met her one night at a nightclub. We knew each other; we had chatted a lot on Messenger, but we had never met. Immediately after seeing her, I knew it was her. I loved her eyes and her smile. How I regret this time in my life. To this day, Susy has been one of my dearest friends, and I know that I can always count on her unconditionally.

Susy...Big shining smile, warmest heart, and twinkling eyes. It was impossible to miss his smile that special night in Acapulco's nightclub, Baby'O, in May 2004. We kept laughing across the dance floor, and I was shy to walk over until he finally came over to me and asked me if I was Suzy Del Vecchio. I asked him if he was Alex Sierra. Some may call it a crazy coincidence, but I call it destiny, and that day I met one of the most special souls in the world, one that today is one of the most significant human beings I hold close to my heart. Alex would impact my life in such a positive way that I am forever thankful to him.

Alex...And I kept living like that, but like the good addict that I am, the use of ecstasy did not stop there. I would call my dealer, and I no longer asked just for coke, but I would also get large quantities of ecstasy. I thought that parties without these drugs would never be the same. Every weekend I consumed both substances, without realizing that the effect of one altered the effect of the other, and the feelings of pleasure I felt when I tried ecstasy for the first time were never the same. I was constantly seeking the high I felt the first time, and despite being almost there, it was never the same.

As a good addict, my tolerance for substances began to increase, so I also had to increase the amounts I used to feel any effect. And when I increased the amounts too much, these ended up producing negative effects: I felt sick; it was almost impossible to sleep; my nose was pretty affected by my cocaine use—it hurt constantly; and it was hard to breathe. A lot of times, seeing my nose bleed and feeling pain, I would flush the coke into the toilet, promising never to use again. But when time passed and I felt good again, the obsession to consume was reborn and thus began a new cycle of "living to use and using to live."

***

Why is there tolerance to drugs? When people use a drug for the first time, they may perceive what seem to be positive effects, and they may also believe that they can control their use. However, drugs can quickly take over a person's life. Over time, if drug use continues, other pleasurable activities become less pleasurable. For example, when a person uses cocaine for a long time, their brain becomes anhedonic; it can no longer derive pleasure from normally pleasurable things, meaning that you stop feeling pleasure, and drugs become necessary for the user to feel "normal" again. Then they may seek and use drugs compulsively, even though they cause tremendous problems for them and their loved ones. Some may begin to feel the need to take higher doses or more frequently due to drug tolerance, even in the early stages of abuse. You never get to feel the same thing that you felt the first time, and you spend your time looking for that magical moment of pleasure in your subsequent highs.[6]

Alex...During this time, I had several girlfriends, all of them lasting a short time because my addiction was the most important thing in my life. I began a relationship feeling the euphoria that any relationship provides us at first—the thrill of the unknown, first kiss, first sex. Those were things that made me feel good, that made me want to stop using on several occasions. But then, time passed, the unknown became routine, and boredom began to appear. Me being addicted to adrenaline, this always ended the relationship so that I could find something new, something to help me fill the void in my life, but everything I found eventually stopped working, and I would sink back again into what I knew how to do best: get high.

Gerardo...In retrospect, I think that all through his teen years Alex was very insecure, and that led him to seek safety in drugs, which gave him security and the image that he—in his fantasies—believed was the Alex everyone wanted to see. He would seek self-confidence, presence, control, women, money, and sadly—little by little—the use of drugs. Motivated by his insecurities, he was taking these wrong paths, easy paths that he never imagined would one day control his life, even though he would try to fight against them and get ahead.

Alex...One day, Andrea called me, saying she had something important to tell me. I was not expecting what she said to me. I still remember her words: "I'm pregnant, and I'm getting married." They felt like a bucket of ice water. Although at that time we had little contact, the news was devastating. Andrea was my first love, and I had the stupid idea that she was going to be there for me forever. But at that moment, I realized that I had lost her, that we would never have the relationship we had dreamed of, and that because of my way of living and acting, we never could have.

She invited me to her wedding. Probably given our track record, I should not have attended, but my ego made me go. I still could not believe that she would never be mine. It hurt me to see her promising her love to another man, and of course, I went to hide my pain behind cocaine, ecstasy, and alcohol.

I am aware that there has been some damage to my memory. I hardly remember things that happened during these years. But in general, I remember just partying, travel, women, alcohol, and the use of all the drugs that I could find. I experimented with cocaine, alcohol, ecstasy, and marijuana. I even went through a time when I injected anabolic steroids to grow my muscle mass. All this was done simply to fill the emptiness inside me. And yet, my use also changed my attitude towards my family and friends.

Juanita...I left the house for some time, and when I came back, Alex had just returned from Canada. I saw him in a very different light. He no longer had the same smile. He was always quiet and thoughtful. He had a different personality. Before, he was very happy. I remember him singing, making jokes, and now he got angry all the time and quickly exploded. He had also changed a lot physically. He asked me to inject him with anabolic steroids on three occasions, telling me that nothing would happen. I guess he then learned how to do it himself because he never asked again. Soon, his parents realized something was wrong.

Clarita...It was probably in the early years of college when Alex had two car crashes where he was miraculously unhurt. One was in Mexico, and Eduardo took the blame for him. Alex was very drunk, and the police would have taken him, so Eduardo arrived to where the crash had been and said he was the one driving. I remember when Alex got home—very drunk and still in shock from the crash. He looked at himself, saying, "God really loves me. I'm in perfect shape. Nothing happened to me."

I let some time go by. I let him continue for several minutes repeating the same narrative until I said, "No, Alex. God loves me because you would be dead and I would be crying."

The other crash was in Ixtapa around the same time, when he turned a minivan upside down. Until then, we were in denial and could not see that perhaps Alejandro had a problem with alcohol, and of course we did not know about the thin line that exists between alcohol and other drugs.

***

Many families of addicts deny the addiction of their loved one for a long time until circumstances push them to face it. Denial is a natural human response to situations that we are not able to face and that we are not ready to deal with.[7]

Alex...In 2005, I traveled with my family on a cruise to the Baltic Sea.

Eduardo...Before the cruise, we visited Amsterdam, and the three of us—Alex, Mauricio, and me—went to a coffee shop, and we had a lot of fun. As you know, it is legal to buy marijuana there, and I've tried it but never liked it. On the ship in our cabin, Alex told me, "Look what I brought, Eddie," and showed me about sixty ecstasy pills. "Girls love them!"

I said, "Look, Alex, we already had some fun in Amsterdam, but right now we are on a family trip. The police can find them." So, I took the bag and flushed them into the toilet. And of course, he hit me. I told my parents about that incident. They were very mad at Alex, but in retrospect, I do not think they fully understood what was happening. None of us did.

Alex...During this time, I dated a girl named Samantha, among others. But it was Sam with whom I spent much of my time. We had a volatile and very obsessive relationship full of lust. I cannot deny that we had good times. We were very sexually compatible, and we were constantly looking to satisfy our sexual desires. I remember one of the reasons why I liked being with her was because she did not mind my drug use. I was free to act and be who I wanted when I was with her.

I constantly wanted what others had. I struggled to get everything I thought of, and with my insistence, manipulation, and perseverance, I always got what I wanted. But nothing satisfied me. I was no longer the same person as I was before. I had a short temper, little patience, and was easily angered. I lost the ability to love myself and therefore the ability to love others. I hid myself in women, giving them power over me. I was constantly seeking their approval. I liked to hear compliments but did not know how to receive them. I did not feel worthy of anything, but at the same time, I wanted everything.

At school, things had already derailed. I left my major in business administration in my third year. Later, I switched to tourism, which I only stayed with for six months, and then in 2006 I switched to architecture, always leaving my studies unfinished.

Mauricio...On one of those occasions, when he was studying architecture at Anahuac University, I was studying the same course at another university. I was very dedicated to school, whereas Alex always looked too laid back. He was just lazy. At that time, we spent a lot of time together. We had many school assignments. We worked in our family room doing them. He used drugs all the time, and it was then when I realized something was wrong, but I never wanted to expose or confront him. Later, he realized on his own that he had a problem.

Alex...I lived in a constant search for what I wanted with my life, but nothing caught my attention anymore. Time went by. Everything had become slow and boring. School did not interest me, my relationship with my family was not quite right. It wasn't unusual for me to steal money from my parents. I forged checks, misused credit cards, and stole all the money I could, just to constantly feed my addiction. I completely lost sight of the value of money. I was constantly shopping online for cell phones, tennis shoes, jackets—all in my quest to fill the void that drugs were causing.

Eduardo...I would always talk to Alex and I would say, "Look, Alex, I think you should try to stop using drugs. It is not fun anymore." Regardless of his problem, Alex was a very high-minded, generous, fun guy. He would give his life for anyone, but he was also very immature, and he thought money and brands were very important. Money was his way of feeling a sense of belonging and security. I do not know where he got that need for things. We were never brought up like that, and it was not the way our parents raised us.

Clarita...At that time, Alex did not tell us anything about his addiction, but he manipulated Gerardo's assistant by asking her to pay the credit card without his father's knowledge. Later, it was Juan Carlos, my nephew, who alerted us to the misuse of our money and a credit card Alex had, which truly surprised us, because Gerardo kept the card in his safe. Later, we learned that Alex had called American Express posing as my husband, saying he had lost the card and needed a replacement. That is how we realized he had another card.

Alex...I remember one day things got really bad, or maybe it was just the first time I realized I was in a situation that did not benefit me at all. I had too many problems and no longer had the capacity to deal with them. I was very tired of seeing what my life had become. I vaguely remember entering my parents' room and asking for help.

I told them everything that was happening. I told them about my addiction to cocaine and other substances and begged them to support me. I told them about my friend with whom I had tried cocaine for the first time and that he had been in rehab and was now clean and sober and enjoying life, something I wanted for myself.

Clarita...It was more or less in early November 2006 when I began to notice that I was missing money from my bank account, so I checked my bank statement and checkbook and realized some of my checks were missing, so I went to the bank and explained my situation. After they looked into it, we found out that Alex had signed some checks. Although I felt awful, I had suspected something because Alex's behavior had changed radically in the last several months.

That night, without speaking with Gerardo first, I summoned my whole family, saying that there was something I needed to tell them. First, I started talking about general stuff, telling them they needed to stop doing some things their father and I did not approve of, about how irresponsible they were with their belongings and how our driver was always solving their problems—the flat tires for driving through potholes after a party, picking up their car somewhere, putting gas in the car. Then, I looked specifically at Alex and told him that I had not raised them to be thieves, that I knew he had been stealing from me, and that he had to hand over his car keys, cell phone, and computer. The next day, I was going to his university, and if I found out he had not been attending, I would stop paying the tuition. He went to his room, and half an hour later, he came back and told us he had a big problem with cocaine and he could not stop.

Mauricio...Alex was not being responsible anymore, and he was not stable in any of his relationships, either with family or friends. He alone made the decision and told my parents about his addiction. I always wanted to do that with him, but maybe as a younger brother it was very hard for me. I did not know how, and I thought to myself, "How could I tell my big brother what to do since I am younger and I also went to those parties?"

Alex...It was around November 2006 when we decided I was going to this clinic on the Mexican Pacific coast. When I arrived at the clinic, I had no idea what was going to happen. I was in detox for three or four days, medicated to help me not feel withdrawal symptoms. I remember kneeling next to the bed and crying for a long time. I knew it was for my own good. I had asked for help, but I was confused, disoriented, and of course, very afraid of what would happen.

After detox, I was integrated with other patients and began what would be my journey into the world of recovery. I was first introduced to the program of Alcoholics Anonymous and the 12 steps. I began to work within myself, and for the first time, I was told that I was suffering from a progressive, incurable, and deadly disease, something I did not believe. I was told that I could never again use any substance that could alter my brain, including alcohol, which I had no intention of quitting.

**

Once past the initial shock of facing responsibility for his actions and the fact that he had missed the chance to finish college because of his drug abuse, Alex realized he had lost friends and had damaged his relationship with his parents and brothers. During his recovery in the clinic, he remained in denial that he had a "real" problem.

Gerardo...In the beginning of his illness, we had no idea what we were facing and that drugs had taken control over our son.

Alex...I went to treatment for the simple fact that the problems in my life were by now too overwhelming—because things did not go as I wanted, because I had already been in car accidents, because of my alcohol and drug abuse. But I remember I was sure it was not because I had a problem with alcohol or drugs. I remember being very insistent with the therapist, telling him, "I came to solve my problems, and by solving them, I am sure I will stop abusing dangerous substances."

The therapist quickly put me in my place and told me I had to first take care of my addiction problem, and by doing this, my problems with life would become normal and easy to solve, but I had to start with my disease. I never liked the way he confronted me. I was sure he was wrong, that my problems of feeling alone, insecure, and full of fear were not because of my addiction, and I was ready to prove it.

Clarita...Perhaps one of my biggest regrets is that I was not well informed about what an addiction meant. Even when we had already decided to send him to this clinic, we still thought it was just a bad habit or bad behavior, a young adult making bad choices in his life. We did not yet understand that addiction was a disease. So, my present regret is that in hindsight, if someone in my family had a serious illness, I would have sought the best doctor at the time and the best clinic for this type of disease. I understood this many years later.

Eduardo...When Alex went into rehab, I experienced it as something external that did not concern me. My parents were not familiar with the topic of addiction, nor were Mauricio and I. Later on, my mother became an expert. And my dad acted on what his heart felt. I think both my parents would give their lives for us and do everything for us to succeed, regardless of the problems we have. I do not think I understood Alex's addiction. I always gave him my support and recognized his struggle, but later, as his addiction got worse, the reality is that I did not like Alex anymore, and I learned that when he was using, it was impossible to talk to him.

Clarita...With time, addiction affects the rest of the family, and they find themselves involved in a roller coaster of emotions. They feel abandoned, angry, and a lot of resentment is stirred up. Often, as parents, guilt and shame do not allow us to see what is in front of our faces. If we see our child healthy and relatively happy, it is very difficult to think he has a chronic, progressive, and deadly disease. Many times, ignorance makes us live in denial until we are forced to accept what is happening. This is easier than facing something as foreign and complex as addiction.

***

Like Conyers says, denial is the foundation of addiction, the fertile soil where it grows and blooms. Denial provides the comfortable delirium that everything is all right, softening the road for addicts so they fall deeper into a kind of spiral.[8]

Alex...As the days passed, I started to feel bored and unhappy with what I was being taught, so I looked for something that gave me the adrenaline rush necessary to hang on to treatment. And I found it in Laura, a girl who suffered from anorexia and bulimia. We began sending notes to each other, then grabbing hands and promising each other eternal love while hiding from the staff. It was make-believe.

I had already lost interest in my treatment. I only cared about Laura, an emotionally lost soul just like me. I was not really interested in her, although she thought differently because of my letters and my way of treating her. She used to write me that she had recovered the will to live and eat because of me. What happened next was what always happened in my relationships: I found a way to make my partner feel good, giving her everything in my power—either emotional or material—while deep down I still felt empty.

During treatment, I was told that I would not be ready to leave the clinic at the end of my thirty days, and they suggested that I stay at their sober living house. Sober living is a kind of treatment where the patient gradually reintegrates into everyday life but continues to live in a safe space where he or she is subjected to constant anti-doping tests. The idea of being away from my family and more time locked up in this kind of place terrified me. Since the beginning, I was firm in my belief that I would be fine, that what I had learned in those thirty days was enough to leave the world of drugs and that I was ready to return to my family.

I never imagined that five years later I would continue struggling with the same thing. Thanks to my insistence, and to my family who was still not very affected by my addiction and did not have much information on the subject, we made the decision for me to return home to them.

Clarita...We did not have enough knowledge of the world of addiction, and we felt we needed to be supportive of Alex. Originally, they told us he had to stay thirty days in rehab. Three weeks later, I went to family week. We were so ignorant that I was the only one in my family who went. Gerardo and my other sons told me, "You go, learn about it, and tell us everything when you come back."

On that occasion, it was the first time I heard the term "codependency" but did not fully understand it. Learning about addiction was a very difficult process. Right there, I was told that my son was not ready to leave treatment, that he should stay in their halfway house for a few months, and they added, "If you let him get out now and go back home, he will end up dying," something that I did not like hearing at that moment and something that is commonly said in the clinics when the patient does not want to follow the recommendations given to him.

We felt that he could receive the same attention at our home as in a halfway house, where he would continue working his program. I told them we thought it was a good family decision because it was Christmas, and Alex, being so family-oriented, would be better at home near his family. Besides, they told me I had to start learning to practice "tough love," a theory with which I have never agreed. I have always thought that it is best to stay close to an addict and give him support and love when he is in early recovery trying to stay clean.

Maybe I am mistaken. It is rather important to point out that at this point in Alex's addiction, we did not have the knowledge or understanding that halfway houses are safe spaces for the addict when he leaves the clinic. Alex obviously created total drama. He convinced me that a halfway house was not for him. He said that he was going to do everything he needed to do to battle his addiction. They say in AA that the person who wants to recover can do it even under a tree. In our little knowledge of what the process of this illness really was and the fact that the clinic had not managed to engage Alex in his therapeutic process, he continued in his denial, and so did we.

Alex...It was December 24 when I returned home. I ran up the stairs, I entered my parents' room, and felt the need to hug them and tell them how happy I was to be back with them and how ready I was to face life again.

On December 31, six days after leaving treatment, the phenomenon of "craving" flared up. Obsession began, and I started to convince myself that a few lines of coke would not do me much harm.

Under the excuse of going to visit my girlfriend, Maria, the one I had before going to treatment, I left my house in search of a little coke to start the new year as I wanted—drugged. I met my dealer and bought a bag of coke, coconut flavor. Yes, I liked cocaine with different flavors, especially coconut. I remember on the way back I asked God to give me a sign if using was not the best idea. And be careful what you ask for, because it shall be given.

I drove down the street going the wrong way and ran into a police patrol car. They turned on their siren and proceeded to ask me to stop. I quickly hid the bag of coke. They said they were going to impound my car. This could not be happening to me. I was supposedly in another place, visiting Maria, giving her a New Year's hug. If I let them take my car, my parents would find out about this, and everyone would realize what I was really doing that night. But since Mexico is full of corruption, I offered to give them my cell phone if they would let me go. Anyone with a little awareness would take this as the sign I asked God for before, knowing that using was not a good idea. But for an addict like me, this was simply bad luck.

So, I took out the bag of coke and started using on the way back to my house.

Maria...One day, he called me on the phone to tell me he was going to rehab, and he promised me that when he came back we could finally be happy. I remember he called me every weekend to tell me how he was doing. He really wanted to get ahead, and I counted the minutes to when I would have him back. The day he got out, he called me on the phone to tell me that he was in Mexico and that he had been told in the clinic that he had to cut all ties from his past so that he could recover. Even though his decision hurt me, I knew that it was for Alex's own good, so I respected it.

Alex...It was a very uncomfortable New Year's Eve. Everyone congratulated me for being clean and sober, for having gone to treatment. Everyone was proud of me, of my desire to change. They gave me so many hugs that I truly felt the love and affection of my family. In a moment alone with my parents, I remember throwing myself into my father's arms and tearfully telling him how sorry I was for all the damage I had done. I promised I would never again make them suffer this way, and even though what I was saying was from the heart and said in good faith, in my back left pocket there was a bag of cocaine. I was apologizing for something that I was already doing again. That was the first promise regarding my addiction that I quickly broke. I started the new year using like I had before going into treatment, or even more so. But in the eyes of the world, I was clean and sober, and I attended AA meetings constantly high.

CHAPTER IV

Crack: A Different Kind of Drug

"My Name is Crack"

I destroy homes…I tear families apart.

I take your children…and that is just the start.

I'm more costly than diamonds, more precious than gold.

The sorrow I bring is a sight to behold.

If you need me, remember, I am easily found…

I live all around you…in schools and in town.

I live with the rich…I live with the poor.

I live down the street…maybe even next door!

I am made in such ways…you can shoot me or smoke…

I used to be called "cocaine…or coke"

The sound that I make, when you're inhaling my stench…

Is how my name "Crack" came to be…(perfect sense)

My power is awesome; try me, you'll see…

But if you do, you may never break free.

Just try me once, and I may let you go…

But try me twice, and I'll own your soul.

When "I" possess you, you'll steal and you'll lie.

You'll do what you have to, just to get "high."

The crimes you'll commit, for my narcotic charms…
Will be worth the pleasure you'll feel in your arms, lungs, and nose.
You'll lie to your mother; you'll steal from your dad…
When you see their tears, you should feel sad.
But you will forget your morals…and how you were raised…
I'll be your "conscience"…I'll teach you "my ways."
I'll take kids from parents, and parents from kids.
I turn people from "GOD"…and separate friends.
I'll take everything from you, your looks and your pride.
I'll be with you ALWAYS…right by your side.
You'll give up everything…your family; your home…
Your friends, your money…then you'll be all alone.
I'll take & take; until you have nothing more to give…
When I'm finished with you…you'll be lucky to live.
If you try me, be warned…this is no "game"…
If given the chance…I'll drive you insane!
I'll ravish your body…I'll control your mind…
I'll own you "completely"…your "soul" will be mine!
The nightmares I'll give you, while lying in bed…
The voices you'll hear…from inside your head…
The sweats, the shakes…the "visions" you'll see…
I want you to know…these are ALL "gifts from me."
But then it's too late, and you'll know in your heart…

That you are MINE…and we shall not part…

You'll regret that you tried me…they always do…

But YOU came to ME…Not "I" to you…

You knew this would happen…many times you were told…

But you challenged my "power"…and chose to be "bold."

You could have said "no"…and just walked away…

If you could live that day over…now what would you say?

I will be your "Master"…and you will be my slave...

I will even go with you…when you go to your grave.

Now that you have met me…what will you do?

Will you try me or not? It's all up to you…

I can bring you more misery than words can tell…

Come take my hand…let me lead you to HELL!!!!

—*Anonymous*

In our need to do anything to make this…sensation of well-being last, we try and do things that continue to put us at risk. It is a kind of inertia, like a spiral without return.

Alex…Around March, a friend with whom I got high and I decided to go to Cuernavaca to my grandmother's house. That weekend, we were lucky because it was the anniversary party of a club called Taizz, and we wanted to join a group of our friends that night and party with them, so we proceeded to buy all the necessary things for that trip: lots of cocaine! That was enough. It was all we needed. We arrived on Friday afternoon very high, because along the way we were inhaling several lines of cocaine without caring that I was driving. I will always thank God that in spite of driving under the influence of drugs and alcohol on thousands of occasions, I had the fortune to stay alive and stay out of harm's way during two accidents in which cars were destroyed.

***

Alex always used to think that he had everything under control, that he was smarter than drugs, and that he could regain control over himself and his life anytime. So, he continued on in denial without feeling that he had a real problem.

Gerardo...I think that Alex's main weakness became his lack of analysis. In the beginning of his drug abuse and his journey into this dark world of drugs, he always thought that he had everything under control, but he was never able to achieve that. He never stopped to think about his problem, and he made bad choices, on one hand because he was young, and on the other hand due to his genetics and the disease that was starting to develop in his brain. Perhaps we did not give him enough time to make the right decisions, for example, when he changed from one major to another. I think Clarita and I were more involved in our work problems, and he, with his extraordinary capacity to manipulate, convinced us that everything was fine. Probably neither one of us made the right decisions at the time.

Alex...We spent Friday night getting high and drinking. It was time to change and get ready to go to the nightclub where we would meet with our group of girlfriends. We arrived with our friends, and it was impossible for us to stay there. We were unable to hide the effects of the drugs and the induced paranoia that we were experiencing, so we decided to go back to the house.

That night, I think neither of us was able to sleep. The next morning, we noticed we were running out of cocaine, so we decided to go out into the streets to look for a drug dealer that could sell us more. Finally, we found a person who offered us "rock" or "crack"—cocaine to smoke. My friend and I disregarded it at first, but with the lack of cocaine to inhale, we decided to see how to use this new drug.

I remember the dealer took out a can of soda. He made some holes in the center, put some cigarette ash on top of the holes, and proceeded to put a yellowish stone on top of the can. He put the can in my mouth and instructed me to inhale all the smoke that I could while he set fire to the stone and the ash. He told me to hold the smoke in my lungs for a little bit and then slowly release it. When I did, I remember I started feeling a strong buzz in my head. It was not uncomfortable. I felt totally at peace. All my fears disappeared at once. It was the best rush of adrenaline that I had ever experienced. It was everything that I had ever looked for. I did not need anything else. I finally found what would become my drug of choice. How I wish this had never happened!

During that weekend, we used this substance several more times. We went dancing on Saturday. We got high continually, we drank champagne, we spent a lot of money, and I paid for it all with the credit card that my dad had given me some time earlier.

On the way back from Cuernavaca, I felt so depressed, so disgusted by my behavior. I was in a really bad mood. I was in a deplorable state. I had gone three days without sleeping or eating. Therefore, I took the plastic that I loved so much, tore it to pieces, and I swore never to use drugs again. I think it was two days later that I was back at the American Express office, asking for a replacement for my card.

***

According to the experts, a recurrent user of cocaine or crack can end up having a great tolerance for these substances, and when he gets used to abusing cocaine, it seems like the person is very active or very awake, even though it is only in appearance. When this compulsive use is interrupted, the situation gets complicated because the addict quickly starts to feel withdrawal symptoms. As opposed to the physical withdrawal from alcohol, crack's withdrawal symptoms are more related to behaviors. It can start with depression, anxiety, and agitation, and sometimes it can turn into paranoia.

As the withdrawal progresses, due to lack of serotonin, there is extreme boredom and lack of motivation. When remembering the effects of cocaine or situations associated with this drug, an intense desire or anxiety for using again is in effect, and these associations provoke a new, compulsive abuse of the drug. The most dangerous kind of cocaine is crack, a combination of cocaine and gasoline or sulfuric acid from which a paste is extracted, and when dried, it is smoked in a pipe or crushed to make a cigarette. The cocaine euphoria is usually followed by a deep crash that lasts thirty to sixty minutes or more, where the user feels tired, anxious, and irritated. Using again gives immediate relief from the symptoms, and then it creates a using cycle, avoiding effects that will not be comfortable. Generally, the more euphoria, the worse the consequences of that fall.[9]

Alex...I called my dealer and asked him if he sold crack because I had already made the decision that this would be the only drug that I would be using from now on. I chose the worst of all drugs, but at the time, I didn't know it yet. He told me he did, that in fact he had a very good quality crack that he cooked himself. We agreed to meet at a certain place at a certain time, and that is how my love affair with this substance began. I remember I spent many hours driving and smoking all over Mexico City. I could not stay in one place. I felt all the cars chasing me, that everybody was watching, spying on me, that no place was safe. I used to park the car for the least amount of time necessary to smoke a little, and then I kept on going, feeling terror every time a car was next to me.

I had the "good fortune" that my parents made the decision to go on a trip to Italy. I say this from my addict side because this would give me the chance to get high by myself without any pressure from them.

It was in June or July of 2007 that they left, thinking that I was well. They already knew that I had started drinking alcohol again. Therefore, before they left, they talked with me and told me that this month would be an opportunity to get back on track and decide what it was that I wanted to do with my life. I don't think they knew that once again I was using cocaine, much less that I was already trapped in the world of crack.

I felt sad when my parents left, because in reality, I had not been well for months. The addiction was again starting to take me to dark places, and I needed my parents more than ever. Unfortunately, I never knew how to ask for help; that is one of my biggest defects. My pride always prevented me from having the humility to ask for help when I needed it the most. What I really felt when they left is that they were tired of my behavior and they needed to walk away from me. I felt abandoned. This feeling of abandonment caused a strong feeling of resentment, and this resentment caused anger and rage, and when I felt this, I was giving myself the perfect excuse to get high.

Many times I have wondered what would have happened if I had told my parents that I was using a new form of cocaine called crack, if I had told them that I was afraid, that I didn't want them to leave, that I needed them. Why didn't I do it?

***

Addicts do not tell the truth about their drug use. We lie repeatedly, and we are incredibly inventive with our deceptions and obfuscations, turning and twisting them to fit the situation. We lie, not because we are inherently dishonest people, but because the nature of addiction is such that we have to lie in order to keep using because our bodies literally need the drug to function. That is the fundamental truth about addiction—when "want" becomes "need," truth, honor, integrity, and decency cease to matter. All that matters is the drug.[10]

Alex...While they were away, my parents left some money in the safe so Eduardo could use it for whatever was needed in the house. Like a good addict, I figured out the combination and was able to use that money for the only thing that I needed at that moment—to buy crack and smoke it. My brother, Mauricio, was abroad in Australia. He was on a student architecture exchange program from his university, and Eduardo was very busy with work, his friends, and his girlfriend to realize what was happening with me. Therefore, I was all alone in the house, getting high all day and night.

I did not eat, I did not sleep, and my mental and physical condition got worse as days passed. I remember I began to have a chronic cough. I didn't stop coughing. I knew it was a side effect of the drug use. However, in front of my nanny, Juanita, who was in charge of taking care of Eduardo and me, I pretended to be very ill. I even went to see a doctor, who took an x-ray of my lungs. He told me I didn't have any problems to worry about, that my lungs looked like they were in good shape. This news only lessened my fear of continuing to do drugs. I felt I was given a green light to keep on smoking. I was doing the same thing that I mentioned before—living to use drugs and using drugs to live.

Juanita...He was smoking a lot of crack because he had a lot of hallucinations, and he was very paranoid. At night, he would call me and tell me, "Juanita, please come here because I feel like they're spying on me. Someone is outside the window." I would try to calm him down. He had a lot of hallucinations. I would tell him, "Go back to sleep. There is no one here," but I had to check and look out the window so he could feel more at peace. Then, the following day, I would find all his clothes covering the edge of his door and windows so nobody would see through those small spaces. After hours of heavy drug use, he felt like he was being watched. I would also find traces of cocaine on the floor, and I would ask, "What is this?" But he would never answer me.

Alex...During that time, the only girl I kept dating was Samantha because, as I said before, she was the only person who knew I smoked crack, and she was okay with it. I loved to have sex with her when I was smoking crack, even though I was very rarely satisfied during sex. My years with cocaine didn't allow it.

Time passed, and it was time for my parents to come back to Mexico. When they saw me, they noticed I was in bad shape, but I think all of us tried to ignore it; neither they nor I wanted to admit the seriousness of my illness.

As time went by, my addiction kept growing. I started lying and stealing again from my parents, behaving very badly, and I became an aggressive person with little tolerance, and I was operating completely outside of reality. We kept going on vacations to Ixtapa, where I did not care about the life I used to like—spending the day at the beach or on the boat looking for girls with whom to go out at night. Now what I liked was to steal money or whatever I could get my hands on, go downtown to buy crack, and go back home to spend the day smoking in the bathroom. It became really uncomfortable. It was difficult for me to look at any member of my family in the eye. I felt watched constantly. I felt they knew what I was doing, but my family stayed quiet. Nobody said anything, and all of us were living in total denial.

Clarita...When we came back from our trip, we found him in bad shape, but it took us a while to understand the severity of the problem. We went to Ixtapa, and even though Alex was not the same, his attitude had changed radically. He managed to lie to us, and he tried to coexist with us. The only one who truly realized what was happening was Mauricio, who would say, "Didn't you see his eyes? Didn't you realize how his jaw was locked when he tried to speak?"

A New Opportunity

Alex...It was a day in September, back home in Mexico, when my dad asked me if I wanted to talk to him. We sat in the family room, and we started talking. I remember being there, sitting in front of him, feeling completely empty. I could not find words to express myself; I could not tell him what I felt, because I did not even have the ability to acknowledge my feelings. I was present in my body and absent in my mind. The only thing that was going through my mind was, "When will I use again?" However, my dad started talking, started trying to understand what I was going through. He gave me a lot of comfort; he was able to connect with my feelings better than me.

***

In his book, Addiction, *Kevin McCauley refers to what AA calls a "clarity moment." Craving subsides for a moment. Consciousness clears a little. The addict suddenly sees himself as others see him. A window of opportunity has opened, but it won't be open for long. Soon the stress will return and craving will resume. However, in this moment, his defenses are down, and it is the chance for the addict to accept any treatment.*

Alex...Let's just say that my dad guessed what I was feeling, and for the first time in a long time, I felt at peace. I trusted him. I felt he understood me. I felt loved, and I think these were the things that helped me summon the strength to ask for help once more. I remember that evening. My parents and I spent it searching on the computer for a rehabilitation center that had the best treatment for me. We spoke with lots of people that knew about the topic who could guide us. At the end of the night, we ended up with the best three options for me. One was in Utah. This was the one my mom liked the best, and two more were in Malibu, California. These three were rated as some of the best clinics in the world.

We called one of the clinics in California to ask for information. They told us about their program. They did not work with the AA 12 steps, and that grabbed my attention because of the experience that I'd had in the previous clinic. After talking to them, I realized it was not for me. Although it had a great program, they focused a lot on individual therapy and in finding the root of my addiction. The cost was super high, an insane amount for us for only thirty days, the duration of the program. Nevertheless, my parents wanted the best for me, and they were willing to do all that was necessary. We also called another clinic named Promises, and even though they did work with the 12-step program, they focused on individual and group therapy. In addition, their way of talking and paying attention to us seemed much more centered.

My Life in Promises

Alex...One day later, we had already paid for the treatment, and I was on my way to Los Angeles International Airport where personnel from Promises would pick me up to bring me to the clinic. I arrived there in August and stayed there until October. Promises, as I mentioned before, has a very good and integrated addiction therapy program. It is the place where several celebrities have gone for rehab. Of course, that was very interesting to me and motivated me to want to attend the program.

Upon my arrival, I fell in love with the place immediately. The treatment and the love I felt from all the personnel made me feel at home, and I knew this was the right place for my recovery. I went through several interviews—with the director, then with two interns who asked me questions about my history of abuse. After that, I went to see the psychiatric team so they could decide whether or not I would need medications, and lastly, I saw the head doctor. I remember he asked me why I was there, to which I replied, "Because this is the best clinic in the world." His answer was not what I expected. He said, "The one who wants to heal can cure himself even under a tree." Those words stopped me short and made me realize that my recovery was going to be my responsibility and was not in the hands of "the best clinic in the world."

Here, I started once again an extensive process of introspection that made me acknowledge what life in sobriety was. I passed the mandatory detox days, and I think it was on my second day when I noticed another person in detox who looked really ill. He didn't stop shaking, sweating. He looked really old. He was an actor in countless movies. It was unbelievable to me, to feel that I was recovering with such important and famous people. It made my addict personality and me feel like we were in the right place and happy with this treatment.

After detox, I was introduced to my therapist, a young and intelligent woman—and I can't help it—beautiful. It was going to be difficult to be able to concentrate on my problems having in front of me such an attractive woman as my therapist. I remember my first session I walked in with a great big smile. She quickly asked me why I was smiling. I told that I was very happy to be there, and she said, "Are you saying that you have been abusing drugs for four years, that you have lost girlfriends, that you have had multiple problems, that you don't know how to live life as it is, that you have lost the trust of your parents, that you have stolen their peace of mind and their dreams, and today you are happy to be in a rehab clinic?"

I felt like somebody had just hit me with a reality check, and for the first time I was sad and confused. She told me not to worry, that that was the reason why I was there, to work with the sadness and be able to recover. That is how my treatment started at Promises.

Clarita...The way that Promises engaged Alex in his treatment seemed fundamental to me. The therapist managed to get Alejandro focused and with clarity helped him get in touch with his feelings and emotions.

Alex...We attended Alcoholics Anonymous and Narcotics Anonymous—AA and NA—meetings every night outside of the clinic, something I liked a lot. The meetings were interesting. The goal was to find the one meeting we felt we could identify with and commit to. That way, I started to like life inside the program. After one week, a new patient arrived. He was a former football player and author. He and I started a very good friendship, but as time passed—and as is usual in my life—the euphoria of what I was living began to fade, and boredom started to emerge.

Moreover, as they say, idleness is the devil's workshop. I was missing what I had always looked for in my life—a partner—and I began to ask God in my daily prayer to send someone with whom I could enjoy this new life. Then again, careful what you wish for, because it shall be given.

Helen

Alex...After a couple of days, a new patient named Helen Marie arrived, an eighteen-year-old girl who was the most beautiful thing I had seen in my life. Her skin was white, and she had delicate features, spectacular green eyes, and a body that could make any model jealous. I fell in love instantly. And this is how my interest in my recovery took a back seat. Now the most important thing in my life was winning over Helen.

Helen...When I met Alex, I was recovering from my nights that I spent drinking alcohol. I was really tired and really resentful because my parents had sent me to a rehab clinic, but there was something in Alex that made me feel immediately that everything was going to be all right and that I was in the right place. I was instantly captivated by his smile.

Alex...It was not long before I started noticing that she was attracted to me, too. She gave me peculiar looks, always smiling at me, and we started having some physical contact little by little—a little hug, a small wink, or sometimes we held hands just for a few seconds. Helen was what I had always wanted in a woman, and it was really a dream come true to have found her at this place.

After thirty days, they recommended that I move on to phase two of the program. In this phase, you could have more freedom, you chose which groups and what meetings you wanted to attend, you could have a car, and you lived in a house separate from the clinic. This time, I loved the suggestion of staying one more month in treatment to complete phase two, because not only was I enjoying the program and my sobriety, but also this would give me the opportunity to continue seeing Helen. Of course, I made the decision to attend all of the therapies for the simple fact that Helen, who was still in phase one of the program, would have to attend all of these groups. That way, we could continue our romance. I felt like a naughty kid expecting not to be caught.

This kind of adrenaline rush gave me the drive I needed for my recovery. The famous Malibu fires happened just a few miles away from the clinic. Malibu's mountain had gone up in flames, and the owner of Promises made the decision to move us to a hotel for a few days in Marina del Rey. We got to the hotel, and we were assigned a room where we would spend the night. I remember calling the spa and setting up an appointment for a massage. Those were the things that went through my mind, that I deserved a massage for the stress I was going through.

The price did not matter. I knew it would be charged on my dad's account and he would never say anything. Like always, the value of money did not exist for me.

When I finished my massage, I ran into Helen in the elevator and asked her if she wanted to take a dip in the pool and the Jacuzzi with me. She said yes. I remember that night as something special. Both of us really wanted to kiss, to hug, to take advantage of this unbelievable opportunity to demonstrate the attraction we had for each other. The night was on our side. The pool was lit with a light-blue light, and you could see a beautiful moon reflected in the pool. Nevertheless, Helen resisted. She resisted in spite of the desire that she had to be with me, and she resisted because she was with someone and didn't want to be unfaithful. We felt so close to one another, but we did not take advantage of the situation. We let it pass. Helen respected her partner and did not want to fall into my arms.

The next day, we moved to another hotel nearby that was cheaper. I imagine that paying for the night in the first one for thirty people was not something the owner of Promises was willing to do for a three or four more nights. But it was here, in the Jacuzzi of the second hotel, where Helen and I could not resist the passion we felt for each other. We kissed for the first time, and once we did, we didn't stop. We took advantage of every moment to kiss, to touch. There was a really special chemistry between us. I felt like the king of the world after having experienced such special moments with Helen.

Helen...During our time in rehab, a fire broke out close to the facility, and we were evacuated to a hotel in Los Angeles. At night, after our group meetings, we decided to go down to the Jacuzzi to relax. We talked about how we felt about each other and how we were so grateful that our newfound sobriety and being in this place brought us together. This was where I thought I could spend the rest of my life with this person.

Alex...After a couple of days, we went back to the clinic. Like I mentioned, I was in phase two of the program where I could have a car. For me this was impossible because my car was in Mexico. Though my dad had sent me the money to get around without a car, I spent the money on useless things. My friend, the football player, lent me one of his cars. To me, this was like another dream come true. I had it all. I was living in Malibu, California. I had the most beautiful girl I had ever seen in my life by my side, and a spectacular car that boosted my self-esteem. I was on top of the world, as they say. Not even for a second did I think about using cocaine, at least not at that moment, when the euphoria was strong enough not to let my illness get inside me.

Clarita...During this time, we did not have the experience that would come later on, where Alex would leave treatment after just a few hours or days. At least this time, this stint in rehab allowed us to have some peace and comfort knowing that Alex was in treatment getting better. We thought, "Alex is in treatment. We are doing the right thing for him and his recovery." We had not yet understood the severity of his disease.

After Alex's third week in Promises, we were invited to a family therapy session where all the family members got to attend, and after that, we had a private session with the family therapist. Alex, of course, told us that it was not necessary to go to the group therapy session. Alex's attitude made us think that he did not fully understand what was happening to him and the gravity of the issue. For that reason, we were upset to find out that he was driving a sports car when he came to pick us up at the hotel to go to the session, knowing that it always bothered his dad and I when someone loaned out their cars. That was part of his temperament. He was in total denial that there was a problem and insisted on continuing to live in a fantasy.

In our denial of what was happening, we thought it was not necessary to go to the group therapy, and we only went to our appointment with his family therapist. Today, I still remember something a doctor once told me: "Parents think that after treatment, we are going to return their loved one washed, starched, and ironed," without understanding that true recovery was going to happen when Alejandro worked with all his thoughts, emotions, and feelings of inadequacy. And we as a family should also do our inner work and go to our own therapy to make changes in the negative patterns that were starting to develop in our family dynamics.

Alex...I was very into my program. I attended all the meetings every night, and I had a sponsor. All was going well, and my family and I thought I had reached the end of my addiction. If somebody had told us that we had just begun, we would have never believed them. Helen finished phase one of her treatment, and her parents did not want her to stay for phase two. They had gotten her into a sober living house exclusively for women in La Jolla, California, where she would continue her treatment for three more months. Helen thought that this would be the end of our relationship because I would stay in Malibu and soon I would go back to Mexico. Nevertheless, I promised that I would find a way to be together. I still had fifteen more days in phase two of Promises.

I remember the day she left. It was very painful to say good-bye to her, but I knew that it wasn't the end of our relationship. I was so happy being with her that I would do anything to continue it. During this time, we stayed in touch on the Internet and through phone calls. I even got a pass to spend a weekend with her in San Diego. However, the pass had certain restrictions: I would have to stay at Helen's house, in spite of her not being there, because she was in her sober living house that I already mentioned. I had met her parents during the family Saturdays at Promises and had made friends with them. They welcomed me with open arms into their home.

One day, I went to San Diego to visit her; she was allowed to spend the day with me. We went to her house. Her parents were not there, and I remember it was then that we had sex for the first time. I still remember the moment vividly, full of emotion, nerves, and adrenaline. Being with Helen was wonderful. We had a good weekend together, and then I had to go back to Promises.

The following weekend, my friend that I mentioned invited me to a Halloween party in a famous mansion, one of the most sought after in the world. I remember we went to a store to buy our costumes. He went dressed up as a soccer player from the Barcelona team and me as a soccer player from the Brazilian team. We were joined by two more friends from Promises, who were grandchildren of a famous German general in World War II. Like I said, I was with famous people, right where my ego wanted me to be. We arrived at the party, and it was something spectacular. However, since we were still patients at Promises, we had to be back at 12:30 a.m. We only spent an hour at the party. Anyway, it was a moment that I can't let pass without mentioning, another experience that made me feel important and special.

Letter from Promises Therapist: November 16, 2007

Clarita,

I wanted to check in with you before Alex's discharge this coming Monday, November 26, and provide you with the recommendations for his discharge and the referrals that I have provided for him. I have recommended that Alex transition into a sober living house. He has reported that he will transition into sober living. I have recommended that he transition into outpatient for a minimum of 3 months. He recently informed me that he is not accepting this recommendation. This recommendation was provided to assure that he will continue his substance abuse treatment, provide him with an individual therapist, anchor him to a recovery community, and provide a place for him to be drug tested on a regular basis. Instead, Alex informed me that he was willing to engage in individual psychotherapy with a private practitioner, and he was given names of a few referrals. Likely, he will only see this practitioner one time a week, which is significantly less than the 5-day IOP program would provide. I have also recommended that Alex attend daily 12-step meetings and continue to work with his sponsor on the 12 steps. I would highly encourage you and your husband to also attend Al-Anon meetings as a means to support yourself through this process. Alex indicated that he will continue to attend the gym and engage in other sporting activities. Until Alex either enrolls in school or gets a job, I highly recommend that Alex secure some commitments at 12-step meetings or begin some volunteer work.

Alex has been provided with the names of individual therapists and psychiatrists for the West Los Angeles area. He was also provided with referrals in Mexico should he decide to return. I have attached a copy of the referral list for you to view as well.

Alex has done a significant amount of work on his recovery since his admission to Promises. He has been a delightful addition to the community, and I have very much enjoyed working with him. It was also a great pleasure to meet you and your family as well. I strongly encourage Alex to continue to engage in treatment, on some level, and for you to consider future family work with Alex. If you have any additional questions or concerns, please do not hesitate to contact the family therapist or me.

Take care, and Happy Holidays!

J.C., Psy.D.

Alex...The end of my stay at Promises arrived, and it was time to move on to the next stage. I had two options. The first one was to go back to Mexico with my family and the second was to go to a halfway house in Santa Monica, California. I, of course, chose the second, which I moved into in November. This was the option that would let me keep living the life that until now had been making me happy, and of course it was the only way to keep seeing Helen. The house was really nice, and I felt very happy during my stay. I spent my days driving through Los Angeles in the Mercedes that my friend had loaned me. I woke up every morning to run. I went to the gym, attended my meetings, chatted with my sponsor, and of course, looked forward to the weekend to be able to visit Helen.

Letter from the Owner of the Sober Living House: November 29, 2007

Dear Clarita,

I wanted to take a moment to inform you of Alex's progress. He has been a wonderful addition to our house, and it is always a pleasure to see his smiling face when I get there in the morning. Regarding his recovery, it seems he is taking many positive steps to change his lifestyle. Yesterday, his sponsor came to visit him, and Tom, the house director, mentioned to me that he knows the sponsor and that he is a great guy, as well as an excellent example of how to stay sober and enjoy all of the wonderful things that life has to offer

Alex attends his NA meetings every day, and he also gets together on Thursdays with the graduates from Promises. I remember how important it was for me when I finished that program a few years back, being close to all those people. It is very important to form these friendships during the first months of sobriety for support and trust, in the good times and in the bad times. One of the things that I would like to stress more is how we have to prepare ourselves for the difficult moments of life, because we cannot run away from our responsibilities and our feelings. Alex, no doubt, is on the right track, and we all are here to help him overcome the difficult moments and to laugh with him during the good times.

Regards

Alex...This is how I spent the next two months of my life. I started to feel the need to be closer to Helen and began to convince my parents to set up an apartment for me in San Diego. December vacation arrived, and it was time to go back to Mexico to spend the holidays with my family. Before going back to Mexico, my friend from Promises asked me for his car, and it was time to give it back. I knew this moment would come eventually.

I went directly to Ixtapa, where I would spend Christmas with my family. We had a great vacation. Our time together was pretty peaceful, and we had great conversations. We made the decision to send my car to Tijuana so that after my stay in Ixtapa I would fly there, pick it up, and cross the border back to Los Angeles. This way, I could have a car to get around in, go to my meetings, my gym, keep up my daily routine, and occasionally go visit Helen without having to borrow a car.

On December 30, I traveled to Tijuana, because on December 31 I could pick up my car and cross the border to San Diego to spend a few days with Helen, including New Year's. I had gone several days without attending my support meetings, and by the time I got to Tijuana, I began to feel the need to use.

Helen...Day by day, my relationship with recovery grew almost as much as my relationship with Alex. They say a lot in the program that things happen for a reason, and I truly believed that God put me in that program at that time to meet Alex. I fell in love with him almost instantly. We both suffered from addiction and found comfort in one another, knowing that this was a struggle we didn't have to go through alone. Through this relationship, I found that for me, sobriety was a beautiful, peaceful thing. I knew that in order for things to stay almost perfect in my life, I would have to stay sober.

I Use Again

Alex...It is impressive how everything in my life was going well. I had a partner with whom I was really happy, I had just spent some incredible times with my family, and my car had been sent from Mexico to Tijuana for me so that I did not need anything. I had been sober and clean for over three months, but in spite of this, at the moment a thought or craving started, I did not do anything to make it go away. I simply let it be, and little by little, it grew until it was impossible to ignore. I convinced myself, as I always do, that getting high that night wouldn't affect anybody, that nobody would know. Anyway, they would not do drug testing until six or seven days after I went back to my halfway house, enough time so that my body would rid itself of the substance, and nobody would realize I had used again.

Therefore, I went downstairs to the entrance of the hotel where I was staying and asked a taxi driver if he knew where to buy crack. He told me yes, and he was willing to get it for me. I gave him the money and sat in the lobby, waiting for him to come back. Thirty minutes later, he came back with some crack, enough to spend a good night smoking and be ready the following day to pick up my car and get back to my normal life, my recovery life in Santa Monica.

Before using, I called Helen to tell her that we would be together again soon. She was very happy with the news. I also called my parents to tell them I had ordered room service and that after dinner I would be ready to sleep. They sounded very happy and proud of me. As soon as I hung up the phone, I felt free from all responsibility, and I lit up some crack. This is how I spent the night. Until approximately three or four in the morning, I did not stop smoking.

I woke up very tired after a very unpleasant night, where once again I felt full of guilt. I failed again, and unfortunately, it was a weight on my shoulders that I could not get rid of until later, when I told my loved ones what had happened. But for now, I would have to live with the secret, a secret that later was one of the reasons why I relapsed.

The next day, I went to pick up my car. I crossed the border and quickly went to the sober living house where Helen was. I remember that we were so happy and anxious to see each other. We gave each other a long hug. We didn't want to let go. I was staying in a hotel in La Jolla that was near Helen's house. We drove quickly to the hotel to have more time for intimacy. That night was New Year's Eve. It was a completely different experience from previous years. This time, I spent it surrounded by people who were clean and sober…and for the first time in my life, away from my family.

It was the beginning of 2008. I spent approximately five more days with Helen before going back to my sober living house in Santa Monica. When I went back, everything went back to normal, as if I had never used a few days earlier. I went back to my AA and NA meetings, I kept seeing my sponsor, I was working my 12-step program, and I kept looking forward to the weekend to be able to drive to San Diego and be with Helen.

Letter from Alex: January 16, 2008

Mom and Dad,

The owner of the halfway house wants me to commit to stay another sixty days here, and in the third month after that, move to an apartment by myself, although I will continue during that month, without paying him anything, coming to the meetings on Mondays, Wednesdays, and Fridays, and he will continue drug testing me. He says that this is the best way to move from a halfway house to an apartment and living on my own. He says this with 17 years of experience behind him. He is trying to get me a volunteer job at least three times a week, and I will find out which classes I can attend. I will also find some kind of job. Anyway, from my perspective, I feel good, and I feel healthy and ready to do a lot more, but like they say in the program, your very best thinking is what brought you here, and really, now it is necessary to follow the direction of people who have much more experience than me. I also want to know your opinion. I understand that it is a lot of money for the rent and all the expenses, but I think that it is something that is going to give us all great results and make us content in the future. I feel that slowly but surely this process I am going through has begun to be rewarding for everyone, especially me.

Alex

***

By now, Alex was really involved in his recovery, listening to all the recommendations, and unfortunately, Helen and her parents started flirting with the idea of Alex moving to San Diego so they could be together. Helen's parents were concerned that if Alex didn't go to San Diego, Helen would leave to go join him.

Clarita...Promises had recommended a period of no less than three months in a sober living house so that later on he could live alone; it is known that if you manage to spend a year clean, you have more possibilities to get ahead. We were very happy because Alex had been clean for four months, and he was in a structured situation. When

Helen's parents and Alex made this proposal, I talked with Gerardo, and it seemed like a good decision because it would be as if Alex were with his own family. I knew Helen's parents, who had promised to take care of him as their own, and he would get involved in the AA program in San Diego.

Today, eight years later, I would have accepted the proposal, but I would have never let Alex live by himself in an apartment. I never thought about all the consequences that this would have. The solution should have been that he moved to a sober living house, similar to the one in Los Angeles. There he would have received the necessary support in the first months of his life in San Diego and where he would have formed a support group like the one he had managed to form in Los Angeles but that he never had in San Diego.

Alex...One day, after coming back from one of my many weekends with Helen, the sober living house owner was waiting for me with all my housemates. He told me he wanted to talk to me. He came at me very aggressively, confronting me. He told me I did not seem to have any interest in my recovery and that the only thing I cared about was Helen, and therefore he was going to forbid the weekend visits for an indefinite period of time. This, of course, got me very angry, and we began to argue very heatedly. The situation became so difficult that I called my parents and told them I did not want to be there a minute longer, that I wanted to move to San Diego. My parents, always concerned about my needs so that I did not relapse, agreed.

Letter from Clarita

Hi Alex,

I am very sorry for what you are going through. As you know, I spoke with the house owner and told him we had already talked with you to make new arrangements, which you were respecting. What has your father and me concerned—and it is not the first time we are telling you this—is that since you are with Helen, much of your time and thoughts are about being with her. You are not living your process; you are living that of a complex relationship.

Now, do not feel that everyone is against you. It is not true, but part of the program and the recovery is to listen to what you are told with an open heart and follow the recommendations. Ours is that you listen to the people that seem to have more experience in these situations and whose only desire is to help you. Listen to them, talk to your group, and if they open another perspective to you, take advantage of it. If you trust in how you are acting and that you are applying all that you have learned, that is good! Do not lose it.

We totally agree and know, even though you do not believe it, that you are going to make mistakes. Neither of us wants you to be a saint, but we do have to pinpoint the fact that you are repeating behavior patterns that are not good. For example, at some point you will have to learn the value of money. Alex, we are not against you or your relationship with this girl. I think I can speak for the whole family when I say that we are very proud of your sobriety! We are, truly, but we are very aware of the efforts you are making, and we see it. Why can't you see that you are not respecting the agreements we made when you came to Mexico? You have not wanted to commit enough to continue your treatment.

Mom

***

Being part of a group and respecting the rules and all the activities that are done as a group foster recovery and commitment, something that Alex was not respecting fully in order to maintain his relationship with Helen.

Clarita...Another reason that we accepted Alex's move to San Diego was the intense fight he had with the owner and his group at the end of his stay at the sober living house. It was a situation that got out of control and could have caused a relapse. When we spoke with him over the phone, we heard the insults directed at him and directed at us, disregarding everything that we were trying to say to calm our son down and contain the situation. The owner even threw all of Alex's possessions out the window and asked him to leave the house. Of course, the following day, the owner regretted his behavior and told Alex he was welcome again. Once more, the circumstances made us act impulsively, and we let him go to San Diego to continue with his recovery. It was like driving with your eyes closed, because if I had known that Alex had relapsed before New Year's, we definitely would have taken him to a sober living house instead of letting him live on his own.

CHAPTER V

The Magical World of Rehab Centers

When we don't feel loved and have a deep emptiness inside us, finding someone to love us will never be a real solution.

—*Gerald G. Jampolsky, M.D.*

***Clarita*...** A very common cliché in the world of addiction treatment centers is that "recovery is not for the one who needs it but for the one who wants it." Under this premise in rehab clinics, when the addict wants to abandon the program, commonly they are told, "If you don't want to stay, go." For me, this is wrong. Who can make a judicious and free decision when they are using? The brain is only focused on getting the next hit. It does not think clearly; it is immersed in the craving. It is difficult for the addict to say, "Yes, I want and need to get sober."

***

There are several ways in which a person ends up in a rehab clinic: by his own decision; because his life is truly already so difficult and his health so deteriorated that he wants to stop using; because he is in a totally hopeless situation where he realizes that he alone won't be able to make it; he is pressured by his family; or because he is already having problems with the law. Then his only options are jail or rehab.

Dr. Kevin McCauley, in his book Addiction, *says, "All addicts want help. Perhaps they may not admit it, or perhaps they ask for some kind of help that is misdirected. For example, "If you want to help me, give me money to buy more drugs. That is what I need." But in the end, they all want help.*

Clarita...My son, Alejandro, wanted to get well. He did not know how to do it, and during his use, he did not have the tools to ask for help. If you gave him the option of getting out of the clinic to go use, he would choose that over staying in rehab and getting sober.

Gerardo...When I think of all the pathways we chose so Alex would follow a treatment, I cannot stop thinking of a lucrative rehab industry for addicts as a marketed product, and I cannot ignore the way that we as societies "create" millions of addicts for later "fixing them." It does not mean that we did not see improvement in Alex, but this is a point that always loomed in my head.

***

Alex entered and got out of different rehab clinics without finding in any of them a place to sow the roots of a lasting and earnest recovery. It is he who personally gives us this brave declaration of the facts, the guilt, the desperation of a young man who—in spite of being surrounded by love and privilege—cannot connect with the luminous part of his being. Therefore, he cannot perform the necessary steps toward healing his mind, his body, and his soul.

A Brief Dream Come True

Alex...After leaving the sober living house, my dad offered to move me to San Diego, stay at a hotel, and start looking for an apartment. He told me he and my mom would come to San Diego the following week, and they wanted to see my five best proposals. That week was very exciting in my life. Helen and I went all over the city searching for the place where we knew we would end up living together sooner or later. My favorite place, and where I liked apartments the most, was in downtown San Diego.

When my mom came, we spent two days visiting the apartments I liked. By the end of the week, my dad came and asked me to show him the two apartments we had liked the best. There was a considerable difference in price between the two, and of course I liked the most expensive one better. After seeing both apartments, my dad made the decision to rent the one that I had liked the most. It was in one of the newest and most luxurious buildings in downtown San Diego, or at least, I saw it that way. Helen and I were happy with my dad's decision.

The next day, we measured my new apartment and went searching for furniture. I remember the excitement I was feeling in those moments. Nothing bad was going through my head; it was all feelings of happiness. We found furniture that I liked, and my dad bought me everything I needed. We spent two days decorating with all kinds of accessories. It did not seem at all like I had just left a rehab clinic three months earlier.

Clarita...In his mind, Alex was very excited in his new home. Having a small, furnished apartment was like getting back to the nest, like recreating the security of home but at a distance. Everything he needed and everything that he acquired were symbols that he was living like a normal person. In his letters he wrote, "Mom, I clean all day. I have the apartment shining." He wanted to look good in front of me.

Alex...My parents were celebrating my sobriety with me and made me see that, throughout this entire experience, they were proud, and that once again they would have some trust in me. The apartment was all set. It was really nice. It was another dream come true. My parents always had the capacity to make my dreams a reality. They wished me all the luck in the world. They gave me a debit card again where they would deposit a monthly allowance. They left me with absolutely all the necessary things to continue with my life in recovery, and they went back to Mexico.

Clarita...After he arrived in San Diego, Alex stayed with Helen's parents while Gerardo and I traveled to San Diego to look for an apartment for him so he would start living on his own for the first time. This was one of the recommendations from the therapists; Alex needed to learn how to be responsible for his own recovery and self-care.

Alex thought everything seemed wonderful when he was fine. Everything was beautiful and satisfying, and perhaps having all those "pretty things" was like feeling healthy again. The apartment was very small, but for him it was a great achievement and obviously a new adventure. We supported him, even though we had the healthy concern that his self-esteem depended too much on external things. We felt he did not want to change his lifestyle—the way he dressed, where he went, and you could see by his actions that he was not humble. We did not notice him wanting to make important changes. We wanted to hear from him, "I can live my life wherever I am and not be concerned about shallow things." We couldn't see that, for Alex, the place where he stayed was very important because it gave him feelings of security and normalcy, besides knowing that he had regained our trust. Reassuring us was very important to him; he did not want to see us suffering. Today, I realize how fear and anger prevented me from seeing all of this.

Alex...A little later, Helen finally left her treatment and her sober living house and quickly moved in with me. We lived a really nice life. We'd wake up, and I'd make breakfast for her. I always liked cooking. We'd spend the day walking through the streets of San Diego, we went to restaurants for lunch, played tennis, exercised together, and attended several meetings together. We focused on our own programs, and neither of us got involved in the other's recovery. We were doing all the necessary things so that our relationship worked, and it went like that for the next several months.

A few months went by. Supposedly I was six months clean and sober, and I was about to receive my six-month chip. We went to a meeting at the McDonald Center in La Jolla, California, a place that we went to every Wednesday. I have to remind you that I had already used on December 30, so it was a lie that I had been clean and sober for six months, but unfortunately, I could not tell anyone. There was, according to me, a lot to lose. The moment to receive the six-month chip came, and I got up, very happy to receive it. I went up to the podium and talked about how proud I was of my sobriety, of the difficult moments, of how— by following the program—I had accomplished this goal and all the dreams I had for my future. I lied to everyone, especially to myself.

***

The two most distinctive features of addiction are lying about the addictive behavior and continued addictive behavior after it has caused problems. Addicts lie, and they relapse to alcohol and drug use, despite their efforts to stop and despite the significant problems that result from their drug use. By the same token, recovery is identified by honesty about the addictive behavior and by abstinence from the addictive behavior.[11]

Clarita...Alex lied to himself. This lie put his sobriety at risk. In the end, the only one affected by this lack of honesty was himself.

Helen...Alex, although he did stay connected with some of the people from recovery and went to meetings with me, he never really built his own community in San Diego that he could rely on. I also went to school, and Alex did not work or go to school, so I think looking back, he had too much time on his hands. But still I loved him and trusted him so much that I did not think too much about it when things started not adding up. There were days when he would tell me he was somewhere, and as I was pulling into the apartment garage, I would see him driving out, getting caught in his lies.

A Dangerous Visit to Mexico

Alex...April 19 was coming up, the day that my brother would get married, and I was going back to Mexico to attend the wedding. It would be the first time in six months that I would go back to my house in Mexico City. I had a really good time during my stay. I was comfortable with my sobriety, so I told my family that while I was in Mexico, I was not going to attend meetings; my recovery, according to me, was in San Diego.

I had been warned to be careful, that recovery must follow us any place we go, a reason why there are AA and NA meetings around the world, always present to give the stability and the support needed, but I felt differently. I thought that the same rules for all addicts in a recovery program did not apply to me.

Helen would not arrive until several days later; she would be my date at my brother's wedding. After the first few days in Mexico, I decided to go to the American Embassy to renew my visa that was still valid until November of that year. But I thought that as long as I was in Mexico and with the time to do it, it was a good opportunity to get it for another ten years and take the weight off my shoulders.

I arrived at the embassy, and at the time of my interview, I mentioned to the American consul that I had been living in the U.S. for several months, that I had a girlfriend, an apartment in San Diego that I had come back to Mexico exclusively for my brother's wedding, and that I would go back there soon. I did not realize that everything I told him was all the information he needed to cancel my visa and refuse to give me a new one. I felt like a bucket of ice water had been dumped on my head when he denied it. I felt that I was being taken away from all the things I had built—my recovery, my apartment, and especially Helen. I left the embassy and called my parents, giving them the terrible news. We were all really concerned because we understood the severity of the issue. For me, being far away from my recovery and Helen could be enough reason to fall back into the abyss of my addiction.

A few days later, when I realized that nothing, not even my dad's contacts, would get me my visa issued, I felt depressed and got high again. Helen had not even arrived in Mexico yet. My brother's wedding had not taken place yet, either, and I was secretly using again without mentioning anything to anyone.

Helen arrived in Mexico a day before my brother's wedding. The next day, when I saw Helen in her dress looking so beautiful, I fell in love with her even more. She looked really spectacular. We had an incredible time at the wedding, even though I admit that I was jealous of my family and friends when I saw them drinking and having a nicer time than the one Helen and I were having—or so I thought.

The next few days are a little blurry. I remember that Helen and I toured Mexico City where I showed her different, beautiful sites, but I was also getting high. I would hide in the bathroom to use, and I remember our nights were not as wonderful as we had both expected them to be because I was stoned.

The time to go back to San Diego with Helen arrived, but I was still without a visa. She left by herself, feeling very sad, and that stressed me out so much that my obsession with getting high grew. I would continue getting high for several months. My parents learned about it, and of course the only thing we wanted was to find a way for me to go back to the United States so that I could continue with my recovery. We all prayed for that to happen.

I applied to several universities in San Diego. My only chance at the time to go back to the States was with a student visa; the tourist visa had been denied on three different occasions while I was in Mexico. I think it was about two months after I arrived for my brother's wedding that I was granted my student visa, and with it, the opportunities to not only get back to San Diego but to also continue with my studies and have something to do back there.

I was once again in my apartment with Helen. She was happy that I came back, and we continued the life we had, except this time my addiction was in full force, and I needed help to stop using. It did not take long before I started using heavily in San Diego. I stopped going to my meetings. I spent my time in the apartment smoking. I left Helen sleeping by herself several times while I got high in the bathroom. I began to push her aside. I caused her a lot of grief and suffering, and she was incredibly sad. Therefore, we decided I should get myself into rehab again.

From McDonald Center to The Landing

Alex...I was admitted into the McDonald Center, where I would go through an inpatient program with the goal of stopping the addiction cycle that I had started in Mexico. I had not been admitted twenty-four hours when I convinced myself that I did not want to be there. I did not like the clinic at all; it made me feel like I was at a hospital instead of a treatment center.

Clarita...Helen's mother called me to let me know that Alex was using again. We went once again to San Diego, spending several days visiting treatment centers so Alex could go back into rehab. Alex decided to stay at the McDonald Center, a place he knew well because he and Helen attended meetings there, and they knew many of the therapists. We did the paperwork for his admission, left him there, and that same night returned to Mexico. A few hours later, after we landed, I got a call telling me he had left treatment.

Then, Helen took him to The Landing, another clinic we had visited during our stay, where he met Kevin McCauley, who would later help Alex on many different occasions.

Alex...My family gave me the opportunity to go to a clinic in Newport Beach, California called The Landing. It was a house on the beach for men only where I would spend the next thirty days of my recovery. Helen took me there and told me she was going to wait for as long as it took for me to come back clean and sober, something that motivated me to go on.

I began feeling good again, going to meetings, to the gym, and spending time with people inside the program. But I also began to realize that I could manipulate one of my advisors to give me money during my stay, and this is how I started working on a plan to leave with enough money to be able to get high the second I got out.

During my stay, I pretended to do all the necessary work to be able to go back out into the world clean and healthy. But in my thoughts, crack was always present—my party companion, my soul mate, my faithful lover, the one who always accompanied me everywhere I went and never disappointed me. Since I missed using, I did everything that my therapists asked of me, expecting to leave that place and get back together with my drug. At the same time, my advisor and I schemed to get money by telling my parents that I needed to have some very important brain tests done. In the end, we pulled it off. My parents paid for the study, my advisor kept part of the money, and I left after thirty days of treatment with $1000 in my pocket.

Gerardo...When Alex and I talked, we had a lot of conversations about his experiences in the different clinics—*anexos*—and hospitals that he had attended. They never worked for him. With time, he became an expert on these topics, and in his own way, he used the information he obtained to manipulate situations. Nobody could really engage him in his recovery, and he never liked those places. I do believe that rehab helped him in some ways. They did detox him physically, but his disease had already changed his brain chemistry; mentally, his illness continued.

Alex...When my treatment ended, Helen came to pick me up. She was very happy to see me sober again and very excited to restart our life together. But the day I got out, I convinced her that I was not yet ready to spend the night with her. I asked her to give me one more day to feel at ease in my apartment and that the following day she could come back with me. All my planning was so that I would be able to be alone that night and get high using the money I had. And this is how I used again, throwing away the cost of my treatment and my thirty days of sobriety.

I continued getting high for several months. This time, things were getting complicated. Helen began noticing a change in me, and she did not like spending time with me anymore, and I, from the sadness of losing her, got high more often. My parents also began noticing things were not right, but they kept sending me money so that I did not lack anything. Unfortunately, I made bad use of the money. I only used it to buy drugs to satisfy my addiction—not for food or to pay my utilities. I began to pawn things when I did not have money, like my cell phone, computer, belts, watches, and when I ran out of things, I started to pawn Helen's stuff. I mean, I began to steal from my girlfriend, my partner. All her jewelry, her camera, and a lot of other things. But Helen was so kind that she kept trying to help me. She overlooked what I was doing with the illusion that someday I would make it and be clean and sober again.

Helen...Things started going missing. He started to get skinny and unhealthy looking, and then he came clean to me and said that he had relapsed. I remember feeling shocked and anxious. I could not understand that with how perfect our life was and how much I loved him, how he could relapse, especially since I knew in my head that if I relapsed, I would lose everything, including probably him, and I could not bear that thought. He told me he would stay sober and go to meetings. I will never know if there was a time that he ever stopped, but not too long after that, I came home and there was tape around the air vent, and our TV was missing. Then my camera went missing, then my purse and jewelry.

New Year's Celebration in Ixtapa

Alex...December arrived, and with it was the opportunity to go back to Mexico to see my family. I went back to Ixtapa and was getting high almost every day. I snuck out at night, and during the day I made up excuses to get away—like that I was going to run at the beach—to be able to go and "connect" some crack and then smoke at night in my room. I would go down to the condominium administrative offices to ask for money from my parents' account, telling them my parents had authorized it.

Clarita...We thought that he was still clean after his thirty days of treatment. When he got out of The Landing, I made arrangements from Mexico so he would continue his treatment in an outpatient program in San Diego. Alex attended punctually and lied to all the therapists, saying that he was clean and was really into his recovery. They recommended that Alex stay in treatment over the holiday because he was at serious risk of relapsing if he were in a stressful situation, such as coming back to Mexico. But, as usual, because he was already using without any of us knowing, he manipulated everyone and came back to Mexico where he returned to his old patterns of using.

Alex...Helen was invited to spend New Year's in Ixtapa with us, and I think it was December 28 when she arrived. I managed not to use for two days while she was with me, but on December 31, the obsession was too strong, and I had to get out of the house to smoke crack. I remember it was like nine in the morning when I kissed Helen and told her I was going for a run, that I would be back later so we could have breakfast together.

But this time, things did not go my way. I decided to smoke on my way back home, and the moment I started using, I became very paranoid and scared of going back and having everyone see me high, so I did not come back until much later. For most of the day, my family and Helen were scared to death not knowing where I was and fearing the worst. They called the police so they would look for me, canceled the New Year's party they were going to have, and there was even a moment when they thought the worst: that I had committed suicide or that someone had killed me.

It wasn't until nine p.m., twelve hours after I disappeared, that I went back to my house, simply because I did not have any more money or drugs and did not have a place to go. When I walked in the house, I immediately felt the tension. Helen did not stop crying. Her face was white with fear, along with the faces of my parents and siblings. And I arrived with my paranoid skepticism, as if nothing had happened. I apologized for having scared them and promised everyone it would not happen again. I asked for an opportunity to demonstrate that this one had been the last one. I also asked Helen to forgive me, and she, with her great love for me, accepted my apology.

The time to hug each other at midnight arrived, and everybody was nice enough to pretend nothing had happened. They hugged me and expressed words of hope. They made me feel again like they loved me and trusted in my recovery. We stayed a few more days in Ixtapa, and I kept finding ways to get high.

Live to Use and Use to Live

Alex...I still cannot understand what it is that made me continue using. I was full of such strong denial. I felt disillusioned and disconnected. My inner self felt the emptiness. It became bigger and more profound over time. It was as if I were digging a hole deeper and deeper. Helen and I went back to San Diego, and the nightmare went on. I went back to the cycle of "live to use and use to live." I could not stop, and over time I got into more and more trouble—trouble that I did not want to face—so I hid under the blanket of my addiction.

***

At this point, Alex found himself in the spiral of addiction where it seemed like he had reached the point of no return. This gives the addict the sensation that his existence cannot happen without using drugs. The problems snowball, making the addict wish that he could submerge himself in his addiction forever because the problems of life seem unsolvable.

Alex...Back in San Diego, I was again pawning all my stuff. I kept misusing my credit cards. I even started stealing from Helen and her parents. And because they cared so much about me, they made the decision to call my parents and tell them what was happening. I was already so far gone from reality that I did not care about anything. I did not go to meetings, I did not see my sponsor, I had abandoned Helen, leaving her completely alone, and even though I could see her sadness and pain, I could not stop. Once more, crack had control over me.

Helen decided to pack her things and move back in with her parents. Again, my addiction cost me the woman that I loved so much. I was alone in my apartment, and of course I continued my drug use, which escalated each day. By this time, I had pawned my television, my computer, and everything else that I had.

One More Time to the Rescue

Alex...My parents decided to fly to San Diego to help me. When they entered my apartment, I could see the sadness on their faces when they saw that everything was missing and that their son was in a deplorable condition. But their great love gave them the strength to keep on helping me. We went to the pawnshop and got back all of my stuff and Helen's. I gave Helen her belongings, and my parents also gave me money to pay her and her parents for all the things I had stolen. Once again, my parents had rescued me even though I didn't deserve it.

One day, while talking with my parents in my apartment, my mom left her purse unguarded, and I took her credit card. That, night I withdrew money several times in order to keep getting high. They arrived in San Diego with all the hope of helping me, wanting to spend time with me, but I constantly pushed them aside, asking for space—the necessary space to get high.

We did not know what to do anymore—whether I should go back to Mexico or continue trying to get clean here in San Diego. I told my parents about Dr. Kevin McCauley, who had all the expertise on the topic of addiction. I met Kevin when he gave a talk at the Newport center about the importance of the first year of recovery. I told them that he had a sober living house. The house was in Sandy, Utah. My parents talked with Kevin, and he decided to accept me into his new house. I would be their first patient. Helen swore to my parents and me that she would wait for me, that I should go and recover in Utah, and that she would be willing to get back together if I was willing to do everything necessary for my recovery.

LeMont Michel: A New Attempt in Utah

Alex...And that's how I drove a car with Helen by my side and we went to Utah. Along the way, we made a stop in Las Vegas where my parents were resting after packing up all of my belongings and cleaning up my apartment in San Diego—with much sadness—leaving everything in storage, waiting for my return. Still in Vegas, my parents treated me as if nothing had happened. They treated Helen and me to a show at the Wynn, something I really did not deserve, but as always, they were looking for ways to motivate me and make me feel good.

Clarita...Perhaps throughout this whole process, the negative aspect of our family dynamic was that it was hard for us to set healthy boundaries, and the lines became very confusing. We kept sending Alex money and rescuing him from many situations, which allowed him to get away with things instead of taking responsibility. Gerardo and I supported him and conceded many things, thinking that this would help with Alex's self-esteem. Everything was done out of deep love, and probably in the process we made mistakes. Even though the outcome could have been the same, we continuously looked for strategies to help him.

Alex...I did not feel deserving of anything at these times. I felt very ashamed for everything that had happened, and something inside me told me that Helen was already so distant that maybe I would never get her back, but I wanted to leave her with a nice memory of our relationship so that she did not forget about me while I recovered in Utah.

Helen...Eventually, he got sent to another rehab center in Utah. At this point, I felt like a dry drunk. I had the same tendencies I had when I was drinking—lying to people I cared about, not being honest with myself. I stopped going to meetings and had horrible cravings. But I knew that I had to stay sober. I knew how good life was being sober, but I could not keep putting myself on this crazy roller coaster with Alex.

Before we brought Alex to Utah, I moved out. I had my best friend come over and pack all my things in both of our cars to move. It was the hardest thing I felt I had done in my life up until that point. I hated the idea of leaving him, even if it was for a short amount of time. After I moved out, we eventually took him to Utah. I went out to visit him once, and it just hurt. I loved him so much, but I was so mad at him, so hurt by him, and slowly getting to the point where we couldn't go back.

Alex...I arrived at LeMont Michel, and I was really astounded with how wonderful the place was. It was a really impressive, big house, with everything decorated to perfection. I felt at home, and that calmed down the desperation I felt to get high again.

Time passed, and every day I was feeling better. My daily routine was to spend three or four hours at the gym, go to my individual therapy, and twice a week go to group therapy. Now my new addiction was the gym. I spent lots of time working on my body, and I managed to get the body I had always wanted. I played golf, I went shopping, I spent time with people in the program, and as time passed, everything was getting better.

Clarita...Alex liked the everyday drug testing that was a set rule at LeMont Michel. The testing gave all the patients in the house the freedom to go about their days doing the activities they chose, knowing every day that they would be tested and would have to be clean. It was not to catch them, but to give them the confidence that if something happened with their sobriety, it was going to be addressed immediately, not many weeks later when their use had already escalated into something more dangerous. This turned out to be an efficient boundary, and a rule that structured him, that kept him away from using while he was there.

Letter from Kevin McCauley: March 10, 2009

Hi Clarita,

Wonderful to hear from you! Alex is doing quite well at the house. He volunteers at the food bank, goes to AA meetings regularly, and is seeing his therapists. I am encouraging him to venture out every day at 9:30 a.m. We like the residents to be out of the house by then and stay busy throughout the day. Alex has made some comments about taking Italian lessons, which I think is a great idea.

He had a small incident with a woman who left her sober living house because she didn't want to be there anymore. She wanted to leave and go use. Alex is, after all, very popular with the ladies. He gave her a ride and then brought it to our attention later. He did not initiate any other kind of relationship with this woman, and he has tested negative on all his drug tests.

The staff and residents all met at the house to discuss the risk of linking up with women like that. Alex was amenable to hearing our concerns and quite graciously accepted that he didn't use his best judgment. I'm very encouraged that he, of his own accord, brought the incident to our attention. I think he knew exactly why this behavior was risky and was looking for us to redirect him. It was a good learning experience for us all, and it was very helpful for the other residents to see that we quickly deal with these errors in judgment.

On occasion, there is some friction between Alex and our resident manager, but they seem to be working it out. Part of the way we designed the house is to create these minor interpersonal conflicts to help our residents practice dealing with them in a healthy and constructive fashion. Alex is handling this very well, and it seems that he and the manager have reached a kind of equilibrium with one another. It's important for our staff to remember that Alex is only a few weeks sober and requires a little more patience. Still, I see his symptoms of irritability and frustration and boundary-testing improving. We are trying very hard not to repeat the head-on confrontations that were part of his last sober living experience and at the same time hold him to the rules of the house. Naturally, Alex is a charming young man, and it is hard not to like him as he learns to cope with his new environment.

We are putting together a report with his therapists. I will forward it as soon as it is ready. Everything looks good so far!

Don't hesitate to contact me by e-mail or phone me anytime if I can answer any other questions you may have. How often would you like me to send you reports on Alex's progress? We aim for about once every two weeks. Does that work for you?

Take care,

Kevin

Alex...Unfortunately, I missed Helen so much. I needed her affection, and not having it stressed me out. On one hand, I wanted to continue recovering in Utah, and on the other hand, I wanted to go back to San Diego and win her back again. I did not know that she was seeing someone else. She was being unfaithful, and I did not know it.

About two months after being in Utah, I got a check from the building where I lived in San Diego, giving me back the deposit my dad had left for the apartment. I used that money to invite Helen to go skiing with me. I was given the opportunity to spend several days with her, as long as at some point during the day I went back for urine testing in order to ensure my sobriety day after day. That was one of the golden rules of the house: you had to have daily testing, something I liked because it regulated me, gave me security, and helped me in not thinking about getting high.

We had a good weekend together, even though I already felt the distance between us. The magic from before was gone. I say again that I did not know Helen was already going out with some other guy in San Diego, but she was not capable of being honest with me and tell me so. She pretended that everything was the same and that she was still waiting for me in San Diego, which made me want to leave recovery even more.

I was so distracted with Helen and our relationship that I lost my car keys while skiing on the mountain. We had to be picked up to take Helen to the airport. My car was parked in that place for several days until a key was made to open it and bring it down. I went back to LeMont Michel one night, days after Helen had left. She called me on the phone, and she told me something that made me feel sadder than ever. She was seeing someone else, and she was about to start a relationship with him. She was just calling to let me know. Then she hung up the phone.

She left me out in the cold. I thought she would wait for me. I had just invited her to ski with me, she had the opportunity to say no, but she accepted the trip, making me believe that we were still a couple. In that moment, she made me realize that I was not the man she wanted to be with. This made me forget everything that I was doing. My pride would not let me stay in Utah while another man was sleeping with the person I loved so much.

***Clarita**...*In May, I went to visit Alex. I was really surprised by how good he looked. He had gained weight, was strong, happy, and working very hard in his program. One day he invited me to hike, and suddenly he got out some papers. We sat down on a rock, and he began to read some words he had written to repair our relationship. When he finished, he said, "Mama, in AA they say that when you repair a relationship, it is because you are ready to never relapse again. I wanted to do this today so that you can be at peace that I will never use again."

During my stay in Utah, I had several meetings with Kevin where we talked a lot about our concern that Alex wanted to leave LeMont Michel and go back for Helen. We knew he was not ready.

Rescuing Helen

Alex...I asked my parents for their permission to go back to San Diego. During my time in Utah, I had started chatting a lot on Messenger with Daniela, a friend with whom I spent a lot of time years earlier because she was dating one of my cousins. I told her my story with Helen, and she also told me about the problems she was going through. We had a great connection, one that would later become one of the best relationships I have ever had, but another one that was lost because of my addiction.

But getting back to the topic of Helen. Neither my parents nor the personnel of LeMont Michel were very happy with my decision. They did not understand what my need was to run to rescue someone who did not need any rescuing. I should have understood at that moment that I had lost her, but again my ego did not let it go. I was sure that if I went back to San Diego, she would realize how much I loved her, and she would be back in my arms.

***

At this moment, Alex's priority was to get Helen back, to win her over again, and prevent her from leaving him for another man. Once more, his recovery came in second place. The urge to run after Helen was more important than the incipient sobriety that he had been accomplishing in Utah.

Alex...My dad decided to invite me to spend a few days with him. I told him about my plans to go back to San Diego. We agreed to meet in Arizona, where I spent some of the best days of my life with him. We talked about many things, we discussed all the pros and cons of going back and leaving Utah, we played golf. We were very happy spending this time together and sharing these moments.

After this, my dad allowed my move to San Diego. I convinced them again that I was fine, that I did not need to be in Utah, that my life was in San Diego, and that I had to go back as soon as possible to get Helen. My dad told me to go back to Utah, pack my things, and then drive to Las Vegas where he would be waiting for me. We would spend a few days together, and then we would drive back to San Diego where my mom had already found a sober living house for me. And that is how one more time I got away with what I wanted. I packed all my things, said my good-byes, left LeMont Michel, and drove my car to Vegas.

When I got to Vegas, my dad welcomed me, and we enjoyed some awesome time together. We played golf, gambled at the casinos, went to the spa to pamper ourselves a little, and on my birthday, we walked down to the parking lot of the hotel, and I saw an orange Lamborghini Gallardo—my favorite car since I was a kid. I had pointed it out to my dad, and imagine my surprise when he told me, "Get in. It is your early birthday present." He had rented that car to spend the whole day driving around Las Vegas. Once again, my dad had made my dreams come true.

My parents have given me so many things that sometimes I do not find the right way to thank them. Like I mentioned before, the shame I carry inside has clouded my capacity and ability to be grateful. It is hard to want everything in life but deep inside feel and believe that you do not deserve anything.

We spent a really incredible day together. We drove to the Hoover Dam. We sped while we were driving. We were like two little boys with a new toy.

***

Unfortunately for Alex, he believed that he was getting away with what he wanted without thinking about the consequences or the risks that he would incur by ending his treatment and his stay in Utah. By putting his wounded ego before everything else, he took the first step toward certain relapse. This attitude of self-deception is very common in people who suffer from addiction.

Alex...Three days later, we decided it was time to drive to San Diego and to my new home. We arrived at Casa Pacifica, the place my mom had found for me. The house owner lovingly welcomed us. She showed us the rooms. There were double rooms and individual rooms that cost a little more. Once again, out of a desire to support me, my dad let me stay in a private room so that I would be more comfortable. The next day, I drove him to the airport, and he went back to Mexico.

That same day, I paid Helen a visit. She was spending the day at the office of the guy she was dating, but not even then could I open my eyes and realize that Helen was not mine anymore. We talked for an hour. She told me I looked good, that she was very happy with my sobriety, that she was confused about us, that she wanted to get back together, but at the same time, she was afraid to relive our volatile times together.

I tried unsuccessfully to convince her that it would not happen again, that she should give me one more opportunity. Very cleverly she told me that she wanted to get back together, but she needed some time to be able to end her current relationship. During the subsequent months, I spent my time going to the gym, I went to meetings, got a new sponsor, worked my steps, and tried to win back Helen again.

On one hand, those months were very good. I made new friends with the people that lived with me. We had good times. But on the other hand, it was very painful. Helen was making me suffer; she was simply toying with me. She did not have the slightest intention of getting back together, but she pretended she did, and I—obsessed with her—let her manipulate me. I spent my nights crying, asking God to get her back, but every time I did, it became more evident that it would never happen. I think we had two intimate moments together where I thought I would get her back, but again, Helen was just toying with me.

Helen...Many years later, I regretted giving Alex false hope then and not being honest. I thought that leaving him would help him mature and understand the reality of our illness. Looking back, I can say now that we were both young and immature. Alex was very special. I will love him until the day I die, and he gave me some of my happiest days. And he helped save my life. His spirit will live on.

Daniela: A New Illusion

Alex...At the same time, my chats on the Internet with Daniela went on. She was the person who motivated me during these hard times, and day by day, I started to get closer to her. After two months of staying at Casa Pacifica, my parents decided to spend the month of July with me in San Diego. They asked me to look for a house that they could rent. I looked for houses all over the place and found one that I knew they would like.

Daniela also told me that she would visit me in July for a few days. She wanted to take her daughter to Disneyland, but she would take advantage of her vacation to come and see me. We had not seen each other for two years, but our relationship was turning more and more romantic, and we both looked forward to being together and seeing whether we had the same chemistry in person.

July arrived, and so did my family. They loved the house I found for them, and I decided to move in with them. Again, I left my sober living house before being ready and went to live with my parents. I had planned to look for a new apartment while they were there. We were all reunited; my brothers also came to San Diego, and we spent some great times together.

We celebrated my birthday and then went looking for apartments. After a day of searching, we found a very nice place in La Jolla. My parents liked it because the people who lived there were mostly older people. The apartment was even prettier than the one we had rented before, and I was very excited when my dad said we could rent it.

Despite all my excitement—the great company of my family and the good times we were having—I was also very sad because Helen kept playing with my emotions, and I idiotically kept letting her play games with me.

The day came when I was going to move in. We took all the furniture out of storage from where we had left it before I went to Utah, and we spent the day decorating my place. It was really wonderful, the love with which my parents and my brother, Mauricio, spent that day working with me. I will always remember it. In spite of not participating a lot because I was distracted by my issues with Helen, I could not help but realize all the love that my family put into this task.

***

Alex once again started an independent life without having completed his stay in Utah and after having abandoned the sober living house in San Diego. Even though he did not have closure with Helen, Daniela was about to enter into his emotional life.

Alex...Finally, the day arrived. I went to pick up Daniela, her sister, and her baby daughter at the airport. I took them to the hotel where they would stay, and I remember staying all night and just talking. There was an immediate connection between Daniela and me. We were both in need of love and immediately started a relationship. We wanted to fill that emptiness and help each other not feel the pain that we both had inside. She was going through a very difficult divorce with a daughter caught in the middle, and I had lost Helen. I also fell instantly in love with her daughter, a precious one-and-a-half-year-old girl. She was the cutest thing I had ever seen, and she had a really special light.

We agreed I would pick them up the next day to take them to Disneyland. We had a wonderful day. I loved seeing the faces of excitement the baby made when she was on the rides, and I played with her as if she were my own daughter. I felt really comfortable with Daniela, and again I had forgotten my problems. Again, a woman had come to rescue me from my inner loneliness. That same day, we kissed for the first time. It was something exciting and special that I will never forget.

***

Despite the unconditional support from his parents, and the loving and constant presence of his family, Alex needed a woman to not feel alone. Be it somebody or something (i.e., the substance), he always needed something to fill the emptiness he felt inside.

Daniela...Our story started with simple online chats. For several months, during which I loved to sit down and message him, we would chat all night, sometimes even until dawn. We consoled each other, we laughed, but more than anything, we understood each other. There was no judgment between us. That is how Alex, living very far away inside a rehab center in San Diego, came into my life and became a very important part of my day to day.

We began to fall in love. As months passed and we grew closer, we decided to meet in person. The idea got me excited and hopeful. However, the doubt was clearly there. Was I really emotionally ready to start a relationship with somebody else? And even if so, with a person who had been fighting an addiction for such a long time? To tell the truth, the answer was no! However, the joy that I felt, his understanding, his vision of beautiful things, and his support made me realize that even though I was scared, I could not help but give myself an opportunity to be with somebody who inspired in me so much love and peace.

My visit to San Diego exceeded all my expectations. I was not only attracted to him physically, but his surprises, his attention to detail, and his willingness to always be genuine awakened in me a kind of self-esteem that had been dead for a long time.

Alex...We went on dating for several days. We went out to dinner, shopping...we really had a very nice time. When Daniela's sister had to go back to Mexico, Daniela decided to spend more time at an aunt's house in Chula Vista. While she spent time with her aunt, I had the opportunity to spend a few more days with my family. Days later, my parents would be going back to Mexico, and I would be moving to my new apartment.

The time came for Daniela to go back, too. But we decided it would be better if she spent a few more days with me. She accepted. I remember that same day we went to a baby store, and we bought a cradle for her daughter so that she was comfortable in my apartment. We bought several toys, and this is how we started acting as if we were a couple that had been together for a long time.

I had some of my best days in San Diego with Daniela. I also decided to ask her to be my girlfriend. She said yes. But since all beginnings have an end, the time came for Daniela and her baby to leave. It was a very sad moment because neither of us knew when we would see each other again. But we trusted that our relationship would go on over the Internet and by phone.

I felt alone the moment they left, and it took a big effort for me to not get high those first few days after they left. But I managed. I kept attending my meetings, exercising, and talking to my sponsor.

Alone Again: The Beginning of a Nightmare

Alex...A friend of mine on the Internet told me that a friend of his was living in San Diego and that he would introduce us so I wouldn't feel so lonely. I agreed to meet up with her, and this is how I met Lucia. We agreed to meet at a restaurant in downtown San Diego. There was a strong chemistry between the two of us the minute we saw each other. My loneliness prevented me from seeing Lucia as just a friend. So, we started a close relationship. Just a few days after meeting Lucia, she was living with me.

She liked to party a lot, and she took me to several nightclubs and parties in San Diego and Los Angeles. This, of course, made me act irresponsibly toward Daniela, and I began to push her aside. This was the reason for our break-up.

***

Loneliness weighed on Alex so heavily that he could not bear it. One after another, women paraded through his life.

Clarita...We went back to Mexico thinking that this time Alex would be fine. He had been clean for over seven months and looked healthy and happy. Besides the sober living house in Utah, he had stayed in another one in San Diego where he had once again found the support of a community. He had a sponsor, he worked his program, he went to therapy, went to the gym every day, etcetera. He had his new dream apartment and had also been accepted at the Culinary Institute of San Diego so he could become a chef. However, he never knew how to take advantage of these tools. Relationships full of conflict were the only things that filled his existential void, but only for a while. When the magic was over, Alex relapsed.

Alex...It was hard to spend time with Lucia at night because, like I mentioned, she liked to party and go to nightclubs to drink. I saw how she drank, and the truth is I began to feel like I wanted to drink like her. But I was careful. I managed to stay strong, although the idea of using was in my thoughts more and more.

One day, Lucia told me that her apartment was ready and that she was moving out. She left me after three weeks of being together every day, after pretending that she wanted a relationship with me, after many good times together. Once again, I was left alone. And in that loneliness and feeling of abandonment, I decided to get high again. And again, the nightmare began.

First, I used all the money my parents had left me. Then I began to get money from my debit card, and when my parents realized this, they canceled the card. I started to pawn all the valuable things I had in my apartment again. I was full of shame and fear. I did not know how to stop, but I did not have the strength to ask for help, either. I began to walk away from the program and my sponsor. I made the same mistakes that I had made so many times. And little by little, I was falling deeper and deeper into the abyss.

I stole from the dealers. I borrowed money from my neighbors. In the late hours of the night, I would remember my parents' credit cards numbers, so I began to use their credit cards more often. I made use of everything I had within my reach. The only thing that mattered was having enough money to get high. And, like always, I got away with what I wanted, stepping on everyone. I even borrowed a very close friend's debit card number, saying that I was in trouble. I used up all the money in his account. I did the same with my brother, Eduardo's, card.

One night I got scared. I started to feel an intense pain in my heart. My left arm was numb, and my breathing had become labored.

I felt like I was about to have a heart attack. I remember I spent about two hours next to the phone in case I had to dial 911, but these pains eventually subsided. I realized I was using again without any regard or respect for myself.

During that desperation, I wanted to end my life. I remember that I wanted to do it like in the movies—slashing my wrists, getting into a hot tub to bleed until I felt asleep, and then die. That night, I filled the tub with hot water. I was going to smoke all that I had and then end my life. The problem was that my addiction was stronger than the desire to die, and therefore, every time I ran out of crack, I went out to the streets to get more instead of fulfilling my original mission. I felt a stronger desire to keep getting high.

I spent three days like this: preparing the tub, smoking, and waiting for the right moment to slash my veins. I did not have any contact with Daniela or Lucia. Helen, of course, was not important. The only thing that mattered now was to smoke until I found the courage to end my life.

On the fourth night, I found the courage to do it. I took a pizza knife and began slashing my wrists. The blood began flowing, and soon I realized that with the little bit I had cut, I would not accomplish anything.

The next day, I called my parents and told them I was so desperate that I had slashed my wrists. I was in such a bad place, and I did not know what to do. I think it was two days later when I heard somebody knocking at my door. When I asked who it was, my parents answered. They came in, and in between sobs, I hugged them. I was overjoyed that they had come to help me. I really needed them. I was desperate, scared to death, and most of all, I did not have any money to keep using.

***Clarita*…**When we arrived and saw Alex, we were really scared. One month after leaving Alejandro healthy, clean and strong—he had been exercising for seven months—we found him skinny and malnourished. Alex had set up his apartment with so much joy, always keeping it impeccable, but now it was a mess. Everything was on the floor, including bags full of groceries at the entrance that hadn't been put away, so all the food was spoiled.

While Gerardo and I cleaned, Alex slept for a while, and then we took him to eat. After eating, we paid the check, and on our way to the parking lot, Alex said he had to go to the restroom. It turns out that he went back in to ask for his dad's credit card number, and without our permission, he made charges with it all night.

Some terrifying days followed where he would leave the apartment and we would chase him through the streets to prevent him from using again, to the point that I slept at the hotel while Gerardo stayed at the apartment and slept on the living room couch to try and prevent Alex from getting out at night. A long time ago, I learned that chasing after an addict does not help. The only thing you can do is pray for his safe return.

Alex...We spent several days together trying to find what would be the best way to help me. During this time, I kept leaving the apartment at all hours of the night to get high. I can imagine their fear and how they were feeling, how I would rob their sleep and peace of mind for so many nights. It is only now, with some sobriety and with a clearer understanding of my addiction, that I can start to be conscious of all the harm I have caused.

My parents called Kevin McCauley, and he was kind enough to take a plane and fly from Utah to be able to help us find a solution to this new nightmare.

Before he arrived, my parents went with me to the pawnshop to get all my things back. I can imagine the sadness they felt having to do this for the second time.

Gerardo...The feelings I had toward Alex's addiction...I could sum it up as terror, sadness, anger, desperation, bitterness, fear, and overall, an indescribable powerlessness that tears your heart out. Rescuing Alex when he was in the process of using was the hardest. I do not think there is any pain as intense as seeing your child consumed by an external force, by something that—though he decided to try it—holds him completely captive.

Alex...Kevin arrived as I had just finished smoking. We sat down in the living room in my apartment to talk, and the only thing I could think about was getting high. I was terrified of having to go back with him to Utah, of losing my apartment, which had been paid for six months in advance. I got desperate to use and told my parents and Kevin that I was not going to go until they gave me money to get high.

After discussing it for several minutes, my parents, supported by Kevin's opinion, decided to give me money and my car keys and went to have dinner with Kevin while I used. And that is how I manipulated my parents for the first time to give me money for crack. I remember perfectly how my dad threw the money to the floor with enormous frustration and anger on his face. It is unbelievable that instead of thinking about the suffering he was going through, I still felt offended that he threw the money and did not give it to me nicely. How sad it is to see how addiction makes you forget your values and morals.

Hours later, afer smoking all the crack I had, I finally said I would go to Utah. I hugged my parents, and once again, I left them alone in San Diego, packing up my apartment for the last time. It is only today that I am able to realize the pain I caused them.

As I write this, tears of sadness roll down my face when I remember such bitter moments in my life and theirs. I hope there is a moment when, through my actions and my way of life, I can redeem myself in my parents' eyes and make up for all the harm I have caused them. For now, becoming aware of it is already a great step forward for me.

***

When he wasn't focused on getting high, Alex could see clearly the harm he had caused by his behavior. The values that he had been taught as a child seemed to return to him when he was not intoxicated.

Alex...Kevin took me to a detox hospital for a few days there before taking me back to LeMont Michel. You had to be clean and sober before you could be admitted into the house. I spent two days in detox when they prematurely released me. I arrived at LeMont Michel, and they gave me the same room I'd had the first time. After twenty-four hours, the compulsion to use again got a hold of me. It was extremely intense. Therefore, I took my car, saying I was going to the gym, and got out of the house. I went directly to pawn my computer that only two days earlier my dad had recovered in San Diego. Again, completely controlled by my addiction, I started the terrifying cycle of getting high.

I quickly found a dealer that sold me crack in downtown Utah. And the next four days were a nightmare. I hope to be able to remember them in the best possible way to give you an idea of what I experienced and what I made my family go through during that time.

Inside my car, I had all my belongings because I had not yet unpacked any of what I had brought from San Diego. In four days, I pawned my laptop, my golf clubs, and gave away absolutely all of my clothes. I started finding a way to use my parents' credit card number that I had memorized to make transactions with the taxi drivers. They would pass the number through illegally and give me money in exchange for a good payoff for them. I asked them for $100, and in exchange they charged $200 on my parents' card, and that is how I got money.

I did not speak with my family during those four days. They did not know where I was; Kevin could not find me anywhere. They contacted the police and moved heaven and earth to find me while I spent day and night getting high, stealing money, and getting high again. Up until the fourth day, I was in a motel where a dealer was living. I sold him all I had left of my clothes. He let me stay in his room to smoke, and when I was out of it, and he offered to buy my car in exchange for crack. I was so desperate that I agreed to sell it in exchange for $2500 in cash and $400 in crack. I went to the car to get the papers and signed them on the back, along with the name of the dealer. When I gave him the papers, he showed me a gun to scare me and told me that he was going to give me the $400 dollars in crack and that would be it. I was so desperate that I accepted it. And this is how I lost absolutely everything that I owned.

The dealer wanted to talk to my parents to make sure they were not going to send the police after the car, that I really had sold it and that nobody would come to find him and get him in trouble. I borrowed his cell phone, and this is how after four nights of hell, I dialed my family's number for the first time. I remember perfectly the terror in my mom and dad's voices. I remember the sadness I felt the moment I heard them. The pain I felt inside was indescribable, but I was anesthetized by the use of drugs. I put the dealer on, and I remember my dad told him not to worry, that the car was his, but he also asked to please take care of his son.

Clarita...The phone rang at five a.m. Just hearing it made me jump. Alejandro was totally out of control, asking us to speak to a person who was threatening him with a knife, telling him that he would kill him if he did not give his car in exchange for the drugs he had already given him to smoke. At the same time, we called Kevin on the other line, thinking in that moment that Alex would give us his location so that Kevin could go rescue him. However, Alex only wanted more crack from the dealer to keep using. He didn't tell us where he was and left us worried out of our minds. Again...

Alex...It is unbelievable how much my parents love me. The only thing they wanted after what I made them go through was to know that I was fine and that nothing happened to me. A few hours after that first call, when I had finished the $400 in crack, I called them back to tell them where I was so that they could send Kevin to take me back to detox. My parents were giving me one more opportunity.

Kevin arrived a few hours later and took me to the hospital. It hadn't even been twenty-four hours when I asked for my voluntary discharge from the hospital to get out and get high again. I remember I walked around barefoot for about four hours in the cold of Utah, trying to get back to the hotel where the dealer lived. I got there, and when he saw me, he asked me what I was doing there. I told him I felt he had been very unfair with what he had given me for my car, and I wanted more crack. He agreed to give me some more, but also without telling me, he made the decision to call my parents to let them know I was with him again. My parents asked him that when I was done using if he would take me back to the hospital where Kevin had left me, and he agreed.

I was in a really deplorable state. I had been using for a long time. I felt completely empty inside. I called my parents from the hospital and asked them to please let me go back to Mexico. I did not want to stay at LeMont. I did not want to be away from them. I wanted to be back in my house with my family again. The rest had become a nightmare. My dad told me it was fine, that they would accept me back into my house, that they would be happy to have me back, and that he would fly to Utah to pick me up. He asked me to please wait for him at the hospital, not to leave again. He told me he would arrive the following day.

Letter from Kevin McCauley: October 2009

Dear Clarita,

I think we are getting close to the end of Alex's run. I am very glad to hear that he's still in Utah. When he shows up, my guess is that he'll want to go back to Mexico. I can do what I can to facilitate that, get him to the airport or whatever. Keep in mind, the minute he gets to Mexico, he will likely go on a cocaine run of unbelievable proportions and will become a real handful.

Can you get him admitted to inpatient treatment in Mexico so that he goes straight there? He mentioned that he was willing to go back to Promises the last time we spoke. That is an idea. I can get him to the airport and the Promises staff can pick him up. There is some danger in bringing him back to California. There is also the option of Cirque Lodge. He mentioned he was willing to go there, too. If he surfaces and is still willing to do that—and if you are willing to support that, and I would understand if you weren't—I can begin the process of setting that up if you'd like.

I still dream that in thirty to sixty days we'll have the old Alex back. We would be more than willing to welcome him back to our home if he can return to the charming young man that he was last summer, the man I know he really is. But I have to say, Alex is about one of the most seriously ill patients I've ever seen.

Please call anytime.

Kevin

CHAPTER VI

Back to Mexico

All battles in life teach us something, even those that we lose.

—Paulo Coelho

***Alex**...*The following day, I couldn't wait until two or three in the afternoon when I was being picked up. I asked again for my voluntary discharge a few hours earlier to go and get high. I went to use by selling the last of my belongings— a tennis racket—and from there went to the hotel where I knew my dad would arrive. He came to pick me up filled with optimism and with a lot of love. As soon as we met, I saw the disappointment on his face for not having waited for him at the hospital and for having gotten high again. But we hugged, and he told me everything would be all right. He went with me again to the pawnshop to get my golf clubs back and my tennis racket. My computer was lost, one more loss because of my addiction. Of course the car and all my clothes had been lost forever. We went back to Mexico.

Upon my arrival in Mexico, my parents had set up a room where I would have all the necessary stuff. I remember they had decorated it very nicely. They had candy, cookies—all that I needed to feel comfortable. I could feel how much they loved me. They gave me a sweet welcome in spite of the difficult moments that I had made them go through because of my addiction.

Everything looked good. I was happy to be back with my family. I was also happy that I could see Daniela again, and we started the relationship we left back in San Diego. For obvious reasons, my departures from home were very controlled at first. Because of this, Daniela came to my house to see me and be with me. I am very thankful for her, and we spent some very nice evenings together.

Unfortunately, I was not doing anything to follow a program and help my recovery. I think it had not even been a week when my aunt and uncle came to visit me. Without anyone noticing, I opened my aunt's purse and stole 500 pesos. After this I asked my parents' permission to go for a run. We have a gym at the house with a treadmill, and we have a beautiful yard where I could have easily run the distance I needed to, but what I wanted was to go out and get high. And this is how I went searching for a hit and once again started the cycle of using. This time, in spite of all the love that my family showed me, in spite of all the dreams we had together to make it, I failed again. I could not keep up with my recovery and the impulse to get high.

Days passed. I cheated on my family. I lied to Daniela and everybody while I used. Stealing money started again, and so did the nightmare.

One day, when nobody noticed, I took my mom's credit card from her purse and went directly to the bank to withdraw money. I withdrew approximately 15,000 pesos with which I disappeared for four days. I checked into a motel where I got high every day. I did not eat anything. I drank little liquid, and once again, I was using nonstop, and I was feeling an overwhelming sadness for having stolen so much money. That, plus the drug use, kept me from calling my parents to ask for their help.

***

Even though Alex felt welcomed by his family and by Daniela upon his arrival in Mexico, his drug obsession—his need to get high— was lurking, wanting to grab ahold of his mind again. A horrendous cycle of use that had started in San Diego and Utah continued its devastating course in Mexico.

Alex...While I was getting high, they were going crazy looking for a way to find me. They took my photo to the police to see if they could find me, and also very wisely, they took my photo to all the nearby motels until they found the right place. I was using when they knocked on the door to my room. I heard my dad's voice and other people's voices, too. I got super scared; I had been getting high all night long. My hands were shaky, and they were burned from lighting my pipe so much. I kept hearing the knocking on the door, but I decided to light up again to escape from everyone. A few seconds though it was, everything disappeared, and so did I.

I opened the door. I did not care about anything because I was in the place where nothing could hurt me. They took me and brought me back to my house where they had a plan to take me to a clinic in Queretaro.

I stayed in the clinic for three or four days. I do not remember how much time passed after my arrival at the clinic before I ran away. I started to look for a taxi to take me back to Mexico, but not without stopping to buy more crack, borrowing money from the taxi driver. I arrived at my house having used once more. My parents took me back to the clinic, where I again escaped.

But it was useless to keep getting high, and after the clinic's recommendations, my parents hired a specialized service that would take me to a psychiatric hospital. They arrived in a van where three people took me to the clinic. Along the way, they stopped to get gas, and I used that moment to get out and run. They started to chase me down the street until I stumbled into a hole and fell. They picked me up and put me in the van, where they proceeded to tie me down. I felt horrible when I saw myself—my body—tied up in a van with three strangers, but that was their job, to take me to the clinic no matter what.

***

Keeping the patient in treatment depends on factors associated as much with the individual as with the program. Because some individuals' problems, such as the severe use of cocaine or crack, increase the probability that a patient prematurely ends the program, it is possible to require intensive treatments with a variety of components to keep the patients who have these problems in the program. The therapist must make sure there is a transition to continuous care, or convalescence therapy, after the patient ends normal treatment.[12]

Clarita...After all the encounters at the clinic in Queretaro, and with Alex's deterioration because of his drug use, they recommended that we bring him to a psychiatric hospital where there was an addiction department. After twenty-one days of treatment, we had a meeting with his psychiatrists, and to my surprise, they told me that Alejandro was ready to get out. I had negotiated a deal with my son in which I promised him that, if after being clean he thought that he was not ready to stop getting high, he could do anything he wanted. I was sure that after being clean he would not want to use.

Unfortunately, I was wrong. As soon as he left the hospital, he waved me off, reminding me of our agreement, and he said, "Ma, I want to keep using." I froze, but the only thing I could tell him was, "It is your decision." I got into the car with Gerardo and went back home. We were just getting home when Alex pulled up in a taxi, saying that he had thought about it, and he would rather be with us. He had drugs hidden in his suitcase.

All this time, I was trying different ways to support Alex. I always had a huge feeling of powerlessness. It was very frustrating that nothing worked, and perhaps already in these moments we began to understand that rescuing or not rescuing, giving or not giving, and supporting or not supporting was not going to change the decisions Alejandro was making. It was probably then that Gerardo and I started the process of letting go of the addiction little by little, although we never did let go of Alejandro. Here is where the fine line begins between how to help your son without supporting the addict. The more informed you are, the less you find ways to help the addict.

During his process of active addiction, we lived a true nightmare. We spent entire nights walking around the house waiting for him to come home, not knowing whether he was dead or alive. We always made use of all the resources within our reach to get him out of those moments. He lost track of time in impressive ways, leaving for three days without us knowing anything, and on the fourth day he'd come back at five a.m. in total angst, asking us to let him come in.

I began to feel like I did not want to get involved in the addiction anymore, because when he destroyed himself, I destroyed myself at the same time by trying to help him in his process. However, what I never lost was my perseverance.

Mauricio...Like any other mom, mine started researching everything. She did not leave things to chance, nor did she trust the stigma around addiction. She instead studied very hard. She took courses, earned certificates; she was really very informed. But you could still see the contradiction between her informed self and her human side that blinded her. She could not implement the information and knowledge she obtained with Alex because her feelings took over. She was always very aware of this—for example, during those times when we knew that Alex probably needed to go to a clinic or a halfway house to start living a normal life with responsibilities. But in as much as they took him to different clinics, my parents ended up throwing in the towel because Alex escaped from all of them.

***

Coming of age is often a decisive factor in addiction cases such as Alex's because it interferes with the patient's recovery. Alejandro was already twenty-three years old when he started his journey through clinics, and it was almost impossible to keep him in treatment without his consent.

Alex...A few days after being in the house getting high and knowing that my parents were desperate, not knowing what to do, I convinced them to give me 5000 pesos with the idea that I could move forward with this money, that I was going to be in a hotel until I was clean and then be able to go back home. I went to a neighborhood called Tepito where I bought 4000 pesos worth of crack, because from the beginning my idea was to go out to get high. Then I went to a dirty, cheap motel where I smoked for the next twenty-four hours. When I ran out of money, I called my parents and asked them to take me back into the house again, and because of the great love they have for me, they agreed.

Mauricio...He used to escape, for example, on a Monday. He'd started smoking, and then on Thursday, very sick after four days of extreme use, he'd come home again—without money, beaten up, and hungry.

***

Like Kevin McCauley predicted, when Alex came to Mexico, the progression of his illness worsened and became very hard to control.

Clarita...Alex disappeared again, and I was left without knowing where he was for four days, until one afternoon his friend, Andrea, called me. Alex had called and told her that he was dying in a motel on Observatorio and wanted her to go and help him. Not knowing how to handle the situation, she called us.

He looked wretched. We called his psychiatrist, who recommended that we get him hospitalized for detox. That is when we took him to the ABC Hospital, where he spent the next four days. When he left the hospital, he got high again. With the excuse of going to the gym, he left and went to a new place in a federal zone called "La Papa" to get crack. Those who sold him drugs had an agreement with the police that if they allowed them to sell, every once in a while they would give back certain users. That was how Alex was detained.

From there, Alex started calling all of his contacts until someone helped him get released; Gerardo and I had decided not to go for him. Later, we talked to a lawyer, who recommended that we bail him out because jail in Mexico was not a good place to be. It is very easy to find drugs there. Gerardo went to get him before he was moved from holding into jail.

Alex came back home, and we called a policeman whom we had met through this process. He sat down and had a tough-love conversation with Alejandro about the consequences of going to jail—consequences not just for him but for the whole family. His words were harsh and incisive.

Alex...After this talk, my dad decided to take me on a trip to keep me away from the places where I used drugs, a road trip to distract me and spend some nice quality time together. We went to San Miguel de Allende where we spent two days. Then we went to Guanajuato where we stayed two more days, but I missed Daniela a lot. I asked my dad to please go back. He said yes, and so we came back after five days. Looking back, I should have taken more advantage of the opportunity to spend more time with my dad, but in the same way I felt an obsession for drugs, I had an obsession to see Daniela.

Gerardo...At this point, we started trying a new tool with Alex: going on little trips. The best, most beautiful moments I spent with Alex were on those trips, and they were useful in getting him out of the drug environment. When we would invite him, he left behind his dark side. His face shone, and at the same time, he saw these outings as a light at the end of the tunnel. These were incredible experiences that we shared together, and I will always remember them.

Daniela: A New Path Toward Recovery

Alex...This is how I started down a new road on my path to recovery, a recovery my own way, without a program and without attending meetings or sessions with a psychologist. I wanted to prove to the world that I could do it by myself, that it was a matter of wanting more than willpower.

***

Again, it was the desire to be with a woman—in this case, Daniela—that triggered Alex's sincere motivation to recover. Again, like with Helen, his priority was to make somebody be with him.

Alex...Everything was looking good, things were working. I got a job at a real estate company named Vidalta. I had a nice relationship with Daniela and her daughter. My relationship with my parents was also improving. I went to the gym a lot. I was doing everything I could to recover. I had also enrolled in a certificate program for interior design, something I had always wanted to study.

Rodrigo Perez del Toro...I met Alex around April 13, 2010 because he was looking for an apartment in the Bosques area for him or Daniela. We immediately liked each other and began talking about life's issues. After hanging out several times, we had developed a friendship, and he asked me if I could hire him for my sales team. I knew he was in rehab, and at that time we were in the midst of the real estate crisis of 2009, but Alex's charisma made him an excellent candidate for sales, and I thought that both Vidalta and Alex could benefit a lot from his joining the team.

On June 15, 2010, he helped his first customer. I felt a lot of empathy for Alex and understood what he was going through because my dad is a rehabilitated addict. I understand how difficult it is to struggle with the illness. Soon after, Alex stopped going to the office because of a relapse, from which he had a very hard time recovering. Because of my fondness for Alex, sometimes I talked to his mom to see how he was doing.

Alex...Looking back, I have to accept that—besides the fact that everything seemed fine—my relationship with Daniela was not easy. She was going through some difficult times dealing with a nasty divorce, and I felt obligated to help her, putting myself in the role of rescuer where I made it my responsibility to help. I did not take care of my own needs as I tended to hers. I assumed responsibilities that did not belong to me, all for the sole purpose of making Daniela love me more, as I always did over the years in my constant search for acceptance and love. We fought constantly, and we would both show our dark sides. They say true love is the one that gets the best from the other person, but a lot of times it was the opposite.

Our fights got worse and worse. I became very impatient and would explode. I was impulsive and aggressive, and throughout all of this, I was keeping everything bottled up inside of me. I didn't feel like I had anyone to talk to. My parents constantly approached me to give me advice, but unfortunately I did not follow it. I felt I could handle everything on my own. It was my own responsibility to look good in everyone else's eyes. I thought that it was my responsibility to make it on my own without the help of anyone. Asking for help is something I had never done. This lack of humility caused me so many problems. And so I went around swallowing my issues, and they weighed me down more and more.

I started to abandon my gym routine. I also started to miss classes. Slowly but surely, my problems began growing, and again I disconnected from my inner self. I was living a reality that wasn't in line with who I was. Thoughts of using again became more and more salient, but I ignored the signs completely. My parents, and even Daniela, suggested that I look for help, that I go see a professional to help me deal with my problems. But of course my ego did not allow it. I kept trying to be strong, pretending to face my problems head on, but unfortunately, they were more than I could handle only a few months into sobriety.

Clarita...Alex was very reluctant to follow his treatment. He abandoned it little by little. He tried making changes in his lifestyle, but he could not keep up with it. At times, he managed to discipline himself, mostly when it was about his image, a fundamental piece of his self-esteem.

Alex...One day, Daniela and I had a big fight over the phone. I remember I lost total control of my emotions, and we both said some very hurtful things. I left my bedroom feeling extremely hostile. I yelled at my mom and even broke a big mirror that I had in my room. My mom felt this anger would make me relapse, and she did everything in her power to not let me leave the house, which made me even madder. I said horrible things to her. I treated her like a son should never treat his mom, and worst of all is that this only made me feel angrier and more guilty.

Daniela...On several occasions, I judged him, setting the bar very high, and with every relapse I became crueler and harder on him. I could not understand how somebody could not fight for his health and for his happiness alongside his loved ones. To me, Alex had it all. And yes, he had it all, including an illness that did not let him be totally happy and peaceful. To me, that was the biggest frustration. I wanted him to understand the damage that he inflicted on us, but especially on himself. As far as our relationship goes, it was not a war I lost. We both lost many battles. In the end, I had to understand that it was not up to me to make him succeed. Because of my own circumstances, we were actually hurting each other instead of helping each other.

Alex...That day, I had my first relapse after five months of sobriety. I got to my house at night, having used already. My parents waited for me at the door. They were very sad and concerned. I apologized to them. I promised that this had been only a small relapse and that nothing big would happen. I asked for the opportunity to continue with my normal life. They again acquiesced to my pleas and did not tell anyone about this relapse.

Clarita...In our desire to help Alex so that his self-esteem did not suffer and so he wouldn't jeopardize his five months of sobriety, Gerardo and I agreed to give him this opportunity, knowing that honesty during this process was the only thing to lead someone to true recovery.

Alex...A few days later, my parents invited me to go to Ixtapa for the weekend. We had a very nice time. I played golf with my dad. We went to the movies together, and I managed to block that little relapse I had had, so we thought it had been left behind.

Days later, I mentioned to my dad that I wanted to invite Daniela to Las Vegas to spend some alone time with her away from our problems, something I could manage because I was earning an income. It would be an opportunity where I could analyze my relationship and really see whether this was what I wanted in my life or not.

We arrived in Las Vegas, and we had a relatively good time. We had some good times, but we also fought aggressively. I even had to sleep on the couch one of the four nights after a big fight. This should have been a clear sign that things were not working out. I couldn't believe that even on a trip away from our problems—where we were supposed to just be having a good time—we did not have the ability to do it. I should have realized that we were two people with shortcomings trying to accomplish something that we were not equipped for. I was very much in love with Daniela, and I feel that it was a relationship we could have taken very far, but unfortunately, we were not ready to give each other what we needed.

I bought a lot of things for her and her baby, all with the intention of trying to demonstrate my love. My expenses were out of control expenses, which made me fight with my parents and become indebted to them again, something that caused me a lot of anxiety in my life. I should have set boundaries that I was never able to set because of my own insecurities.

We got back to Mexico, and life went on like normal: I kept going to work, sometimes to the gym, but now the most important thing for me was my relationship with Daniela. She was, like I mentioned before, going through her divorce, and that complicated our relationship. I tried to help in all possible ways, but I felt at times that my help annoyed her. However, out of insecurity and fear of losing her, I kept pressuring her and insisting on helping. I should have realized that there are moments in life where everyone has to face their problems and that I simply should have been there in case she needed me.

***

In spite of not getting high at that point in time, Alex could not see that the one who needed help was himself, that as long as he had not completely recovered, he could not establish a solid relationship with anybody. He could not see that his obsession had just changed names, from crack to Daniela.

Change of Path

Alex...My parents had planned a trip to the California coast with some of their friends. They had postponed this trip because they did not want to leave me alone at home, but given the fact that I could halt my relapse and that everything looked normal, they decided to do it. I told them not to worry about me, that everything was going to be all right, to leave and enjoy their trip. The truth was that, like before when they went to Italy, I needed them more than ever. My problems with Daniela were pushing me to the edge of relapse, but again, the inability to express my emotions left me to face my problems alone.

Daniela...Probably our relationship would have had a future if I had been able to understand or imagine what he was going through. Codependence with a chemical substance is a more complicated issue than what one can see or imagine on the outside, and I lived that frustration in the flesh. Alex tried to explain to me that his problem belonged to him. He explained that it did not have anything to do with me, and that even worse, it was something bigger than him and something against which he had to fight every second of his day. Today, I understand that at that time what he wanted the most was to overcome his addiction and live a fulfilling life next to me and my daughter.

Alex...Not even twenty-four hours had passed after my parents' departure, and I was already getting high. Then I started the cycle of "live to use and use to live." I stopped talking to Daniela. I lost my relationship with her. I also lost my job. I had quickly used up all of my money, and then I started stealing from my parents, everything that was within reach. I initially stole two computers and pawned them with my drug dealers. A day later, I got a call from my job, and they told me I had my first check for commission. First thing I did was to get the computers back, and I spent the rest of the money on drugs. And this is how I had money to get high for a while. Once the money from the commission ran out, I started selling my clothes, belts, jackets, shoes, T-shirts, and then I began stealing my parents' household items. All of this left me feeling worse than before using.

My brothers did not know what to do. They felt the need to tell my parents what was happening, but at the same time they did not want to ruin their trip. They gave me one day to end my use, and if they saw I couldn't, they would call my parents. Of course I couldn't, so calling them was inevitable. My parents talked to me and asked me to stop getting high, to not keep ruining my life this way. They asked my brothers to take all the car keys and close all the doors of the house, except for the one at the entrance and my own room so that this way I did not have access to their belongings. But I quickly found a way to open the doors and continue stealing.

Juanita...I saw traces of crack. There were some little balls wrapped in colorful paper, and inside there was a transparent stone like glass. He used a can of Coca-Cola and some pipes to smoke it. Alex told me, "I do not have money to go get drugs." Even though his mother scolded me, I did give him money for drugs because I could not say no. He liked to relapse when his parents were not at home, and he loved that he could be alone for a month.

As soon as they left, he went to buy his drugs. He could spend eight days without sleeping when he was getting high. I bought him Yoplait and Coca-Cola because he did not eat anything else. There were times that I slept upstairs with him because I was afraid something bad would happen to him because he was out all night. He'd finish what he brought and would go out again, so I hid the car keys from him, per his mom's instructions, so that he did not drive while using. They did not let him use in the house, and sometimes he lied to his parents that he was clean. When they realized he wasn't, he had already locked himself up in his room to get high. He was very elegant and loved to look good, but when he used he seemed like he was another person. He'd put on pants, tennis shoes, and a hoodie and went out to get high.

Alex...My brother, Eduardo, who was already married, decided to stay a few days at home to try and help me with my addiction, but it did not work. He did not know what to do with me. He saw how I went in and out of the house all the time, and he was desperate, looking for ways to help me. Unfortunately, when I am in my cycle of use, there is nothing—nor is there anyone—that can help me.

Eduardo...I moved in with Alex, because every time my parents left for a trip, he relapsed. I do not know whether he did it to get attention or what, but that is what happened. During this time, the experience was too taxing. I had to go to some horrible neighborhoods to rescue his iPad and watches, and it was very risky.

Alex...There came a time when everybody was too desperate, and my parents made the decision to shorten their trip and go back to Mexico. My mom was the first one to arrive at the house. The idea was that with my mom there, we could find a way for me to stop getting high and then we would meet my dad in Vail, Colorado to spend a month together, or the necessary time to give me another opportunity to quit using on my own.

The first night, I managed to not get high. I was so happy to have my mom with me that I made a huge effort to stay in my room and not be disrespectful and escape from the house. But the next day, I couldn't help it. The desire to get high was too much. I convinced my mom to go with me to the place where I buy my drugs so that we could get back all the things I had pawned. My mom said yes.

We got to the place, and she gave me the money to get all the things back that I had stolen. What she did not realize was that at the same time, I bought more crack to use back at home. When I got home, I locked myself in my room and got high again. After this, I could not stop anymore. Days passed, and I could not control my addiction. Therefore, the trip with my dad was canceled.

A few days later, my dad came back from his trip, very sad because he had hoped that I would manage to stop getting high and that my mom and I would meet up with him. But my addiction was out of control. I have only a vague memory of the days that followed, but what I do remember is that those days were full of use, theft, lies, manipulation, and mostly, a lot of sadness for my family.

They looked into a clinic in Idaho, and I agreed to go. They bought the tickets. We prepared my suitcase, and we were all ready to go, but something happened. I do not remember it well because my addiction was so strong, but I told my parents—a few hours before the trip—that I was not going anywhere. Once again we lost the money from the plane tickets. Again I had no consideration for my family.

It is incredible, but drugs completely numb all of my feelings. The only thing that matters when I am getting high is to keep doing it. It is like a survival instinct.

***

For Alex at that point in his life, drugs became something as indispensable as oxygen. He could not conceive of his life without getting high. The problems generated by his addiction were already impossible to face, and once more, the substance was his means of escape.

Alex...I was being given medicine to tranquilize me. This, combined with my use, had me completely disconnected from reality. My parents found an expert who owned a clinic in Tijuana. This person flew in from Tijuana to go to my house and do an intervention—I mean, help my family with my admission process. The day he came to my house, I was truly sick. I was having a seizure on the floor. My jaw was completely locked. I could not stop writhing on the floor in pain. I had mixed all the anxiety-lowering medications that the psychiatrist gave me with crack.

When I managed to calm down a little, after much medicating, the owner told me a little about his clinic, to which—I imagine out of desperation—I accepted to go, but not before convincing my family to give me money to get high one more time. And so it was, how after using for the "last time," my dad took us to the airport. It was a sad good-bye. Once again, I would check myself into a clinic to try and cure my illness.

What happened in the hours that followed is erased completely from my memory. I have only a few recollections. It seems like I began drinking beer on the airplane, which made for a very potent combination with all of my medications. I went to the restroom on the plane and lit the pipe, which I had hidden in my sock, to try smoking any residues of crack. The smoke alarm was triggered, and when I got out of the restroom, a flight attendant was waiting for me. Apparently they were going to report me to the authorities because smoking in an airplane restroom is a federal crime involving several years in prison. I do not know how, but the clinic's owner managed to convince the pilot not to report me to authorities, saying I was on my way to a recovery clinic and asked to give me an opportunity. The pilot agreed to let it pass. I was saved from getting arrested when I got off the plane.

I arrived at the clinic, and they gave me medication to help me sleep. The next day, walking by the detox area, I saw a space in the window that I could escape through, and so I did. I escaped the clinic and quickly took a taxi to buy more crack. I borrowed money from the taxi driver with the promise of paying double when he brought me back to the clinic. I do not know what happened in the hours that followed, but I do remember walking through the streets of Tijuana when a taxi came by. I had avoided the first one.

This driver let me in and very nicely told me that he would take me wherever I wanted to go and that he would lend me money to get high. I do not know how it happened, but this taxi driver already had instructions from the clinic's staff, so they caught me. We were getting gas, when suddenly a van stopped next to us. Three individuals got out, held me down, and put me in the van. I was totally drugged and did not know what was happening or how they had found me. But they had done it. They took me directly to my first *anexo* and threw me in a detox room where they gave me a blanket, and I heard the words, "Welcome to your new home."

I woke up the next morning not knowing where I was. I was scared, surrounded by people I didn't know. I felt a sensation of terror, and that is how I spent the next five weeks, locked up in an *anexo* where they made me do manual labor every day and where AA meetings lasted up to four hours. It was a nightmare. If you behaved badly or did not follow the rules, they punished you harshly, and they made you do the dishes from all the patients in a really filthy room. Every week, people from the clinic came to visit me. I saw them, with the illusion that they were going to get me out, but it was not like that. They only came to ask me how I was and whether I needed anything, although I never got what I really needed.

In the third week, they gave me permission to receive a phone call from my family. I thought they would be the ones giving me the news that I would get out, but I was in for a surprise. My parents told me absolutely nothing. They left me crying and sad without any answers. They just said how sorry they were about what I was experiencing, but it was for my own good. They did not really have answers. They said that I was in the hands of the people from the clinic and that they did not have any power over my situation.

But finally, after thirty-five days, they came to get me. I was really excited, swearing never ever to get high again because I did not want to be a situation like the one I had just been in. I arrived at the clinic, and it was seven days before I felt like getting out and going back to be with my family.

One day, I went down and told one of the advisors that I did not want to be there anymore, that I wanted to go back to my family. They let me call my parents. When I talked to them, they said they were not yet ready to have me. They asked me to stay longer, that they would come to the clinic within fifteen days and get me out. After thinking about it for a whole night, I decided to wait for them, but the following morning, I felt desperate and decided to ask the staff to be discharged. My idea was to take my passport, buy a plane ticket, and go back to Mexico. But I was in for a surprise. My parents authorized the discharge, but they did not authorize them to give me my passport. They did not even authorize the staff to give me back my suitcase with my clothes. That was not what I had planned, and when I left, I was alone in the streets of Tijuana.

I found the first phone I could to call my family. Talking to them, I thought that I could convince them to let me come back home. My dad told me to call him in twenty minutes; he was going to call the owner of the clinic to decide what to do. Twenty minutes later, I called him, and he told me the only option I had was to go back to the clinic and wait for them there, that they would be there the following weekend. Very reluctantly, I accepted this and walked back to the clinic.

When I went back, the owner and the team of therapists decided to have a meeting with all the patients. During this meeting, the owner explained what had happened, that I had asked for my discharge but

I had come back and asked them if they would take me back. He put this decision in the hands of the other patients. Everyone accepted my return. But then he went on, attacking me verbally in front of all the patients. He said that I was a selfish person, that the only person I thought about was me, and that I was sucking the air from my parents. When I started hearing this, I got desperate. I got up from the chair, saying that I did not go into a clinic to be insulted. The owner did not take this kindly and threatened to send me to another *anexo* for three years. After several minutes of aggressive interaction, the meeting was finally over.

I was very afraid and wanted to leave more than ever before. Minutes later, I saw the opportunity to escape, and I took it. I jumped a fence and started running. It was about twenty minutes later when, unfortunately, they found me. The owner took me by the neck and literally forced me into the back of a car where he told me that I was going to an *anexo* again, this time a harder one.

And this is how I ended up in the CRREAD, the *anexo* where I am right now. Four days ago, I thought my family was going to visit me. I learned they came to see me, but they were not allowed to come in because I had not been here the necessary fifteen days to be able to have visits. When I learned about this, I was very depressed, and the idea of ending my life went through my head.

***

The failed attempts to rehabilitate Alex in lucrative clinics in an attempt to achieve a much-desired sobriety left his parents exhausted and distressed. It was very frustrating for them to end up with clinics that promised to be experts in relapses but that did not have the training to take on patients as complex as Alejandro.

The circumstances obligated them to take action in other ways, with the hope that something different would happen in order to gain control over the self-destruction of their son. It was with much pain that Clarita and Gerardo decided to leave Alex in that anexo *in Tijuana. The reasons they had to do it were explained to Alex in a letter. Here is part of it:*

Hello Alex,

We decided to go over the facts, our only hope being that they help you remember everything that has happened in the last few years. We do this simply to help you take responsibility for what your life has been. To be honest, we would like to think that most of this has been forgotten because of your drug use, but we know that is not so.

Chronology of facts:

Three failed careers: business, tourism management, and architecture. No interest in or dedication to your studies because of your drug abuse. Your car: total loss when you drove it while intoxicated at a very high speed. When we traveled to the Baltic, you had drugs, as well as on the trip to Argentina. You overturned the SUV in Ixtapa due to a lack of responsibility when driving drunk and using cocaine. Result: total loss.

In Las Vegas, you used the credit card to gamble and see if you could win all the money you owed. More stolen money, stolen checks, and an indiscriminate use of your credit card. You stayed in the first clinic for 35 days, and you left to get high. You worked at the real estate company and were totally irresponsible and uninterested. Thousands of lies.

While we were in Italy, you started your journey into the world of crack. You stayed in Promises for 60 days, and in the halfway house in Los Angeles, while you lived there, you did not want to participate in anything other than your weekend trips to visit Helen. Improper use of money and credit cards, lies. "I am walking by Malibu," when you were in San Diego with Helen. You abused your friend's trust when he lent you his car, and you used it like you shouldn't have. You left Malibu and what you called your recovery to go to San Diego with Helen. We set you up in your first apartment in San Diego totally to your liking, wanting to celebrate your sobriety and help you form a healthy life. And what happened after a few months? You came back for Eduardo's wedding.

We think that after this relapse you started your most marked path toward self-destruction that we are experiencing today. Loans, credit cards, theft, poorly used bank accounts without any consideration of others—all for using.

You went back to San Diego with the idea of trying to study again. We agreed to let you and Helen join us in Las Vegas because according to you, everything was better and you both were going to start school in September. A few weeks later, you relapsed, you kept stealing from Helen, her parents, us. Once more, you abused the credit card. Overdrafts. Pawnshops. You hit your car again, and that had to get major repairs.

After getting high for over three months, we went back to San Diego because Helen's mom called us, worried about your condition and her daughter. You chose to go recover at the McDonald Center, but you left a lot of debt at the building where you lived. You abandoned the McDonald Center irresponsibly because you did not like the place and moved to Sober Living by the Sea. You stayed for a month, during which you planned how to steal from us to get high again the day you left. You did so, and you immediately got high with the money you got from our credit card, telling us the money had been used for blood tests and who knows what else.

You came back to Mexico, and during the ten days we spent in Ixtapa, you borrowed money from the management office to keep up with your addiction. You lost your tennis shoes and God knows what else. Helen came and you disappeared on New Year's Eve, getting high all day, causing all of us indescribable panic and fear, thinking about all the bad things that could happen to you.

You convinced us once more to let you go back to San Diego to your apartment, arguing that you did not need another clinic, that you could do it by yourself by following the program, attending meetings, and exercising. Helen supported you. She said it was your responsibility, and we accepted with the condition that you go get your urine tested three times a week and that if you were clean, we would not take you to any other treatment. You never did the drug testing. You were not clean ever. Helen packed her stuff and went back to her parents' house. We, once more, came to rescue you, packed your stuff, and fixed your overdrafted bank account. With a lot of sadness we packed up your apartment, and you left for Utah with Kevin.

In Utah, you were fine for a few months. You took a class to know yourself and to learn to love yourself, forgive yourself, and teach yourself that your recovery should only be for you. You did not take advantage of it, and the only thing in your head was going back to get Helen. We invited her to go skiing with you so that you could be with her again, but she was already dating somebody else. You were so distracted that you lost the keys to your car, and it was quite a hassle to be able to get another key to get the car from where it was. Once again, you manipulated us, convincing us that you had to go back to San Diego. You went back there to Casa Pacifica, near Helen. In the summer, we went to be with you, and we once again set up a new apartment for you very lovingly. You started the relationship with Daniela, and at the same time you dated Lucia, abusing the credit card indiscriminately and irresponsibly.

Once more, after almost eight months of being clean, you went back to using. Again, because you failed to follow up with a program that helped you have a healthy life, because you used money that did not belong to you, and because you were getting involved in relationships for which you were not ready, you used again.

You used the "speed pass" for personal use, lying to everyone, especially to yourself. You lied to Eduardo, calling him in Spain to give you money. You called a very good friend for the same reason. You broke the car's windshield (we paid for a new one), you used the credit card to pay for cab services that gave you $200 in cash when you paid them $400 with the credit card, and your addiction was really brutal. You lost everything—the rent, the furniture, etc., etc. You went back to Utah with Kevin, managing to manipulate us, saying that you would only go if you could get high one more time. We had to accept this and give you resources to buy crack before you got into the car. This is a strategy that has worked until now—using our desperation and our sadness from seeing you like this, wishing that somehow you would accept the help that you need so much.

In Utah with Kevin, you detoxed in the hospital for three days, which was extremely expensive, only to escape the next day by lying to everybody. You took the car and went out to get high. You gave away all of your clothes, shoes, jackets, again you pawned your computer, cell phone, camera, racket, golf clubs, just to buy more crack and use. Again you abused our credit cards, borrowing money through them in tire stores, restaurants, and cabs. You disappeared for four days, living in a motel where there were other users and dealers, totally cut off from your family, without caring about the concern, pain, and fear you caused us and Kevin.

You showed up when you wanted to lie to us about being threatened with a knife and God knows what else, but the only thing you wanted was for the dealer to know we were not going to come after him if he kept your car. You hung up the phone on us, leaving us in panic from your story, and four hours later, you called to give us the address where Kevin could go and get you. He took you to another detox from which you left two hours later and walked for I don't know how long to go back to your dealer because in your head, you felt he had not given you enough crack for the price of your car. Once you smoked again, he took you back to detox. You stayed four days, again with a high cost of hospitalization, and you told us you did not want to live this way, for us to come and get you, that you wanted to live with your family. Your dad went, and before he arrived, without waiting for him, you left detox and went to smoke, selling the last things you had.

You came back to Mexico, and with that came more lies. The second day after you arrived, your Aunt Paulette left her purse unattended, and you stole money from her to go and get high. Another cycle of constant theft started again.

Twice in clinics in Queretaro with the same results—escaping from them without caring about the fact that they were already paid for. Between one clinic and the other, you stole credit cards and went to cheap motels without caring what you caused whole family, not hearing from you.

Over these last few years, we have lost an endless list of things: cell phones, cameras, watches, sound systems, shoes, glasses, belts, and jackets.

Your reasoning is always the same: "I can do it by myself. Leave me alone," and when you get high, you always come running back to us to rescue you once again. Because of this, you ended up in a psychiatric hospital for three weeks, and when you left that same night, you went to smoke, of course! After using, you came back to the house as always. You started back up with Daniela, you managed to stay clean for 45 days, but you had problems with her, and you stole 16,000 pesos from us. That money was hidden in the house.

You made the caregiver that we hired from the psychiatric hospital to be with you all the time get out of the car, and then you took it and drove to a cheap motel to use. Of course, when you ran out of money and you felt bad physical and morally, a friend of yours called us because you called her so that we would come to your rescue. You were so sick that we took you to detox at ABC Hospital. You were there for a few days, and after leaving, you escaped. A few hours later—for the first time—the police caught you. After many hours and phone calls that you made to your contacts and us, we took a call from you and decided to go and get you, because if not, you would go to prison.

We went to pick you up, but you started getting out all the time to sell everything you found and to steal from taxi drivers and drug dealers, etc. Again, the police caught you, and your dad negotiated with them. From there, we took you to Narconon, but 48 hours later, you left. You came to the house and went with your dad on a trip to the country. One more time you "tried" to get ahead by yourself. You could do it for a while, very possibly because you were interested in Daniela and the baby, but again you relapsed because of arguments with her. This showed us that your recovery has never been either firm or solid. You believe you have the tools to make it, but since you have never truly cultivated them, you have not been able to get clean. Whenever anything triggers something negative, you go back to using to medicate your pain and the huge emptiness that little by little has formed inside you.

This last story is as terrifying or worse than the rest. We came back from our trip because we were informed you had relapsed after six months of being clean. We went back to living horribly destructive days and nights. You went back to stealing everything you could get your hands on, and we tried to help you by sending you to a clinic in Idaho. We had our luggage packed and our airplane tickets paid for, but in order to keep getting high, you broke your promises again. We did not leave. The trip was canceled, and the plane tickets were lost.

Back to smoking day and night, taxi drivers charging us for all the money you stole from them, more selling of clothes that were not even yours, your mom's bracelets and rings, your dad's cufflinks, a lighter that belonged to your grandfather that was now Mauricio's, electronics, your mom's cell phone and watch, alcohol bottles, and again, the credit card.

The owner of the Tijuana clinic came to get you committed and again—the trick that never fails—you asked for money to get high, and if not, you would not go. You started smoking on the plane, escaping from rehab two days later. They took you to your first *anexo*. You went back to the clinic, saying you were convinced you wanted to leave your addiction. You left again a week after arriving there. You went back, and that same night you left again, on the condition that if they found you, they would put you in another *anexo* for six months. They found you, they put you in the *anexo*, you hurt yourself by cutting your wrists, and the owner decided to give you another opportunity. He took you to the clinic, a clinic you left again, signing your voluntary discharge. It hadn't even been 24 hours when you called, saying you were in jail, stabbed and beaten, which was a fabricated story because they looked for you in every jail in Tijuana, and nobody found you. You went back to the clinic because you again wanted them to pay your taxi driver. Nobody told you to, but you decided to go back. You were sent back to the *anexo*, and again today, there you are.

Your Mom and Dad

***

Alex's journey through the magical world of rehab clinics had ended. Now he was in a very different place. Isolated, without any comforts, alone, and with lots of time, he started writing for hours on end.

Perhaps isolation, deprivation, and loneliness could help Alex. His parents knew that after trying everything, they would not miss this chance for their son.

CHAPTER VII

The Darker Places

> Insanity is doing the same thing over and over again and expecting different results.
>
> —*Albert Einstein*

With immense sadness, but also with the hope that in the Tijuana anexo *Alex would finally find a solution, Gerardo and Clarita decided to leave him there, in spite of the extreme conditions in which he was living and his insistence on leaving that place.*

Clarita...I have learned little by little to focus in my life, it has not been easy. It has taken me years to understand all of this. If anyone had told me at the beginning of Alex's addiction that I would have to detach myself from him, I would have turned around and thought, "What parents leave their child without any support?" Today, I know the best thing to do is to walk away when he is using and stay very close when he is clean and trying to recover, but always be careful to give him his space. As Beverly Conyers says in her book, *Everything Changes*, "We must try not to destroy our self-worth or our values trying to solve an addiction."

***

Alex tells the difficult experience of being inside the anexo *and the unorthodox methods of treatment they used there.*

Alex...CRREAD, as I mentioned, is a center to help low-income people with addiction problems get back into society and live a life free from enslavement to alcohol and drugs. I never imagined ending up in a place like this, a place where day after day you live in sadness and grief caused by a life filled with bad decisions. The *anexos* are places characterized by their strong, and on occasion, violent therapeutic methods—if we can call them therapeutic—to treat their patients. Not long ago, if a patient did not cooperate, his hands and feet were tied, and buckets of ice water were thrown on him until he screamed that he was going to comply. Sometimes, a staff member would hit him if he behaved badly. There are several *anexos* that to this day still work under those conditions. Thank God, the *anexo* where I am has stopped working this way. Though the philosophy is a little lighter, it is still a nightmare.

I sleep in a small bed with a blanket that barely covers my body. The floor of the room is usually dirty and infested with cockroaches. The condition of the restrooms I would rather not talk about; I leave it to your good imagination. There are no showers in the center. If you want to take a shower, you have to do it with a bucket of ice water. The food is not the center's forte, either, because they use waste that they collect during the day in what they call "the panel," an old, dirty van that leaves in the morning and goes to different places like supermarkets to ask for food donations for the center. You can see cockroaches walking by the dining room while you are eating. But the human body gets used to all of this. If, in my days of active addiction, I could walk barefoot through the streets looking for my next dose, sleepless for several days and not having eaten, why not be able to do this? This is what I have to repeat to myself every moment of every day in order not to lose my mind. I don't think that anybody deserves this kind of treatment, but unfortunately, my family—because of the harm I have caused them—think a little differently.

Clarita...Throughout this whole process, Gerardo and I were so desperate and our pain was so immense that we wanted to show Alex "tough love" to see whether this theory would work. Even though we wanted him to have the experience of living in an *anexo*, we never abandoned him, and we still wanted him to receive some kind of therapy, along with visits from a physician to look after his health. On Sunday visits, a couple of friends of ours, Angel and Becky—who provided unconditional support for us, even more so for Alejandro—were a contact with the outside world that helped him not feel so lonely during those difficult times. They brought him food he liked, books, candy, and chocolates.

Gerardo...In retrospect, having put Alex in the *anexo* was the worst thing we could have done, but it was part of the dynamic and what we were recommended; however, I would insist on not sending addicts to those places.

***

Alex spent the following four months inside CRREAD in Tijuana. How much did this particular way of treating the illness of addiction help him? It is something that cannot be measured. However, he was clean during his stay, away from drugs. He finally reached his limit and, fed up with the confinement, contacted his parents, asking them for an opportunity to get out of there and be taken back to the clinic where he would follow his treatment properly. For this reason, Alex wrote a letter to his family where he committed to a series of tasks, which he thought would keep him away from using. He also mentioned in the letter that, in case he did not fulfill his commitments, he would deal with whatever consequences his family decided he should face.

Letter from Alex to His Family: January 24, 2011 (Tijuana, Baja California)

Sierra Family,

First of all, for what it's worth, this letter is written without any kind of pressure and is therefore absolutely valid.

The past several years have been full of pain and suffering for everyone. You have been the main victims of my terrible disease, and today that is something that hurts me, and I know it has left marks on all of us. I think that asking for your trust would be ridiculous after this last episode, where for one reason or another, I broke my commitments, commitments that you were firm that I keep as proof of moving forward on my road to recovery. Today, it seems that this has put you at a crossroads, and for this, I apologize.

To me, these six months have been really hard but no doubt filled with growth and learning. These six months have not only given me back my sobriety, but they have also awakened in me a new desire to live. They have awakened in me the value of family, and for that, today I have the humility to tell you that I need you. And it is not that I love you because I need you, but I need you because I love you. But today, the decision to open the doors of your home to me again is in your hands, and I know it is not an easy decision for you. But if it helps, I have asked God to light my way and give me clarity to make the right decisions. Because of that, I know that if God brought you here already, it is because it was His time, and if we have faith, we are going to make the best decision between you and me.

As far as my commitments, I think it is of the utmost importance that they are realistic and I what I can see doing is the following:

- Attend AA, NA meetings, or group therapies in order to build new friendships and relationships.

- Go to the gym every day in order to continue detoxifying my body and feel better about myself while having a little discipline.

- Go to my weekly therapy sessions with my psychiatrist to continue my process of personal development and continue with my medications.

- Have a healthy and enlightened relationship with all the members of my family at home.

- Look for a job within the first two months to learn to value money and understand what it is to work for my things.

- Look at the possibility of continuing my studies in order to feel more prepared for life.

Not fulfilling these commitments will result in losing my family's support and facing the consequences that you find appropriate.

I think there are a lot of things to talk about, and I would love to have some kind of family therapy that could help us all grow. I think we are a family with a lot of love between us, and we have been touched by this terrible illness that has left us in a very uncomfortable position. I think that frequent communication could be a good tool to recover what each of us has lost because of my illness.

I understand that with this decision I am playing my last card, and trust me, I have thought about it a lot, and I have analyzed it from every angle.

I am convinced it is the best decision I can make, and I think it is one that gives me more motivation and strength. There are risks both here and in Mexico. Only God and I will make this recovery possible with a great effort on my part. And, rest assured, by giving me the option to make this decision, you are giving me a great gift.

In conclusion, I assure you that my intentions have always been finding the best for me and for you.

I do not want to justify what I've done, but my behavior has been, in large part, due to my disease. Remember, when I don't get high, I am still sick. Using is only a symptom of my illness. I am going to need a lot of your support, and I hope to have it as I always have.

Today, we are finally closing a chapter on this illness that I hope we never again have to open.

I ask you for faith, a lot of faith. God has taken us down this path, and I personally do not think it has been a mistake. I promise to give all my effort. I do not want to live a life like the one I've been living, nor do I want you to have to go through the terror again that my illness has caused for you the last few years.

With lots of love,

Alejandro Sierra

Clarita...Even though Alejandro was aware of what was necessary to keep up with his rehabilitation, something in the chemistry of his brain had changed so deeply that, although he had the best intentions to continue with the program, he could not. One question I still have today is why Alex, with this illness, did not have the discipline that other people do to recover? How could he not adjust and practice all the steps he needed to follow to achieve well-being? Was it that part of his personality where he felt invincible, the one that held the most weight and did not allow him to be disciplined, bringing him once more in line with risky behaviors? Was it his personality or the change in brain chemistry? Maybe drugs made him feel more whole, and even with his most earnest desires to change and not cause us more suffering, at the end of the day, the most important characteristic of the illness of addiction won out: to keep using regardless of the consequences.

***

Alex's words seemed to come from a sincere desire to continue down a newfound path of recovery. Maybe the experience of having been deprived of the comforts he was used to, along with the feelings of isolation and loneliness he experienced in Tijuana, had given him back the desire to live clean and sober. In his letter, he expresses sincere repentance and a serious commitment to himself and to his family.

Alex...A few days later, my dad and Eduardo came to talk to me, and my reality convinced them I had been clean and sober for almost six months and that I was ready to go back and follow through with everything I had promised. At the time, I felt that this experience was the best that had ever happened to me. I really saw what this illness was doing to me, and I also saw the suffering that it inflicted on my loved ones.

Gerardo...I always acknowledged his efforts, and everybody criticized me when I told them, "It is not that he does not want to get better, it is just that he cannot stop. It is totally different." And if he could not stop, it was because he could not…because [the substance] had dominated him. Therefore, acknowledging when he managed to get better was very important; it required a brutal inner strength.

Alex...Going back to Mexico, I dialed Daniela's phone number to meet her, to try and get back together. I was a different man, and I wanted to move forward. She rejected me, and between the anger I already felt and the resentment for having been in that place, I decided to do what I did best: get high.

***

In spite of the written promises from Alex, Daniela's rejection and his resentment toward his parents for having confined him made him use again. Alex did not know how to express the anger he had for feeling abandoned in the anexo. *That, plus the failed relationship with a woman, caused him incredible frustration. It only took one phone call to find enough reason to throw away the sincere promises he had expressed in his letter.*

Alex...When I got home a few hours later, my mom told me I could not stay in the house. That was what we had agreed if I got high again. So, I went back to the streets to keep getting high. When I went back, my parents did not open the door, and for the next twenty-four hours, during which, of course, I lost the notion of time, I went to borrow money from all my neighbors and smoked crack.

A neighbor told me she would not give me money, but she would pay for a hotel room for me to spend the night and eat something. She took me to the hotel and told my parents where she had left me. My dad and my brother, Mauricio, came to see me at the hotel, and there I begged my dad to give me another chance. I was already tired. I asked him to please not confine me in any other place, to give me a chance, and they would see that in four days I was going to be clean again. My dad accepted and paid for the hotel for four nights under the condition that I stayed there to detox and rest without leaving.

Like every other time, my addiction had grown, and I could not resist for even a couple of hours. I left the hotel and stayed out all night. Since I did not have money, I borrowed from the guests in the hotel. They began to complain, and the manager called my dad. Then my dad, without discussing it with me, decided to call another *anexo* and send me there.

They came to get me in a taxi. Four men held me down in order to take me to this new place. It was one of the most horrible feelings I have ever experienced in my life, seeing how my dad allowed them to take me. I only screamed, "I am your son! Please do not do this to me. You promised me you were going to give me four days," but I don't think he could hear me anymore.

This new *anexo* was in the area of Xochimilco. The conditions were worse than in the previous *anexo*. I slept with twelve men, and we peed in a bucket that they did not take out of the room until it was filled. The food was spoiled. What I can tell you is indescribable. I write these experiences to try and change the concept of the *anexos* where a human being loses all of his dignity.

After fifteen days, my parents were allowed to come visit me, along with my brothers, Eduardo and Mauricio. They were really horrified when they saw this place, and they took me with them immediately.

Of course, I left promising to go to a clinic in Idaho that was working with something new that my mom had read about—cognitive behavioral therapy. I knew I needed help, but I did not tell the others. I promised my parents to go wherever they wanted if they let me use one more time. I had already learned this new way of manipulating them. My parents and my brothers, in their desperation, agreed to give me 1,000 pesos to go use. I packed my suitcase to leave the following day with my dad, and I went to get high.

Eduardo...When I accompanied my parents to see Alex at the *anexo* in Mexico City, he had an expression of terrible hatred and vengeance, and he told us, "Don't even worry. When I leave this place I am going to use." I could not believe it. I felt frustration, anger, and incredulity. All the consequences of Alex's addiction concerned me so much. I was speechless.

Gerardo...Some of the most difficult moments were when we tried to convince Alex to go back home, or go to a clinic, or go to the hospital. Alex was dominated by the power of his illness. His relapses were brutal. Sometimes his reactions were violent, out of desperation not to be confined again. Physically he was so pathetic and depleted that it only caused unreal feelings of sadness when we saw him. What do you do? Try to convince him to quit using? Sometimes we managed to do it and he'd go back home, only to leave later on. He'd convinced us using his extraordinary capacity for manipulation. It's possible that neither of us made the right decisions.

Alex...I went back the next day. We left for the airport, and we spent the night in a hotel because the flight was very early the next day. Since I had used throughout the previous night, my brain was obsessed with continuing to get high. I could not resist, and I escaped at the airport. My dad and Mauricio waited for me in the hotel room for a few hours, and since I did not come back, they went home.

Mauricio...My dad and I took him to the airport. We couldn't have him at home because we wouldn't be able to stop him from leaving to get high, so we left at seven at night and stayed in a hotel room right there. We went down to have dinner, and suddenly, Alex says, "I am going to the bathroom." I said, "I will go with you," and while I washed my hands, he took off running. He had done that several times on other occasions. My dad and I went running all along Airport Boulevard, but he was not there.

Alex...I did go back some hours later to the hotel room, knowing it was paid for and that they would not be there. The next day, I went to the front desk and made up a story where I told them my dad had agreed to be charged for two more nights. Even so, because of the drug-induced paranoia, I was very nervous that they would find me, so I chose to leave the hotel and go to a very dangerous part of Mexico called Tepito, where drugs were cheaper.

To be able to keep using, I asked for money from taxi drivers. My strategy had worked other times. I'd ask them to lend me money for drugs, they took me to buy them, and they waited for me there because then I would take them to my house where I would supposedly pay them. That was where I escaped. I think I was going off of a high adrenaline rush, but I did not care. But once, I was not so lucky and the driver caught me. He put his gun to my head. Then the police arrived, and he told them I had stolen from him.

The police took me immediately to a police station in Alvaro Obregon, and from there I called my parents, promising that if they helped me this time, I would go to detox for three days at the Sanatorio Español. It was four a.m., and my parents came to get me, but as they were on their way, I called them and told them I would rather meet them at the hospital entrance and that I had already taken care of everything. I took a taxi that again took me to buy drugs, and when I got to the hospital, my parents paid for it, thinking it was the trip fee. Again I managed to get away with what I wanted, or so I thought.

We waited for my psychiatrist to hospitalize me. I was very quiet, knowing I had drugs in my suitcase. They gave me a temporary room, and I said I wanted to shower. When I locked myself in the bathroom, my parents realized something was not right. My dad came in and saw I was about to light the pipe. They stripped me of everything I had, and I was admitted there for three days. I was so angry at myself because I had agreed to the hospitalization, and I didn't think that I'd be able to escape this place until the doctor discharged me.

They came to visit me the entire time I was there, and on the last day, when I had agreed to go to a long-term clinic in Dallas, the psychiatrist told me that no one was going to take me. When I was truly ready to go—he said this based on my history of escaping or looking for ways to not go at the last moment—I had to go to the airport where they would leave my passport and my ticket at the airline counter. Or, if I decided not to go, I would have to find a place to live by myself in Mexico.

I decided not to go to the clinic. Per the instructions of my psychiatrist, my parents paid for four days in a cheap motel while I looked for an apartment to live alone in and see if this way I could become responsible for my life. They left me at the motel, and I immediately went down to the front desk, and I asked for the paid money back, arguing I was going to stay only the first night. With that money, I obviously went to buy crack; I felt there was no going back. The following morning, after not having money, I went to my house and told them I was going to the clinic in Dallas now.

Since it was a long-term program, I packed all my stuff, and my dad very kindly decided to take me to Dallas. We arrived at the clinic, I was admitted, and my dad went back to Mexico. Two days later, I asked to be let out. At that clinic, if you do not ask for your discharge three days in advance, they do not give you your belongings. Instead they are sent immediately to your house. Obviously it was a therapeutic strategy to convince us to not abandon the program, something I did not care about because in my mind, the only thing I wanted was to leave and use again. I did not care that they did not give me my stuff, and the only thing I had taken with me were three boxes of cigarettes, which helped me get by and buy my first drugs again.

After I decided to leave, I started walking when a truck passed by. The driver gave me a ride to a Dallas neighborhood where I could easily find drugs. I got what I needed, but it was a very dangerous place. Some men pointed guns at me, and among the five of them they beat me up. I tried to run away, but I hurt my knee, and I ended up in the hospital.

I was alone and in lots of pain. Then I dialed the number of the clinic, asking them to admit me again. I then decided to leave the hospital to go buy some more drugs before going back. I asked the cab driver that was taking me to call the clinic, asking for the number of a credit card to pay him. At the clinic, they refused to pay the cab driver because he told them he had taken me to buy drugs, and then they halted my readmission process.

Again I was alone without options, on the street, without sleeping or having anything to eat. I decided to go to another hospital for detox. I stayed there for two days, and from the hospital they called my family in Mexico. I thought my parents would save me again, but they only asked the hospital personnel to call the clinic. Personnel from the clinic came to pick me up, and like the good addict I am, I tried to convince the guys in the van to take me once more to buy drugs. They obviously refused and took me directly to the clinic. I arrived on crutches, very hungry, only wanting to sleep and rest for a while, but at the clinic they did not allow me to sleep. They said I had to start right then and there working on my recovery, taking responsibility, and facing the consequences. I did not like that. I got angry and decided to leave and never go back to this place. They gave me all my belongings, and I went directly to the neighborhood where I had found crack.

***

What Alex is about to experience in Dallas represents a visit to hell, an episode that if somebody had told him years earlier when he was an intelligent, young boy full of life and unfulfilled promises that he would experience, he would have thought it an impossible scenario. However, "crack" came across Alex's path, the substance that possessed his soul, cut his wings, and dragged him to the depths of a well from which he never seemed to be able to escape. His description of those months in Dallas also shows another perspective on the illness of addiction. It offers the insight of seeing the addict as a victim of obsession that strips him of his ability to discern and completely deprives him of his freedom of choice. There is no other way to live other than using and continuing to use.

***Alex**...*Those two months on the streets of Dallas were a nightmare. Pleasant Grove was the perfect place to get crack and continue getting high. It was one of the most dangerous neighborhoods in the city. Some days I slept in an abandoned apartment, where some people let me stay. Other times, I lived in Jesse's car, a man about sixty years old who was an addict like me. He let me live in his car in exchange for me going to get money to buy crack. I realized I had an enormous ability to collect a lot of money within a few hours, making up stories and lying to people.

At night, Jesse and I got into the garages of homes and stole lawn mowers, tools, and anything that we found. One day, a police patrol car stopped us, and they took my friend's car. Since we did not have any money to get it out from where it had been impounded, I was left literally without a place to sleep and without my things, because everything I had owned was in the van.

Then I decided to go to a church where they gave me a blanket, and almost without realizing it, I started to sleep behind a dumpster from that day on, where there was a small roof to protect myself from the rain. I was living on the streets, and I did not care.

From then on, my life became a routine. Every day I woke up, begged for money at a gas station, and as soon as I had enough, I walked for hours to get some crack. I went back to my place, smoked, and repeated the same thing over and over again all day long. During that time, I did not communicate at all with my parents in Mexico. It was only much later that I learned about their despair as a result of not hearing from me.

E-mail from Clarita to Alejandro: April 11, 2011

Hello Alex,

I decided to write you e-mails in case you ever see them so you know how much I love you and how much I miss you. It has been very difficult for everyone, and I imagine for you too, but that was your decision.

You are always in my thoughts and in my heart. Every night I pray for you and ask God to guide you so that soon you can make better decisions. When this happens and you truly want help, call us or send me an e-mail.

Take care, and may God keep you and guide you.

I love you,

Mom

Clarita...We were scared to death for a long time, yet every time he called and asked for help to go back to Mexico, I told Alex, "Why don't you go back to the clinic that your dad has already paid for? There they are going to support you." After we made contact several times, I did not hear from him for a month. Every day I turned on the computer, looking at Dallas city web pages, where I could find out hospital numbers and county jails to see if my son was still alive.

Alex...There was a moment where I did not have any strength left to keep living this way. I did not have shoes. My feet were full of blisters and fungus. I did not have clean clothes. I had not taken a shower in many days. I ate only one McDonald's burger a day, given to me by the manager of the place in exchange for washing her car. She also allowed me to go into the bathroom to brush my teeth and face. I lost everything, but my toothbrush? Never. Sometimes, when I looked at my reflection in the mirror, I thought, "I do not recognize that guy. I know it's me, but I do not see myself in him."

Between the exhaustion and the emotion that it took for me to find so many good people that tried to help me, I decided I no longer wanted to keep living this nightmare. I had known many compassionate people during those months that helped me, thinking they were giving me money to eat.

There are no words to describe the experience I had. I tried to call the clinic several times, but they did not want to admit me. On occasion, many good people did help me. I looked for jobs every day, but because of my appearance or whatever, nobody could get me anything. I did not have anything.

One day, I was begging for money as usual at the McDonald's traffic light, when a woman and her daughter stopped in an SUV. I got close enough to ask for something, and the woman refused to help me. But I saw how the little girl asked her mom to give me money. The truth is that it moved me a lot. I don't know…it was the innocence of the little girl and the way she looked at me. That was one of the moments that maybe moved me the most. I wanted to go back to reality. I was so moved by people's kindness that, although they saw me high, helped me. The visual contact was very strong.

I am not really sure, but I think it was then that I started to think about what I was doing with my life, besides the desperation I felt seeing the kind of condition I was in. Among the good people that helped me was Armando, a Mexican who lived in Dallas and tried to help me by taking me to his home to have dinner, lending me money to spend the night in a hotel and be able to rest in a clean bed and take a shower, and most importantly, he lent me his computer to be able to read my e-mails and contact my family and ask for help. I contacted my parents to tell them to please help me go back to Mexico. Nobody deserved what I was living. I told them I missed them with all my heart. I hoped they would find in it their heart the desire to help me get back to Mexico. I missed them so much.

They sent Mauricio to see how I was doing.

Clarita…This whole time, Gerardo and I stayed in touch with Kevin McCauley. We really valued his opinion. It was so hard to leave Alex on the streets. I thought about Alex all the time—Alex there alone, without food, without a roof, without a bathroom, and at the same time, we felt the powerlessness of not being able to do anything anymore. The last time we had talked with Kevin, he told us we were doing the right thing, that it was time to let him go. Little by little, we had been left without tools. It was extremely painful. It would be like playing our last card, knowing it could be counterproductive. On one hand, there was hope since this experience seemed to have moved him in such a way that he decided to ask for help and would go for treatment. On the other hand, there was the terror that he could end up in jail or dead on the streets of Dallas.

Gerardo...The stories that Alex and Mau told us about the experience in Dallas leave me no doubt that a spiritual power, somebody from up there, was always with my son.

Mauricio...A few weeks had passed since I learned that Alex was living on the streets in Dallas. At that point in my life, I was reading the Bible and a lot of religious material, and I found a passage that spoke about saving your brother, your neighbor. Then I said, "How am I going to live my whole life knowing I have a missing brother on the streets of Dallas?" I didn't want to live like that. If my mom was desperate not knowing anything about him or where he was, I had to find him.

I sent him messages through Facebook, and one day my mom called me and told me Alex had called to ask for help. He had left his friend, Armando's, phone number to be able to contact him. I called him. I told him I was coming and left the name of the hotel where I was going to stay.

Alex arrived at the hotel with his Mexican buddy. He had lent him his computer. Really a great guy that later I treated to dinner as a token of gratitude for having saved my brother's life. It was fate, because finding him in Dallas would have been impossible.

I found Alex like we had thought—tired, with a beard, and his feet were very hurt, filthy, and stinking. The first thing he did was shower and shave. The next day I took him to have a haircut. Then, clean, with his new haircut and shaven, he told me, "Let's go shopping." I could not believe it. After having lived in the street, begging for money, stoned all day, and sleeping on the floor, his attitude really left me dumbfounded. He told me about his experience as if he were talking about an action novel.

Clarita...In one of the many books I have read about addictions, I remember a phrase that says, "All addicts tell their experiences as if they were war battles." I remember it now because when he came back from Dallas, it was shocking to listen to his stories while we were eating, as if they were simple adventures. It got us very angry to think that the experience of living on the streets had not impacted him deeply. However, today we understand that Alex had a very hard time connecting with his pain.

***

The reunion between the brothers was very emotional, and Alex says so in the first letter that he sent to his parents by e-mail.

Letter from Alex to His Parents: April 29, 2011

Dear Mom and Dad,

Meeting with Mau was one of the most incredible things in the last few months. Mau arrived with news somewhat different than what I expected, but overall he told me that you are not interested in helping me anymore, much less helping me return to Mexico. I understand that, because of what we have gone through, this is what our relationship has come to. Trying to describe to you what I have experienced in the last two months would be close to impossible. Simply put, there are no words to describe it. Yes, luckily I have not gotten high for over twenty days. I cannot tell you the exact time because when you live on the streets, the notion of time is lost a little. Anyway, I managed to do what I had always wanted—to find within me the decision to set drugs aside and try to get myself a life.

Now, it is important to mention that the opportunity for work for a person who does not have any place to live, nor is legal in the United States, is not as easy as it used to be, and less so for a person like me. If I was a mechanic or knew about construction or manual labor, perhaps there would be an opportunity, but for someone who does not have any idea about hard work, it is nothing short of impossible. I am very skinny, malnourished, with heart pain. My heart really hurts when I breathe and when I stretch my left arm.

Anyway, the truth is I do want to go back to Mexico. If you do not want me to go back with you, that's fine. If you do not want to help me, either, it also seems fine to me, but the truth is I do not want to stay the way you want me to—in a homeless shelter and go out to look for a job here in Dallas. The truth is, this is not what I want from my life.

I have been very close to God for the last month. I think it is He who has protected me and taken care of me. I met all the policemen in Dallas. I met so many people. I had so many experiences—good and bad—and I think it is time to go back to my country. I am not homeless. I have family. I love you, I miss you, and I feel that despite the fear you feel about me coming back, the truth is that sooner or later I have to go back.

In fact, one day before you replied to me, Armando—who I am sad you thought used drugs and gave me money to get high when he is simply a hard-working Mexican who felt sad seeing me in the street and helped me every once in a while. Anyway, he was going to take me to the bus station, and he was going to pay for my return to Mexico.

I do not know what to ask of you. I do not know what to tell you. I want to reiterate that what I have experienced in the last few months has been terrifying. Not picking up the phone when I called and letting me live on the street made me realize you really have given up on me, and I do deserve it, but here I am. I survived, for better or worse. I made it, and the truth is, I want to go back to my country.

I don't know what to tell you. I am tired, I am really sad, and I'm telling you what I think with the hope that you understand that life here in Dallas ALONE WITH NOTHING is not really a life, and that in spite of me being the one asking for countless opportunities and that I have to be responsible for everything I've lost, I feel that you did not bring us up this way, did not prepare us to end up alone in a homeless shelter.

Anyway, I do not want to go around in circles. I do not want to bother you. I want you to know that, one way or another, I became a survivor, and now I want the opportunity to survive in my country. Close to my family. If you want to help me with the basics, I would appreciate it, and you would make my departure from this nightmare a little easier.

Later we will talk on the phone and continue talking.

That's all for now.

Alex

Letter from Clarita to Alex: April 29, 2011

Hi Alex,

First of all, it is not that we did not want to reply. We were in Ixtapa. Unfortunately, it did not occur to you that, being Holy Week, we would be there. I imagine that what you are going through must be very hard, but without wanting to be hard or hurtful, it was what you chose to live. You had been asking us for a long time to leave you alone, that you wanted to make it on your own.

Unfortunately, we did not listen to you before because we wanted to rescue you again and again, but you said to us very clearly, "If I do not want to, nobody can do anything about it." The truth is that, even with all the pain we are experiencing, we understand that it is best for you to empower yourself, knowing you can do it by yourself. You are a 27-year-old man, and you have the right to live your life as you wish, the same way that I'm sure you realize that we cannot keep living the experience of your addiction, either.

I am confident that the day you truly get tired of a life of self-destruction and use, you will really ask for help. You will do what is necessary to move on. There are, like you say, very good people willing to help you. You just have to wish it with your heart. To tell you the truth, I do not know whether you called the clinic or not. They say that after leaving with your clothes, you did not call again. Or maybe you did, it but it was like the tale of Peter and the Wolf: nobody believed you anymore.

I already gave you referrals to good people who truly want to help, just like you've wanted. Also, we have given you the opportunity to go back and get treatment in a clinic, which is what you really need. Truly trust in the power of God and of your mind, and I am sure you are going to succeed. That you own nothing is true. For years you have given crack the power over all of your material and emotional things. Unfortunately, you have given over your life to it.

It is really sad, but I am sure that if you try, you are going to pull through. You are always in our hearts. We love you and miss you too, but Alex, something has got to change. We cannot go on like this. I do not think it is fair, either for you or for us.

Your Mom

Mauricio...Later, we walked through the places where he had been. I visited the church that put a roof over his head. He took me to a McDonald's and introduced me to the lady who gave him a burger for washing her car. We walked from there to the house of the dealer to see the route he walked daily. Currently, when I see a homeless person, I help them, because after that experience, I see in that person my brother, Alex, living like that in Dallas.

In Mexico, I had planned a strategy, along with my parents, to keep him clean a few weeks before taking him back home. I had inspirational books, the Bible, and a routine to bring him back to reality. The plan was to keep him in the hotel room to read some of the books together that I had brought and then do some charity work. I told him, "Look, Alex, here's the thing. We are going to go to meetings daily. We are going to try to do some charity, and then we will go to bed early."

Letter from Gerardo to Alex

Hello Alex,

I am convinced that you have something important to do in your life, but you have wasted the opportunities with your relationships and with your behaviors that have not helped your personal growth. Instead, they have been to keep taking advantage of us and of someone up there who continuously protects you.

Our powerlessness is beyond belief and so is the frustration of thinking that even though we try to help you pull through, you relapse continuously. We are saddened in a way that I do not think you can understand. I know the drug you use is terrifyingly violent, and we have lived through it these last several years. We do not want any more ups and downs, and I am sure we will find a definitive solution, with you or without you. You will take it or leave it. It is in your hands to decide your destiny. You have a new opportunity, and I pray to God He lets you reconsider, and in your deliberation, you can find strength to go back home.

You already know this, and I do not want to repeat to you the consequences you have faced because I want to leave you in this e-mail only positive ideas of what you can, if you want to, achieve in this life—happiness and inner peace and everything else that comes with it.

Your Dad

Mauricio...Little by little, he began to understand, and together we looked for a group where there were meetings every day. We also found a place where men between thirty and fifty years old lived together, all of them rehabilitated addicts who were dedicated to working on a little house. The following day, we brought them food, and we worked with them all day. The next morning, we went back, and Alex told me that he did not want to be there anymore. The situation was uncomfortable for him.

I didn't want to push him, but then it occurred to me that we could go to the supermarket and buy food to give to people in need. My intention was to make him see where he had been and the gravity of the situation he went through. However, I don't think he could grasp this.

In the meetings we attended, far from just listening to others' stories, everyone was motivated and said very nice and sincere things with the intention of helping others. The only bad thing was that Alex was not very receptive, and he made it clear that meetings did not help him. He has always said that, and to be honest, it was hard to make him change his mind. I told him to try, starting at that moment, to do something different from the past, because what he had done until then had always ended in relapse from not having the foundations, or anything else, to sustain him.

On the spiritual side, the truth is that it was very difficult to get through to him. Like it says in the Bible, "Whoever has ears, let them hear," and I truly think that Alex was unreceptive in that sense. He told me he had his own spirituality that worked for him.

We went for pizza, and then I took him to another meeting, but every time I proposed it, he told me he wanted to go only because there was no choice, but the reality is that he was enthusiastic.

I told my parents. In an e-mail I explained to them how he was doing, that I was running out of options. I even asked them for new ideas. The fact is that I never ran out of desire or hope in helping Alex become more proactive in his recovery, but I do not know if—at that moment— future plans were what Alex needed.

On several occasions, we discussed that there must be a transition from the situation he was living in on the streets to going back to a life of comfort, but I don't think it yielded any results.

***

Crack addicts live with so much hopelessness, truly so devalued, that evasion becomes their perfect defense mechanism to not keep feeling so much pain.

Mauricio...This experience was very useful to me, and I am sure for Alex, too. Although he never said anything to me, he never said, "Thanks for coming to rescue me. It is so good you came," but I don't think there was any way Alex could feel otherwise. Maybe Alex did hit rock bottom, but at that point, his illness had progressed so much, which prevented him from objectively seeing the crudeness of the life he had been experiencing. Sick people like him do not even realize where they are. It is funny, but it would seem that homeless people live very freely, very peacefully.

***

After being rescued by his brother from the street, Alex was again willing to change his path and start, once more, the process of rebuilding himself.

Alex...I could have kept surviving on the streets; one gets used to everything. I did not call my parents at all or look for them because I was so saturated with drugs. I also did not call them because I had no choice, or because I wanted to be rescued. I had looked for them and called them since the day I arrived in Dallas because, like always, I love them and because they are and always will be my family. For better or worse, I will adore them, and no matter what happens in my life, no matter what I do, I will always look for them, and I will never forget them.

For a change, I found myself in a moment similar to many others, where I stop getting high, I say that I am going to change, I ask for help, I want to succeed, and as time passes, I go back to the same. Then, of course, I understand the fears and doubts of my parents and brothers. I did not know whether this time it would be different because only time and my attitudes would determine that, but what I did know is that my life on the streets was much easier when I got high than when I stopped using. The only thing I would really like is for my family to acknowledge that I could make it on my own without anyone's help.

I was happy to have been reunited with my brother, but I was still sad to feel the distance between my parents and me. Yes, distance that I had created, but at the end of day, it HURT the same way.

I did not know what my parents' plans were, nor did I know whether they were going to support me, or how much they wanted to get involved, but I was committed to pulling through and pushing forward, regardless of their decisions, because what I had experienced in the streets had been one of the most difficult experiences of my addiction, one more nightmare in my life. It might have been the worst of all. I was tired, malnourished, and sick in a lot of places, sad, and full of desperation. At that point in my life, any small thing or act of compassion filled my heart with happiness and hope.

***

Gerardo and Clarita decided to support their child and welcome him back to Mexico. The first condition of his stay was that he get a job immediately so that he had the means to live with dignity and start to build a future based on his own efforts. He came back in the beginning of May to his country where he found a job and started repairing the relationship with his mother and the rest of the family.

Letter from Alex to Clarita

Clarita, Clarita the most beautiful mother…

Hi, I have been thinking for two or three days about what I wanted to say in my Mother's Day letter, and I ended up writing it at 2:33 a.m. We have written each other so many letters with such lovely sentiments, filled with optimism and advice and dreams, and I think all of them at the time made us feel good and loved. Even if later on I didn't strictly follow through—or in my case, not at all—does not mean that the words written at the time were not from the heart with lots of love.

What a couple of months! I believe that neither the stories nor anything else are going to be able to describe what I experienced, but the most important thing is that there is no way that I can imagine what you have lived, Mom! I think the system is not designed so that a son makes his mom suffer in the same way that my decisions and actions have made you suffer. Because of this and many other things, I will always be indebted to you. I will always question why life made us go down this path, because in spite of saying that it was me who chose it, I feel that there is a bigger plan for all of this to have happened, all that has happened up until now.

I can confess that, more than having felt the coldness and bad vibes of using people to get money, what inclined me to quit using was the necessity of having my mom by my side. It was not the streets, it was not the loneliness, it was not hunger, it was not being uncomfortable, it was not the beatings, it was not the guns, nor the smell of trash. It was knowing that day after day I was walking away more from my family, from the people that I have told countless times ARE WHAT I LOVE THE MOST!

Mom, one of the biggest pains that my illness has caused me is having the relationship that you and I have today. It does not feel natural. Yes, I have earned it all. But in the end, it is the same: I miss my mom. I want to go back to being a son for you. I hope you understand what I am referring to.

Thanks for moving heaven and earth to take care of me, and above all, I am sure that there is nothing stronger than a mom's love. That is what took care of me, the love of a mom like YOU. Thanks for always being there for me. And rest assured, at 3:38 every day, just as you did, I was thinking about how much I missed you.

Happy Mother's Day!

I LOVE YOU

Gerardo...An important lesson is to always be by your sick child's side, supporting him, understanding him, acknowledging his or her efforts day after day, trying to find a solution and see if in one of those attempts, he or she finds the way out. Never stop having faith; never stop being an optimist.

Alex...One of my parents' conditions for returning to Mexico, that they communicated through a letter, was to find a job immediately. I know my life experience during the past several months made me value the most basic things—counting on a shower, having toilet paper or a warm meal. My parents, they gave me the things I needed to start. It was very important to me that my parents knew that I was interested in changing, in being in Mexico with my family, where I belonged. I think that in the end, we all wanted to leave the Dallas nightmare behind.

***

And so it was, showing incredible willpower, that Alex, with renewed energy, started a period of drug abstinence that filled his family and him with hope.

Alex...Like I mentioned before, I went back to Mexico with lots of gratitude—to life that was giving me this new opportunity, and to my parents and brothers. My cousin, Juan Carlos, helped me find a job in a movie production company. It was tedious because it required lots of precision, and honestly, it was a trial by fire. Because I am so restless, it was very hard for me to stay focused. It was tiring, but I was very happy to be doing something productive. Besides, I liked what I did, and I got along very well with my boss. He told me I was doing a good job.

At the same time, a friend of mine invited me to handle public relations for a nightclub. My job was to take people to visit the place. Everybody thought I was crazy by getting into that environment, but I felt very confident in my recovery. I felt very peaceful when I left at night, and I had fun without drinking. When it was four in the morning and everyone was really drunk, I was thankful to God that I was not like that. I could talk to the girls, and I got great reactions when they saw me sober and coherent, instead of drunk and trying to flirt with them. I woke up the next day without the feeling of having to call a friend to find out what I had done the night before.

About a month later, my brother, Mauricio, and my cousin, Rodrigo, threw a party at Mau's home, and another cousin brought his girlfriend's girlfriends. There I met a girl that charmed me. She had beautiful eyes. I left the party, but when I was on the road with my friends, I thought, "What am I doing if where I really want to be right now is at Mau's house with that blond girl?"

So, I went back. I spent the night with her and told her a little about my addiction. I went out with her three more times, and I was very happy with this new relationship. She was a girl who was very different than all the others I'd met. We decided to spend a weekend in Ixtapa with my cousin and his girlfriend. I had the best three days that I had had in a long time—laughter and good, clean fun.

Marimar...It was very funny, because when Alex arrived, I turned to my friend and said, "Look how handsome that guy is," and she replied, "That's Alex, the one I wanted to introduce you to." He only said hello to everyone and left. Then he came back, and several of us went to a bar. I spent the whole night talking with him. He opened up immediately. I loved that from the beginning he was so transparent. He had just given a talk for teenagers, along with his mom. They had been invited to speak by the association Convivencia sin Violencia, and he told me about how the talk had helped him. He took me to my house and asked me for my phone number. I was thrilled. He was a charming and fun person. Made me laugh a lot. Maybe it was because of his intensity, but immediately he started planning a trip, and I was amused. The following week, we saw each other every day. Then another week passed, and we left for Ixtapa.

On the trip, I noticed how he enjoyed everything with such passion. At that time, I thought his shows of happiness were exaggerated, but he valued and enjoyed everything much more. "I am happy, I am happy!" he repeated to me. Later, I understood it was because Alex was reborn after having lived on the street. It had been two months since his arrival from Dallas.

On Saturday, he asked me to stay and meet his friend José, who was coming to Ixtapa for work. Up until then, I hadn't realized that it was very important to him that I meet his friend. That same Saturday was incredible because he lit candles all over the apartment and played a song—our song—"I Will Always Love You." We had a great time that day. It was fun and romantic. He was very passionate. I liked his energy a lot.

Alex...One month after my arrival from Dallas, I got a call from one of the owners of Valentina telling me he had bought the place and was looking for some partners to remodel it. I told my parents, and they jumped down my throat, saying that I couldn't meddle in the business of a dance club where I had started my use of alcohol and drugs. At the time, because of my experience in Dallas, I was clean and sober. So, little by little, I kept talking to them and convinced them that there would always be Discos. Why not remodel this one and make it a safe place for youngsters where they were always watched, even with a safe service to bring them and take them back home?

For this job I thought of a very good friend, my lifelong friend, José, who was an architect. He built and remodeled restaurants. Very excited, I called him to tell him about the project, and I said I wanted to invite him and his girlfriend to Ixtapa for the weekend. He told me he would meet me there on Sunday by himself to see what could be done with the project since his girlfriend had other plans.

Clarita...When Alex told us his idea, I thought it was the wildest thing, a fantasy in his head, and once more, it showed his lack of awareness in understanding that this should not be his world. Gerardo suggested the idea of going with José to look at the place to see what he thought. My husband liked the idea of creating a place where parents could go for dinner where, at the same time, there was a space for young people, that is to say, a safer project.

Alex...As we had planned, on Sunday night I left Marimar and my cousins at the airport and picked up my friend. I introduced them. I told him, "Look, José, this is the girl I am going to marry."

We went back to the apartment and started watching a soccer match. The game was so exciting that we decided to watch the second half at a bar called Mr. Frogs. When we arrived, José said, "Bro, aren't you going to organize my bachelor party for me?" He was getting married in three months. I thought it was a great idea, and we left to go to a "table" in Zihuatanejo, a bar where there was table dancing. That weekend, we had been advised not to go to Zihuatanejo because violence was intense between the *Zetas* and some other cartel, but I ignored it.

When we got to the place, it was empty. We were told that everything started after midnight. We did not feel like staying and left to go for a pizza. We then wanted to go back to the table-dancing place, so once more, making bad decisions, we left for the "bachelor party."

When we arrived, there were a lot of people. Someone brought some girls, and we stupidly asked how much it was to take them dancing somewhere else. The place no longer looked the same. Some guys at the bar did not stop looking at us, and I began to feel very uncomfortable, but we ignored it. We paid what they asked for and left with the girls.

When we arrived in Ixtapa, I realized someone was following us. Suddenly, they intercepted us with a car, cutting off the road in front of us. When I tried to back up, I hit another car that was already behind us. At that moment, some men with guns of various calibers got out of the cars and pointed them at us. Because I didn't know what they were going to do, my first reaction was to escape. José yelled at me to speed up, and I instinctively pulled onto the street, trying to escape toward the other side. It was then when they started shooting. Thousands of thoughts went through my head. They want to kidnap us. They want to steal from us. I saw myself cut into pieces and buried on a mountain. I felt like I was in a horror movie. We were scared to death. We did not understand what was happening.

Today, now that I reflect on it, I do not even know how I got to the first hotel I saw and got out of the car, yelling to my friend, "Get out because they are going to kill us!" But he never answered me. When I looked down, I realized I was bleeding profusely all over my body. At that moment, I asked for help and passed out in the arms of an American man. Later, I was told that some tourists helped me and brought me inside the hotel lobby, and from there, they called an ambulance. I woke up in the ambulance as it was already going toward the Zihuatanejo General Hospital. I was desperately screaming, "Where is José? Where is the person who was in the car with me? Where is my friend?"

I never saw him again.

Clarita...Alex was shot five times on different parts of his body with different caliber guns, and his dear friend died immediately from a shot to the stomach. After this experience, the pain of having lost his best friend was such that Alex stopped writing. It was even hard for him to talk to us about that experience.

Alex and Eduardo 1985

Disneyland, Mauricio and Alex 1987

Sunday with family 1987

Christmas 1987

Brothers

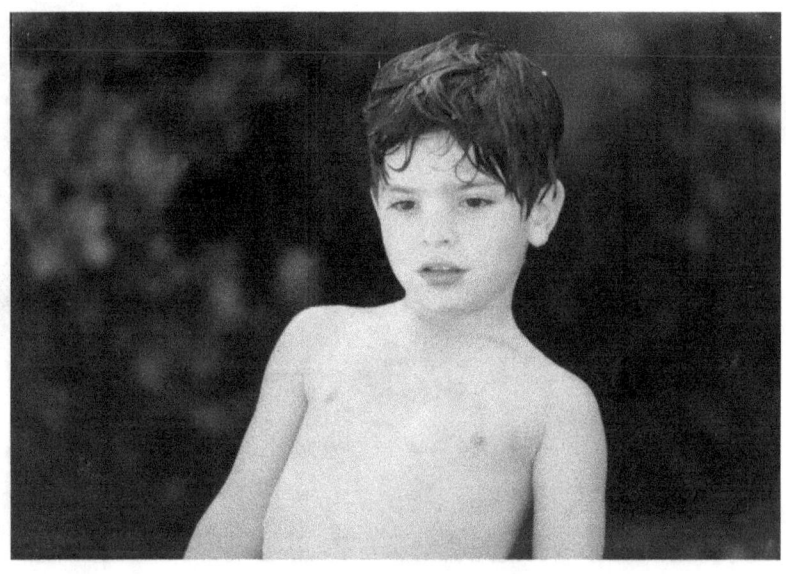
Alex, Cuernavaca

Alex and Clarita and World Cup 1994

Golf Outing

Alex and Gerardo

High School Graduation

World Cup 2006

Cruise in the Baltic Sea

Eduardo´s Wedding 2008

San Diego 2009

Eduardo´s Civil Ceremony 2008

Alex with Mickey Mouse

Clarita´s Birthday 2012

Mauricio and Alex

Golf	Vidalta 2013

Alex and Marimar

Alex´s Last Birthday, July 11, 2013

Farewell Ceremony Ixtapa, February 22, 2014

CHAPTER VIII

The Happiest Moment of My Life: Marimar

Alex had a huge heart. I would have loved to have his kindness.
I wish more people could have this quality.
Our world would be a better place.

—Marimar Planas

The soil teaches us that sometimes we think all is dead; however,
with lots of care and love, everything is born again.

—Pablo Neruda

Marimar...It was terrifying. I woke up on Monday to go to work and saw Alex's message and several missed calls. He told me, "I am at the hospital. Some drug lords intercepted us, and they shot at us. José is dead." After that, there were no more messages. I was frozen. The shooting was on July 11, the day of Alex's birthday.

Clarita...As days passed and when he was ready, Alex started getting out his feelings about the tragedy a little at a time. It took him a long time to overcome the shock that he was in. He could not believe what had just happened. He wondered every day why José and not him. He tried to be close and in touch with his friend's family, but it was very hard for them to relive that moment. Alex commented how that silence hurt; he wanted to be near them so that he could be close to his friend. But he understood the parents' pain.

Letter from Alex to His Parents: New Year's Eve, 2011

It is clear that this year has been complicated, full of the unexpected and almost surreal experiences. The last several years have been filled with hardship. It has no doubt been difficult for everyone. The reasons why all this happened may be easier to understand after a while. But for the time being, the learning experience has been substantial; the lessons are clear and strong. And one of the easiest ones to see—that has been the most important thing we have—is our family.

Today, during mass, the priest invited us to thank God for our times in darkness when He had put a light at the end of the tunnel. Although my illness has brought much darkness, there is not the slightest doubt that you have always been that light. What happened on my birthday was terrifying. It was an experience that I shall never forget, and it was something that marked the day my life had to change.

Yes, there are many things to fix, to keep growing up and maturing. It is clear the road is still long, but thank God, it will be a road on which I will be totally present. With all my heart, I thank you for your patience and your great love that you've shown me for so long. I thank you for everything you have given me, emotionally and physically. And I want you to know that in some way, I will always try to give you back part of what I took from you. It was a good end, 2011, and I am sure it is a preamble to a great 2012. May it be filled with health, love, friendship, and success for you. But as always, the biggest of all successes is to be part of the great family that you have formed with so much love.

Love you,

Alex

***

Like we mentioned, Alejandro stopped writing. From this point forward, his family—with the support of his girlfriend, Marimar, and the people close to him at this stage of his life—continues the narration in recognition of Alejandro's significant contributions to this project and his interest in shaping a legacy that could help others. So, with e-mails, letters, and personal experiences, they wrote the last chapters.

Alex was on the brink of a new horizon away from drugs and by the side of somebody to love. After existing in the dark underbelly of his addiction, sober life in Mexico seemed to welcome a more luminous stage of his existence.

***Marimar*...**I went to the hospital to visit him every day. I asked a girlfriend of mine to join me, and that is where I met his parents. He made me feel very special when I saw him again. He was there for like, a week. Everything got complicated because a lot people were intervening. E-mails went back and forth from people who suggested that I walk away from the situation. My parents, my friends, everybody pressured me and asked for explanations. Those who were giving their opinions really did not know him; it was just gossip. I felt I had to be there for him, and I was convinced that I wanted to give our relationship a chance, so I pushed aside what everyone else was saying. I felt alone against the world. Those pessimists actually made our relationship grow much faster, because as we talked, our feelings deepened. Our relationship was definitely starting in a very profound way.

***Clarita*...**As a part of his recovery and because of the shock that Alex was in, it was recommended that we take him away from Mexico for a while. A friend lent us an apartment in Colorado, and we went there with him—Mauricio, Gerardo, and me.

It was a month filled with recovery, for Alex as much as for the rest of the family. We spent a month all together. My sister also came with her granddaughters and her daughter-in-law. This way, Alex could enjoy seeing the kids and spend some fun times with them. Eduardo also told us that we were expecting our first granddaughter. In the midst of so much pain, it was welcome news of hope and love.

Alex was recovering day after day, but I kept feeling angst and restlessness in my heart because my son could not express the pain of his friend's death, the shooting, or the awful trauma he had experienced. Many months later, Alex managed to tell me that that had been one of the most difficult experiences of his life. It had been so devastating that he could not even talk about it. "You know, Ma? What happened with José was an experience that I will never forget, and it marked the day that my life would have to change. I have had to live with it, and I will have to live with it forever."

***

During Alex's stay at the hospital, Rodrigo, his former boss, went to visit him and offered him his job back. The harsh experience of the shooting made him cut ties with many people and allowed him to start living again.

Clarita...In spite the tragedy, things were calm, and together we were spending what would turn out to be some of the best moments of Alex's last years. After that month, since Rodrigo had offered him a job, Alex started with that new project, which made him really happy. The income from his job at Vidalta opened up a path to economic independence besides bringing back his self-confidence, knowing he could do things and do them well.

Rodrigo...Alex always brought joy and energy to the office. It was very fun to work with him, although sometimes his hyperactivity made me nervous. He always marched to a different drummer. He had ten thousand ideas per second, and although several of those ideas weren't viable or did not yield results, there were two or three that we have implemented to this day. His motivation to work as a team and have cordial and fair relationships with everyone encouraged us to implement a bonus-per-sale for every member of the team. This allowed me to keep my sales team together and lower the high turnover rate that I'd had until that point. If it were up to Alex, all the earnings would have been distributed evenly between everyone. I think I learned a lot from Alex—some good lessons along with some difficult and deep discussions. He was not quiet when he didn't like something and would defend his point of view by all means necessary.

Marimar...After the accident came a very complicated period that became more intense after news of the incident got picked up by the media. I obviously wanted my parents and friends to meet Alex without judging him, but when they saw the news on television, everybody worried a lot.

Then summer vacation came, and Alex's family took advantage of the opportunity to go on a trip. Every night he called me on the phone. When he returned from Colorado, he became my boyfriend. It was August 10, 2011. He came back with a lot of presents, which made me feel very spoiled. He gave me a feeling of absolute peace and tranquility that moved me so much because I had never felt like this with anybody. Even when we were just sitting there watching a movie, there was a feeling of absolute connection between us. It was so strong and striking. It was something I did not want to miss. In one of the many letters he wrote me, I loved this one comment he made: "You know, Mar? With you I have the feeling that I am with the person I should have always been with."

One day, I went to have lunch at his house with his parents, and they patiently began to explain to me a little more about Alex's history and his disease. In the beginning, I did not know how to treat Alex. I mean, I did not know what to watch out for, maybe because of the stigma around the illness. Clarita recommended that we try to have the most normal relationship possible. I think we openly spoke about addiction over the course of the meal. Obviously, I was nervous about the issue, so I started doing my own research about addiction and crack since his parents had explained to me that this was a "different" kind of drug.

Now that I look back, the reality is that nothing can prepare you. It is good to be informed, and it is useful to know a little more about what you are getting yourself into and the risks that exist, but the reality is that living through the relapse of a loved one is terrible, and the way it wears you down emotionally is very powerful.

My parents were still very concerned, and although we had been together for only three weeks, Alex's parents decided to invite them over to their house to meet each other. It was a very formal dinner. I think everyone was nervous. Gerardo and Clarita were very honest with my parents and told them all about addiction and the clinical aspects of the illness. My parents were very interested in knowing what had really happened because there were many conflicting news stories, and they did not understand the relationship between the accident and Alex's addiction. They were more at ease after having met the family and hearing the explanations that Alex's family shared so openly. After that, my parents sent me some e-mails, sharing their point of view. My dad even told me the story of a relative who had an addiction.

Letter from Alex to Marimar: October 4, 2011

Mar,

I think there are so many things I have already experienced in my life! Many experiences that perhaps other people will never have! All of them have molded me and have made me the person I am today.

I can tell you that in spite of my history, I have NEVER experienced or felt what I am experiencing and feeling with you. I thought I had been in love before, but I was wrong. In you, I find all that I've ever looked for but never thought was possible to find. I feel loved, very loved, and you have no idea how I thank life for this spectacular sensation. I was constantly looking for something else, something better, something to fill the void I sometimes felt. And you came into my life to fill that void completely, to stop that search, to—for the first time in my life—make me feel at peace and completely fulfilled by what I have. Now, I not only feel that there is nothing more to look for, but now that I have so much—thanks to you—I feel indebted to you. I hope I am able to give you as much as you give me day after day, sometimes without realizing it.

You are teaching me so much: to give myself completely without fear of getting hurt, to be able to trust in the good and the bad that I have inside me. You are a person that I know will not use anything against me. With you I feel protected and cared for.

I believe you came into my life at the perfect moment, and although at the same time it was a difficult moment, throughout this whole thing we've both managed to realize that we are willing to work together. I have discovered this woman that has crossed my path—strong, attentive, observant, sensitive, vulnerable, affectionate, and with a capacity to love and trust, which at the time was hard for me to believe. You are really beautiful inside and out. That beauty you have inside radiates around you constantly. You have no idea the light I see in you and the purity and love that show in your eyes.

I am really lucky to have you in my life. I hope we can share it together for many, many more years to come. I will fight for you constantly, and I will do everything in my power to make you feel how important you are.

I LOVE YOU

***

As he expresses, Alex had a deep, long-lasting emptiness that was being filled with Marimar's love. That space of love, along with his job, his family's love, and his follow-up treatment, put him in a better place.

Everything was going well. However, relying on somebody else to fill his personal void was dangerous; the emptiness should have been mended from the inside out. His vulnerability was ever-present.

Clarita...I do not have any doubt that, even with all of the hardships in his life, Alex had many moments of happiness and feelings of peace. I am sure he felt happy when he could help others, enjoy the beauty of nature, and appreciate being near us, but for some reason, these moments did not last, and little by little, he went back to feeling uncomfortable, riddled with pain and fear. With these fears and feelings of inadequacy, he probably could not perceive the good in his life. Neither could he trust in the possibilities of happiness that he had.

Marimar...Starting from there, everything started to improve. My friends met Alex and loved him because Alex was always trying to be liked by others—always generous, super thoughtful, and spontaneous. Alex met someone, and he gave all his attention to that person. Besides, he was constantly focused on helping and looking for ways to support people. My friends used to call him "Alex Productions" every time they saw how he planned or made something small or unimportant into a big, magical event.

I loved the spark and energy he had; he was always smiling. I think all of that made people love him. With my siblings he was really nice, and he spared no expense when trying to give of himself. One of the things that defined him most was his generosity. He was very spontaneous. I have several stories about that. For example, we used to go to McDonald's to eat, and he'd buy six extra burgers that he gave to the guards who watched the entrance to the gated community where he lived, the guards on my street, and Juanita and Mary. He was always thinking of who else he could give something to. He was like this every day.

He loved candy more than anyone in the world, and I remember one Tuesday we were at his house, and he said, "Mar, let's go for candy." We went to the little town of Vista Hermosa, and he started buying plastic bags filled with candy. He asked me to fill them, and then he said, "Now let's give them to all the children we meet on the street."

When he had something, he always had to share it. For example, at the moment he earned a commission, he wanted to give it away to his loved ones. He enjoyed making people happy. I learned from the affection and attachment he had with his family, something I had lost a little but got back through him. I valued my family and the communication I had with them again. I also liked seeing how he defended the people he loved the most. And when he told me about his life on the street, it made me appreciate so many things.

He made me laugh all the time; he was so funny. When we talked, I loved the way he respected what I thought or believed, although sometimes I did not agree with his particular way of thinking. I loved seeing how he overcame challenges from within—his fears, his limitations, and his ability to always be a better person. His sensitivity towards everything was really unbelievable. It was something really special—a childlike innocence—and that was one of the things that I liked the most about him.

In the beginning of our relationship, things would get a little complicated because sometimes Alex would get aggressive. When he got mad, he had a short temper. And then he regretted it and asked me for forgiveness. I knew the aggression was not directed at me—it was just general aggression—but his reactions still scared me. One of the things he taught me that stuck with me the most was, "Mar, we are already mad, but it's over. Let's enjoy the rest of the day." But it was harder for me to let go of the anger. It was very difficult to adapt myself to his unbounded passion. Nowadays, that way of thinking has helped me a lot. Trying to choose what really matters and letting go of what does not. After those times when Alex exploded, he would apologize to me and explain himself through his letters:

> I know I have big flaw. I do not like feeling like a bad person or feeling guilty. I keep absolutely everything bottled up inside, and it settles into a place in my being where I become so uncomfortable that the only thing I know to do is attack and scream, and then I rationalize everything on my own terms and try to succeed in making myself feel good. I am sorry. I am working a lot on my character. I am trying. I am in the best stage of my life right now in terms of security and strength. I ask you to be patient with me.

Clarita...When a person is using, all his emotions are anesthetized. His masks are on, and his shields are up. His defense mechanisms are in place. With these, he can handle any conflict that comes his way and avoid pain. Early in the recovery process, the addict is naked and doesn't know how to act in the face of his emotions and feelings, in the face of his frustration. Not knowing how to handle them is brutal.

Alex did not know what to do with the impulses he had, nor did he know where they came from. To put it simply, he did not know how to adapt to life without using. He continually felt defenseless and fragile. That is why he was so desperate for anything.

I would like to point out the profound difficulties that Alex was facing. I don't think that any of the therapists managed to see it. It was necessary to work with him much more deeply and beyond his addiction. It was important to think about why Alex had started to numb his emotions so early in life. Why his anger and pain?

If we are assuming that the addict in the early stages of recovery is naked, why not explore where all that intolerance comes from? On occasion, Alex himself thought that it came from what had happened in his brain, and that was probably part of that emptiness he had prior to using. And it is precisely for that reason that he relapsed again and again. Nobody was working on the part that existed beforehand. It is very difficult to be able to overcome oneself after having a life of false control. It is very complicated to let go and understand that a superior strength is what has the true control.

***

Through all of his writings, we see that Alejandro let out his frustration and aggression in his relationships. He kept feelings buried deep inside, and he never wanted to talk about them or work on them. For him, it was very important for people to see him as likeable person so that everybody would love and accept him. Perhaps his lack of control and feelings of inferiority led him to want to take control or verbally abuse others and himself.

Letter from Alex to Marimar: December 11, 2011

Hi my love…Yes, I can see that what happened before sunrise on Saturday was influenced a lot by drinking too much. I can also say that it is because of certain character flaws that are still a part of my personality, as is a short temper. Sometimes, I don't see situations realistically, and I don't always understand the significance of certain events. But none of this is an excuse to disrespect you in such a way. You have my apologies, and they are from the heart, with a huge personal sorrow and sadness. But that doesn't fix the damage I can cause you.

The only thing that can heal you is a true change, which I have promised but have not accomplished. I am worried. I'm very afraid of losing you because of something that somehow gets out of control. You are right; it is essential to look for ways to avoid the situations that can take me to that place. This is my responsibility. Although I ask you for your help, it has to come from me because you cannot be my nanny, and like you said, you trust in me and my decisions. I hope from now on to make the right decisions.

To say that I love you is just not enough. Loving you for me is like a prize. I do not know whether I deserve it or not, but I do commit to fighting to deserve you. You are a gift that any person would want, but I have it, and I thank God for that every day.

For a long time, many people have told me I have an angel watching over me, and I am sure that angel is you. I have also lived for years hearing how God takes care of me, how I am so lucky, how life has given me everything, and today, seeing you by my side only reaffirms what I have said. God put you on my path, and you have straightened it. You have filled it with light, and my life today—thanks to you—has a very special meaning. I love you without asking you for anything in return. I simply love you and will keep on loving you forever.

LOVE YOU

Alejandro Sierra R.

***

Alex keeps trying to find himself, but he does not understand that he has to separate himself from certain past behaviors that he continues to repeat, like drinking alcohol, if he wants to move toward a true recovery.

Clarita...When Alex came back from living on the streets, and after José's death, he started a relationship with Marimar and returned to life before addiction—the "good, clean" fun. He felt different and uncomfortable when he was not drinking alcohol like everybody else. So, he started drinking, trying to belong, to fit in socially and get back to the "healthy" way to party instead of the darkness of his addiction. Once more, I saw in my son this denial of his illness, a reason he should not drink again. However, since he had so little experience being clean, he went back to his old, familiar patterns without realizing that these could again become a gateway for using crack, although he always insisted that alcohol was not his drug of choice.

Marimar...There were some things that we disagreed on, and I must confess that there were times when I hit him right where I knew it would hurt. It was a process, working with both our personalities. I learned what to say and what not to say. We were getting to know each other and seeing how we could get along in the best possible way.

We had to talk a lot, and that made me work on my own character, on things that I normally wouldn't have ever noticed or discussed. Alex's attitude toward life, enjoying things that I took for granted, helped me a lot, and I grew a lot because of this thanks to the work that both of us did. We grew up a lot.

Ours was a powerful relationship in every way. We took a lot of trips, went to all the concerts. That is how the first year was. My friends loved him more and more, and my parents were more at peace with our relationship because they were getting to know who Alex truly was, and that was what I wanted people to see. In fact, my friends from the university and my siblings didn't know he had an addiction until after he died. As an addict, he was always aware and didn't hide his condition, always knowing that people are not defined by their addiction. He gave me that capacity to see God in everything because I had a more traditional religion. He used to say to me, "God is in you."

Spirituality and Recovery

Clarita...Jung says that craving can be compared to, on a certain level, a spiritual thirst, "to feel complete in the union with God and with our spiritual identity." Alcohol, drugs, a piece of cake, games—none of these momentary solutions can alleviate this thirst.

Alex always searched but was never able to feel complete. Always an idealist, a dreamer, sensitive, empathic, always talking about helping others, he could not deal with the demands of life. Alex always felt different, lonely. He perceived himself as inadequate, of lesser importance than everyone else, always wanting something more. This yearning drove him to damaging patterns, destructive relationships, and substance abuse. Always looking for the last piece of the puzzle. In the beginning, he denied and rationalized his behavior. Sexual encounters, alcohol, and drugs momentarily filled his existential emptiness. This is very common for addicts. When addicts are talking about their first experience, you hear: "I felt all my troubles disappear," "I felt at home," "A new world up opened to me," "This is what was missing in my life." But unfortunately, soon they are wrapped up in an addictive pattern, and they lose control over their drug of choice.

I do not know what Alex experienced in the AA program. Since he was very spiritual, I think he focused more on what other people said and did instead of working on his own program. I want to think that he never understood the meaning of the 12 steps, and for that reason, he never really worked on them in depth. Deep down, he was always in denial. He was never able to see his spiritual capacity. With his drug use, he deteriorated physically, mentally, emotionally, socially, and spiritually. The spiritual recovery is the last one to take place, and because of that, there are so many relapses. Alex was never able to rebuild himself completely, and with every relapse, it was more difficult to see himself as a whole being.

***

That's right. Spirituality is an essential factor in the study of addiction. It is intimately connected to the core—the very nature of addiction— and serves to fill the existential void that addicts suffer. When the inner being is damaged or distorted, its spirituality is also damaged, resulting in destructive behaviors and addictions.

The world of spirituality, according to Godlaski, refers to the human experience, related to the purpose and ability to give relevance to things and the deep connection we have with ourselves, with others, and reality.

Puchalski's definition of spirituality is "the part of the human being that searches for a transcendent meaning and purpose of life that allows the human being to transcend without difficulties and sufferings." Whitfield's definition of spirituality is "a personal relationship between the individual and a superior or transcendent force, a supreme being, an energy, or the universe."[13]

Recovery requires commitment, courage, and patience. It is not something that can happen overnight; it is a continuous life on a spiritual path. Often, recovery can seem tedious, and it is then that we must resort to the mantra "one day at a time." That phrase allows us not to let our mind wander into the past or the future, into what would've, could've, or should've been and the "cannots." Rather, it teaches us to live in the here and now.[14]

Luckily, there are many tools to be found in our spiritual practice. In general, it could be the 12-steps program from AA; practicing a religion; or going to therapy to get out all of our repressed emotions, memories, and experiences that are acting against the possibility of having a healthy and happy life. Spending time in nature—we know this has restorative power. Creative expressions—mental clarity and perception are more acute when we give ourselves the opportunity to express ourselves creatively. Without recovery, it is impossible to approach that creative side we all have inside of us. And this creative expression can be very healing.

Paying close attention to diet, exercise, and rest is important. Often, addicts abuse their bodies by using drugs and alcohol, during which they may skip meals, not eat, not sleep, and exhibit inappropriate sexual behaviors, so it is very important to watch over these aspects of their lives. Like they say in AA, it is vital to pay attention to HALT (being hungry, angry, lonely, and tired) because these are red flags for relapse.

Time for meditation serves to center the mind and let go of the ego, thoughts, and mental noise, along with practices like yoga.

Learning how to overcome plays a fundamental role in our spirituality. Our attachments to people, partners, children, our expectations, and our foolishness in thinking that it is our point of view that should be followed—these do not allow us to go beyond ourselves, and therefore, they prevent us from letting go of our suffering. We complicate our lives when we are rigid, stubborn, and proud. Our anger grows until it has nothing to do with our initial anger. Part of overcoming ourselves is to let go and put ourselves in the hands of God and have the serenity to accept the things we cannot change, as it says in the "Serenity Prayer." It is very important for the addict to surrender to the inevitable fluctuations of life, to stop living other people's lives, and understand that there is an energy or supreme power that guides us. This does not mean that we do not have control over certain things, but it is releasing the ego.

Our mind can be our best quality or our worst enemy. Alex spoke about the inner voices that gave him advice and directed him, voices that reminded him of his fears and his shortcomings. These voices project the future and make us live in the past tense. [15]

Overcoming Ourselves

The process of hitting rock bottom and letting go of the illusion of control over our situation is a fundamental step in abandoning the pain of addiction. The experience of "defeat" is the ultimate key to finding redemption, the door to recovery, healing, and discovery of our spiritual potential. It is the watershed moment of transition from a limited experience of who we are toward an experience of integral consciousness, and it can happen to people in many different ways.[16]

Marimar...Alex was adamant that he had found in me the balance and peace he needed, which I think was due in part to the communication we shared. Another thing he told me a lot was that I had seen his spirit from the beginning: "It is a relief that somebody sees me, not the gossip, or my problems, or addiction, or stories about drugs, but really how I am." Then he looked me in the eye and said, "Mar, you do see me."

I think he really liked my spiritual side. We understood that he had a void he needed to fill, so I began to encourage him, for example, to look for volunteer work, because that is what I thought could help him in dealing with his own emptiness—seeking a sense of well-being from doing things for others. We never had a specific project. Sometimes we went to addiction institutions, but it didn't work out too well, maybe because Alex was not yet strong enough in his own process to help other addicts.

We also went to an orphanage and brought Christmas presents for all the children. Alex loved that. He enjoyed it a lot. It was unbelievable to see how he did it, with so much enthusiasm and love. Part of giving yourself to others is forgetting about yourself, and that could also help him in his own process.

Clarita...Undoubtedly, there are many elements of personal growth that an addict can follow. The part where the addict overcomes himself and says that he no longer wants to live that life comes from his spirituality, and that is an aspect of the process that made more sense to us as a family. Once his spiritual growth was strengthened—that if Alex fortified his spirituality—we would start noticing some changes in his daily life and in his recovery.

In addition, there were other changes in his personal growth, which sometimes Alex could stick to, and other times he could not, such as diet, exercise, altruism, and providing support and strength to his family. Slowly, Alex started to neglect his treatment, which consequently put him in a vulnerable, unprotected position. In his impulsivity, Alex would want to get everything done in a day, and perhaps that made him relapse, but at the same time, he started doing things that we thought would be impossible: being successful in his job, which allowed him to give an engagement ring to Marimar; planning a wedding; and starting to dream about and build a future. For me, it was my wish for my son—to find happiness in being a productive man and seeing his dreams of starting a family take shape—was coming true.

***

Marimar was certainly a reminder that Alex was not his addiction, that he could have a "normal" life next to somebody who really loved him. It was a moment of vivacity and hope.

Red Flags

Marimar...Throughout the first year of our relationship, Alex exercised and attended therapy so that he could feel good and make changes. One day, we even went to couples therapy so we could understand each other's point of view. In our relationship, Alex's addiction was never taboo; we spoke about that all the time. Obviously, I had never experienced anything like it personally, but he told me, "I already know myself in regard to the red flags that start emerging." He even had his checklist to remind himself of the signs. Alex used to tell me, "If I suddenly stop going to the gym or I stop doing something like that, I start seeing how my brain is beginning to fool me, because when I start being lazy, that is when a relapse can happen."

Clarita...[In this respect], Alex gave lip service to what he needed to do, but deep inside was a great denial of his problem and the belief that he was never going to relapse again. He continually refused to attend group therapies that were part of his recovery. This made me think that since Alex had become accustomed to a solitary life, his ego always deceived him. Developing a sense of belonging to a group was so hard for him, let alone a therapeutic group where his beliefs would be confronted, like in AA.

At the same time, he felt that he could handle everything on his own. Deep down he knew he couldn't, but in his addicted state, he used to say, "I know that if you leave me alone, I'll do it by myself."

Our purpose in everything that we did, like leaving him on the streets, was not so he would suffer but so he understood that he needed help. The only time he went to a clinic willingly was to Promises because his crack use had scared him. He would get back in shape so quickly that withdrawal did not scare him, and then he tricked his brain by telling himself that he could do it alone.

Marimar...I remember that Alex constantly explained to me that at one point he had seen his darkest side, and he had made his family see it, too. He felt that when he was doing well, he had to try twice as hard. He used to tell me, "I feel that I have screwed up so much in my life that sometimes I think I have to compensate for my behaviors, and because of the way I've screwed up, I have to double my efforts with my parents, with my brothers." I think that's the reason that Alex lived with such intensity and felt the need to show affection toward everybody.

***

The road to recovery can be thought of like quicksand. Besides fighting for his life against his illness and looking for tools to escape addiction, Alejandro wanted everyone to like him. He felt that he had to explain and justify everything for everyone. In his recovery process, day in and day out, that feeling must have been exhausting. He was constantly confronted by his self-image and his self-perception, and that's exactly what might have caused him to get trapped again.

Clarita...His was an everyday struggle. He suffered from low self-worth, and there were many times when he said he felt like a piece of shit: "If I had to talk about everything I did, I'm not going to be able to. I don't deserve anything." Then came the overcompensation. He wanted to look good in front of everyone. I think my approval was always fundamental in his life. He'd look for me all day long. Sometimes he even told me things that a man his age would not normally share with his mom. He really could not let go of me.

Marimar...Alex told me there were wonderful things he could appreciate after coming back from so much despair. However, he also used to tell me, "I have to show the whole world, even those closest to me, that I am worth it, that I am a good person. It is always the people closest to you that you hurt the most. No matter what I do, I cannot fit in with anybody." He told me that all the time, that he was very affected by what people said. How exhausting it must have been for him. He had it hard because it was like an internal struggle. He felt alone, and on top of that, he felt he had to fight against society.

One Frustrating Relapse

The first definition of relapse is nonspecific. It can be applied to any illness. Relapse is returning to the previous state—to the active phase of the disease—after a short recovery. It is important to point out that unless there is a short recovery, it is impossible to relapse. The second definition more specifically applies to addiction. A relapse in this disease is to go back to the attitudes, thoughts, feelings, emotions, and behaviors that take you back to the active addiction.[17]

***

It was only three days before Alejandro's birthday, a complicated date because it was also the anniversary of the shooting and José's death. Then Alex had what everybody thought of as a "slip."

Clarita...That day, Gerardo and Alex went to a golf tournament where Alex won. His golf buddies were drinking during the whole tournament and at the award ceremony. In the end, they invited Alex to keep celebrating at a restaurant, something that worried Gerardo for obvious reasons, and he even suggested that Alex not go so he wouldn't be exposed. Later, we learned that Alex started drinking in that place, and when he was offered cocaine, he also accepted it.

After coming back from the restaurant, we talked with him again about the danger of drinking without having the understanding of the direct link between drugs and alcohol, and the concern we had that he continued to put himself in those risky situations. However, Alex couldn't understand that any kind of addiction, even if it wasn't crack, could alter his state of consciousness and become the precursor to a relapse.

***

One day before his birthday, he surprised everyone and disappeared.

Marimar...It was very powerful, because in theory, he had been clean for a year, although he sometimes drank during that year, something he should not have done. The memory I have is horrible and awful, because things were perfect one day, and the next day he vanished. We did not know where he was, and he had turned off his cell phone. I had my cell phone next to me at all times. Uncertainty is the most frightening feeling in the world, and the whole time you think the worst. Although I had read about addictions, which had helped me a lot not to take things personally, it was still very difficult to understand, and yes, it did affect me deeply.

In the solitude of her room, Marimar sent texts constantly from her phone:

- My love, if you see this, please call me, please let us know that you are okay...I need you with me. Please do not leave me all alone!

- You do not understand the torture this is. It is horrible not knowing where you are, how you are doing, whether you are alive or not, whether you need help or not. I ask you to please let me know you are all right. We have so many plans. Don't make bad decisions that will only make you ruin your life. I love you.

Of course, I did not sleep at all. He got in touch at dawn or in the morning the next day through a chat. His first message was, "Forgive me. This has nothing to do with you." And then he arrived at his house.

***

They all spent the day of his birthday together at home, trying to convince themselves that it had only been one night of bad decisions. Gerardo and Clarita, after celebrating with Alex, were supposed to leave for Europe.

Clarita...After the relapses that occurred every time Gerardo and I left for a trip, obviously it scared me to leave Alejandro alone. At that time, Gerardo and I had planned a trip, and the fear and restlessness invaded me again. It was as if Alex, in a state of permanent adolescence, looked for an opportunity to feel "free" every time we left and go back to using. But as they say, hope is the last thing that dies, and although that small relapse was unsettling, seeing him so happy—having had a year clean with a good job and Marimar by his side—we wanted to see these as good signs that would let us leave feeling a little more at peace. I was lying to myself, because from the moment I got onto the plane, I was already very nervous. Today, I realize that as we prepared for our trips with excitement, Alex's cravings began, and with this, the longing to use again.

***

As soon as his parents left, Alex had one of his worst relapses. Most likely, neither Marimar nor Alex nor his parents thought that already having cocaine in his system would be the catalyst. Marimar left for a vacation in Cozumel with her family, and Alex met up with her there to spend a few days with them. The reality is that it was very hard for him to leave home because he was using again, although nobody knew it. Alex was happy knowing that he was going to have the freedom to use for a whole month. There was no way to stop him. His brothers and Marimar tried to support him the entire time.

Juanita...As soon as his parents left, Alex went to work, and then he came back one hour later happy, saying, "Wow! I have the entire house to myself for a whole month!"

Letter from Alex to Marimar: August 7, 2012

Mar,

The illness is wining today. It is blinding me to all the beautiful things in my life and has me in limbo. I know I will get out of this, but the truth is I don't know when.

I don't want to hide anymore. Telling the truth is the only thing that will help me get out. Only in knowing what I can lose is there the possibility of recovering my life. And only in recovering my life will I be able to recover all that I have lost. Having experienced this illness hurts my soul. It hurts to have lost so many important things that I will never get back. It pains me to know all the harm I have caused to the people that I love so much. They have placed their love and faith in me so many times, and I was not able to keep my word. I disappointed them. I already know there is no going back in many respects. I want you to know that I never meant to harm you, that with you I managed to do things that I never thought I could do, that you gave me love I never thought I would feel. I love you with all my heart.

I know you have to walk away, that you cannot be by my side and see how I hurt myself, because that makes you suffer.

If I lose you for this, it will be something with which I will have to live my whole life, and it will be one of the worst nightmares I'll have to face, but I understand that you do not have to experience it.

***

In spite of all his pain and knowing what he could lose, Alex could not stop getting high.

Marimar...For our anniversary, I gave him twelve little boxes, and in every one of them there was a thank you note for different things. He opened them one at a time, and it was very hard because when he saw everything, he started crying, and he said to me, "Mar, in these moments I feel I am just the opposite of everything you tell me I am." I just wanted to make him feel good, to forget the past, and I thought these gifts could help him recover. At the time, I still did not understand how drugs can take away your freedom or how addiction worked. I thought that as soon as he saw the boxes and a video I had made, magically everything was going to be okay again. Alex, who could not stop crying, started to explain to me how addiction affected him:

> In my head, I know what I have with you and how much I love you, but right now I cannot feel it. Addiction erases all feelings. You can make others suffer and not feel anything. When you are sick, your only objective is to use more. I cannot run away from myself. I cannot analyze whether this is the life I want for me or for my children. I carry this illness, and when I am fine, the only things I think of are the good things you and I have talked about and experienced together. Every time

I have put more effort into my life, I am glad that I've done it. There are probably things that I still need to do, and I can only think that life sends me these relapses over and over to open my eyes to a different life.

Sometimes I feel lost. I do not know where to go. I do what I can, and sometimes I feel pressured by the people who ask me to do more. I will spend the rest of my life with this Dr. Jekyll and Mr. Hyde, and just like in the book, the moment comes when Jekyll controls Hyde. However, Hyde never disappears because he is part of the personality of both. I am more than certain that that moment will come. I wish with all my heart that every time I relapse, it is the last time.

I asked him to explain to me why he couldn't stop. Even in his moments of addiction, I felt he was worth it. He insisted that I not take it personally, but for me it was terrible. I felt like he annihilated me completely and literally broke my soul. I was really confused. My head screamed at me to walk away from him, but my heart told me to run behind him, not to leave him. I wanted to make a wise and realistic decision. I think that Alex never really wanted to acknowledge his relapses or feel the pain deeply, so he blocked it out for fear of relapse.

He wanted to fix things soon. He did not understand why I needed to keep talking about the topic, to incorporate it into our conversations. He didn't understand why we encouraged him to speak about it, but we believed that when he understood the harm he caused, other relapses could be avoided more easily. However, Alex avoided the topic every time. Obviously, for the family a relapse is terrible, but the one who is most affected is definitely the addict, because as soon as he realizes the harm he has caused, he feels an inexplicable pain.

Clarita...I called Alex from Europe, and he did not answer. I got a recording that said his phone was out of service. I called the house, and Alex told me that it was true; he had lost his cell phone, but he was going to buy another one. Then I talked to Eduardo, and instead of telling me the truth, he confirmed Alex's story. Not only did I stay calm, but I also went on a cruise where I stayed without Internet for several days. I only could communicate when I arrived at ports, but my children told me everything was all right.

When we got back from our trip, we realized that *nothing* was fine. I arrived at the house, and Eduardo and Mauricio opened the door with desperate looks on their faces. This confirmed what I was feeling during the ride from the airport to our house. At that moment, I saw Alex coming down the stairs. His face was a mixture of sadness and pain. In it, I saw that he had failed us once more.

I went upstairs to my room. I closed my door and sat down on the floor to cry. The pain was indescribable. I could not understand how, after all that we had been through, he could relapse again. It was like a horror movie. The house felt dark and ice cold.

After several days, he could not stop getting high. We didn't know what to do. Then we decided that Gerardo should take him out of Mexico to see if, while he was far away, he could manage to stop using and finally end this terrible illness.

***

During the trip, Gerardo and Alex talked a lot. They looked for alternatives and played golf. Alex was "good," he "put in effort." His physical and emotional resilience was impressive. Seeing how quickly he managed to get out of that dark place and get back to reality greatly impacted his family and Marimar. From one day to the next, he was perfect; he did everything he had to do to be well and with the best disposition.

Alex also writes several letters of apology. Among them, he writes to his brothers, who were by his side during that last month of anguish:

My Dear Brothers,

I write this little letter to you today, a few days after having stopped using. First of all, I owe you a huge apology for all the bad times I've put you through and for the worry, anger, and helplessness. I know it's not easy, but I'm asking you to find a way to understand that when I am in my cycle of use, my priority is to use, and unfortunately—because you have supported me during my relapses—I have walked all over you.

I made lots of promises back then. I told you many lies, although probably deep inside you knew what they were because they always caused false hope and then new disappointments. I imagine it must be very unpleasant having to spend time with me during those periods.

And now comes a part that is probably more difficult to understand, the moment when everything has already passed and we go back to real life. In the beginning, these are the hardest days because of the guilt and thinking about the hurt and pain from my failures and the harm I've caused. There is also the desperation to use, and with it, the freedom to do all the activities that at some point were impossible to even think about.

I thank you from the bottom of my heart for your patience, love, and care for always sticking with me despite the rejection you got from me. I want you to know that all the times when I told you, "This is the last one," and "Tomorrow will be a better day," were not only lies to you and me, but also, deep inside, I was trying to give you hope so that you did not leave me. And I am thankful you were with me to the end.

I understand that there is pain and that things are not so easy to forgive. I know that after what we have gone through that you cannot understand how it is possible to have allowed a relapse like this. But the only thing I ask of you is to open yourselves to the idea that through effort and hard work I can earn your friendship and trust again. Although this illness darkens everything completely, my relationship with my family has always been the most important thing I have. I hope that over time we get those relationships back on track and cultivate them so they are always improving.

I love you much.

Alex S.

Marimar...On one of those days, Alex wrote me a letter that started, "I, Alejandro Sierra, promise to...Sorry, I will never fall again..."

And that letter was found by my parents, so Alex—by that time he was already fine—went to talk to them to explain and give them information about addiction. They were concerned, and he wanted to reassure them. I was struck by the love he felt for me, because even though it was hard to talk about this topic—it was like being naked in front of them—he patiently went about explaining to my parents what his situation was. We wanted to do things right, because for him, family is the most important. I remember that with my commitment letter in hand, very calmly I told his siblings the things Alex had promised me, and they looked at me and said, "Mar, it is not that simple. We know from experience."

Clarita...Like Kevin McCauley says, we are not responsible for our illness, but we are responsible for our recovery, and the reality is that Alex never put to use all the resources and tools he had. He was not disciplined. He felt like he was Superman. I don't know the reason, but he allowed his "cravings" to occupy all of his thoughts, feeding them, and allowing them to also affect the conflict-free areas of his life. He said he could get better on his own; however, he kept needing us. He lived in our house with us, and we were on the receiving end of all of his moods. If Alex wanted to live with us, we needed a minimum commitment on his part, and that is what we asked from him. However, I lived in constant panic, not only as a mom, but also as a therapist, knowing and recognizing that he did not commit and did not change his lifestyle. Even in understanding that he was solely responsible for his recovery, we were unable to dissociate ourselves from his behaviors.

***

After the relapses, Alex followed his treatment for a few months, but little by little he abandoned it.

Marimar...Alex did his treatment, but he was very desperate. He did not see change with therapy or with the meetings. I don't think he ever stayed in therapy for a whole year, and maybe because of that he did not give the therapies a proper chance. It was difficult for him to speak about profound issues; he only spoke about things on the surface. As soon as they were going to touch a nerve, he resisted and abandoned the session. This was an excellent defense mechanism. He did not give the tools he had a chance to work, nor did he understand that his process was long term.

The first several days were very delicate. When he was fine, communication became very difficult because I didn't know what I could help him with and what I should or should not say. Sometimes, I didn't know if his recovery was actually requiring that much work or if this was his way of avoiding that commitment. It was hard to respect him and give him the space he asked for during this process because I wanted to ask from him as much as I could; I wanted to get the best of Alex so that he would pull through and be fine. I reminded myself constantly of the saying, "Not to demand the best from a loved one is indifference."

We had meetings with his family to vent about everything and where Alex wrote never-ending lists of everything he was going to do. During those times, we reminded him how complicated it was to dialogue with him when he was all right. When he was sick, he was a softy who promised and was committed to everything, but once he was fine, he started abandoning those commitments. I remember how we constantly chased him to say, "Alex, what is going on? You haven't been going to your therapy anymore," to which he would answer, "Leave me alone. You are pressuring me all day long, and you want me to be perfect on the first day?"

***

Perhaps for the addict, going one day to the gym and another day to therapy are small but very important steps in achieving recovery. However, sometimes the family sees the effort without realizing the difficulty in achieving those goals.

Alex...I feel so much pressure from you all the time. You do not understand the huge steps I have taken. For you, it can sound like something normal that I get up daily to go to work, but for me it means an immense effort.

Marimar...The reality is that the first year of our courtship, we felt so good together, and I unconsciously felt that our relationship would produce a real change to save him from this addiction. Maybe because of that, the impact of the relapse was so terrible. I had to understand that nothing depended on me. I knew he was making an effort, but for me, it was like starting from scratch, because I trusted him fully that he was always going to be fine. When the relapse suddenly came, it was a very hard hit. I stopped feeling like the savior. I could do a lot to help him feel lighter and accompany him, but even though I had previously told him I was not his nanny, after this I started understanding better that his recovery did not depend on me or on anyone else but him. That first year ended well, with the family together. However, for me it was a watershed moment. The veil was removed from my eyes.

***

After a relapse, recovery comes...

Marimar...For New Year's, we went to Ixtapa with his family to celebrate there. The beginning of 2013 was good. Alex started doing very well at Vidalta. He sold a lot, and at the same time, he also started working with an uncle selling real estate. He was very active in his job, which meant economic independence. For him to be able to separate from his parents in that respect was an impressive achievement, and it obviously also helped him in his recovery because Alex really enjoyed what he did. At work, the office environment made him feel very good. He was the youngest, but he became very good friends with his coworkers because he was very empathetic.

***

Besides his job, Alejandro was slowly gaining back Marimar's trust.

Clarita...For my birthday, in March of 2013, Gerardo and I decided to take a trip with our children. We looked at several places. I don't know why, but without thinking it through, we decided on Las Vegas. It was a very nice trip, except that Alejandro started drinking in front of us, and when he sat at the betting tables to gamble, he was excessively nervous and anxious. After going back to Mexico, we realized this had caused a lot of anguish for him and the family.

Eduardo...I remember we went to Vegas to spend my mom's birthday there. I imagine maybe we chose a bad place to celebrate because

Alex drank, and it did not seem at all dignified to me. I had started a new job in January, so I left for Vegas after my family did. When I got to the airport in Vegas, I called to let them know I had arrived. Alex was drunk when he answered the phone, which put me in a very bad mood. Of course, he always said that one thing had nothing to do with the other, but I did not share that idea because I have alcoholic friends who never drink or gamble.

Trip to Dr. Daniel Amen's Clinic

Clarita...After getting back from Vegas, Alex entered a stage that was by then very familiar to us—a red flag. He was anxious, depressed, and very afraid of a relapse. So, we decided to go see a doctor that had been recommended to us, Dr. Daniel Amen, who scanned Alex's brain to look for possible damage. It was a really positive trip because we could spend time with Alex and Marimar, and besides, we got some answers.

During the visit with Dr. Amen, he gave us an overview of what was happening with Alex, something that was very important to him. We discovered that indeed there were already several lesions on his brain. There were parts that were turned off where there should normally be activity. This could explain the depression he was feeling since his years of drug use had lowered the levels of serotonin and dopamine that his brain should have been producing. He also found that some areas that should be at rest were unusually active in Alex's case. Much of this was in the brain centers of pleasure, feelings, and emotions.

Marimar...Alex did not finish an activity. He would already be thinking about the next thing, and then the next. He could not stay still. It was as if his brain were running at a higher speed. I told him, "Enjoy," and he would say, "I *am* enjoying." He had not yet finished eating lunch when he was thinking about dinner.

When he had the scan done, we confirmed the reason for his hyperactivity. I mean, his brain did not rest. The part that was usually turned off for other people was almost always turned on for Alex, which explained his impulsiveness, anxiety, and insomnia. He had three different studies done, one of them with a contrast liquid to see how his brain worked. The three different study conditions were normal, under stress, and almost asleep. They ran different tests, and afterwards, we all went to the meeting with the doctor to hear his explanations. He was amazed with Alex. Because of his ten-year history of using and since crack was his drug of choice, the doctor told him, "Your brain scan does not match your history, and it is a miracle you are not that sick."

In the frontal part of the brain, where decision making and learning from mistakes is located, there was a hole. It was an area where oxygen was not getting in well. It was like an off switch. There was a lesion, and that is why it was so hard for him to make the right decisions. The doctor told us to see Alex as if he had just had a very complex brain surgery and had to rest for a year. He gave us a list of many things that Alex had to do. There were many areas that could regenerate so for everyone there was hope. With all that talk, Alex breathed deeply after a long time. He told us, "See? This is what I was trying to explain." Seeing it physically made it clearer for everyone, because it was not just a lack of will, but a real impossibility.

Clarita...After the study results, I remember Alex's exact words: "It gave me so much peace to understand why I act like I do." Such treatment consisted of neurofeedback sessions to learn how to regulate brain waves and have better brain control; hyperbaric camera sessions for better oxygenation; cognitive behavioral therapy; group therapy; cardiovascular exercise to oxygenate the brain; supplements; a healthy diet with green tea and omegas; massage; yoga; and meditation.

The doctor really explained a lot of things about his behavior and recommended that he not to go to clubs during the first two months to prevent overstimulation and obviously to keep from drinking alcohol. If he did all of this for a year, his brain could be considered to be in remission. If he kept doing it for two years, his brain could look like anyone else's.

We had arrived at the right time. We knew Alex's recoveries had been complicated because of his lack of commitment, but this gave us back hope, because we also saw in Alex the desire to follow his treatment.

We all got back to Mexico and were pretty excited, because for the first time, we had seen clearly and could understand not only the location of the genetic damage, but also the location of damage caused by his drug use. My niece, Natalie, who is a nutritionist, created a comprehensive treatment plan that consisted of IV pushes, vitamins, and supplements. Alex also understood that, although he could restore the lesions, his genetic predisposition and the damage caused in the pleasure area would always be there. Therefore, it was very clear that he should not drink alcohol again. Although it was not his drug of choice—nor were other potentially addictive substances—it could lead him back to his former path. The reality is that Alex started off very excited.

Marimar...Alex arrived with his batteries charged. At this point, we were talking about getting married, and of course, I was nervous because I feared he could have another relapse. To me, it was very important that I went to the doctor because it helped me understand that if I wanted to be with him, I had to help him take care of himself, that it was going to be a team effort.

After we got back from the trip, Alex showed my parents his scans, and they were very hopeful. We also explained to my friends and Alex's so that they understood the situation and stopped putting pressure on him at weddings or events when we had to leave early or when Alex did not want to have a drink. Over the first few months, we stopped going out almost completely. He had an energy therapy for about four months, which made him feel very good. He also went out about twice with Monica, a consecrated friend of mine who facilitates spiritual healing through prayer. It was very nice to see how one day, after his therapy and time with Monica, he called me over the phone, crying, and he said, "Mar, I feel they are taking a big weight off my shoulders. It has been many years since I felt like this. I feel happier emotionally, and for the first time, I am feeling an internal freedom.

Letter from Alex to His Dad: June 2013

Hi Pa,

How are you? CONGRATULATIONS!!!

Father's Day: I think it is a very important day to celebrate the person who has been a friend, a great protector, a great example, and a great man with a great heart.

It saddens me to remember having wasted so many years in that useless life instead of having taken advantage of every second of every opportunity to grow up alongside a great one.

I am thankful for the new opportunities. I am enjoying being able to share with you these important moments of my life.

I love you.

Alex S.

***

For the first time in a long time, the magic of family togetherness that Alex talked about so much was reestablished. Everyone was feeling good. Trust between everyone is reborn, along with a deep desire for Alejandro's brain to heal.

August: Happy Engagement

Marimar...On August 17, it was the second anniversary of our relationship. He gave me the ring, and we got engaged. I did not really suspect anything. It was amazing. He, as usual, with his "Alex Productions," had made an appointment for me at the beauty salon so that I looked great. I knew he was going to surprise me, but I did not know what it was about. He even took my cell phone away so that nobody would ruin it. I did not find it weird because he was very thoughtful, and he surprised me all the time with romantic and beautiful gestures.

First, we went to have lunch, and then he told me the celebration was at his house. We arrived there, and he asked me to wait for him upstairs. I think I was there for over three hours. Then he came to get me, covered my eyes, and took me to the terrace. There were many impressive flower arrangements and candles scattered all over the place. We were so excited that he started to record everything. When I saw him looking nervous, it made me nervous, too.

At dessert time, he came up with a spectacular fondant cake that represented the house we were going to live in. He sat me in front of him and opened one of the roofs, and while he said, "I want to spend the rest of my life with you," he pulled out a keychain with the house keys, and from another roof he retrieved the ring. We hugged each other for a very long time and cried for ten minutes. We gave everyone the news, and people started arriving at his parents' house for a toast. It was very beautiful.

After that engagement day, we started planning our wedding. His remission date given by Dr. Amen was March of 2014, so we chose to get married in May of that year. During August, September, October, and November, we spent our time on the preparations. It was a lot of fun. Every weekend we went shopping for the house. By November, we had the master bedroom ready, and the rest was quite livable.

Eduardo...In October, we went to San Diego to watch an American football game, and I invited Alex to join me and my buddies. We had a great time. To me, it was like a reunion trip with my brother. It is remarkable how kind Alex was, because during the trip, I told him I was worried that I was not making enough money. He told me he would lend me money from the commission that he had just received. I told him not to worry, that I would ask my dad for help. I am impressed by how generous he was!

***

It is important to recognize Alejandro's growth and accomplishments throughout 2013. His achievements were undeniable. Economic independence, a good job, participation in the construction of his home, helping an uncle when he needed it, supporting a driver's daughter with the her tuition payment, committing himself to the wedding preparations, and with the dream of a life spent with Marimar, Alex had a life that he never thought he'd have.

CHAPTER IX

Struggling for Life

The pains that you suffer, the loneliness that you encounter, the experiences that are disappointing or distressing, the addictions and seeming pitfalls of your life are each doorways to awareness. Each offers you an opportunity to see beyond the illusion that serves as the balancing and growth of your soul.

—*Gary Zukav*

Unfortunately, Alex failed to change the patterns that had always led him to relapse. There were only promises that never came to fruition, and little by little, Alex abandoned his treatment once more. He his self-worth was dependent on how other people saw him, and he did not seem to realize his own good qualities. He always perceived himself through somebody else. In all these situations, we kept seeing that Alex's illness and denial continued, and with these was the impossibility to solidify his recovery.

In November, situations arose daily that started to cause Alejandro anxiety. Looking back, they were significant red flags, but inside the family environment, it was very hard to make Alejandro see them because he had the need to prove that he could do it all. For example, organizing a wedding, which can be difficult but manageable for a common couple, for him became an extreme situation.

Marimar...I remember that Dr. Amen had explained to us that too many emotions, regardless of whether they were positive or negative, could cause a relapse. Alex had different pressures at work, and I imagine that planning the wedding and honeymoon were also something that caused him anguish because he wanted everything to be spectacular.

Around November, we started arguing. I imagine this again was a red flag because he got very upset. One of these arguments was about the flowers. He told me, "Tell them not to show us anything because there will be no wedding." And I remember he yelled something like, "I am going to go use," or "I am going to kill myself." I have blocked it out, but it was very powerful. By that time he was not exercising anymore, and he had pushed aside the activities that had been recommended to him as part of his treatment. That's what always happened. He was so concerned with his job and the commission to pay for all the expenses of the honeymoon that he forgot about all of his tools.

After that explosion, I probably should have told Clarita and Gerardo about it, but I did not know up to what point that was normal, and I felt it was part of the intimacy of my relationship.

He would constantly tell me he felt unworthy of things going well and for all the things that he had. He felt guilty. This, without a doubt, was another red flag.

Clarita...I believe Alex cared a lot about looking good in front of us. He always thought that whatever Gerardo and I said was very important, although he always ended up doing whatever he wanted. Since the day Alex arrived, excited to tell us that he wanted to give the engagement ring to Marimar, I remember we all thought it was very risky because of the stress of planning a wedding. We felt he was still very vulnerable, and we tried to tell him it was not the right time. But, as usual, Alex tried to convince us it was and ended up doing what he wanted. In spite of that, once he made the decision, it was very exciting, seeing him navigating the Internet every night looking for the most perfect engagement ring. All the preparations were coming together, with both dreamlike and stressful moments.

In the case of the honeymoon, something similar happened. He had the money to pay for it, but he knew that coming back home from the trip it was going to be complicated to pay for the expenses of the house and his newly married life. When we expressed to him that it was a very expensive honeymoon and that he had to think about the future, he understood, but at the same time, he got excited by the idea of going to the places and dream hotels he had chosen—places that were a little out of his league. All those situations were mixed up in his head and caused lots of noise.

***

With all these changes, almost imperceptibly, Alex began to feel the commanding need to use again.

Alex...When I began to feel that obsession for using again, my lack of humility and my resentment would cloud my mind, preventing me from asking for help when I needed it most, even though I was having one of the best times of my life.

Clarita...We will never be able to explain this obsession. Alex started to relive in his mind the moments of getting high. His body trembled just remembering it. These are the moments when you must ask for help. He had the sweats and a lot of anxiety that he tried to counter by going downstairs to the refrigerator to see what sweet thing he could put in his mouth. After so much anguish and those terrible, unimaginable obsessions, he was progressively making room for the craving until it got a grip on him. Then he reached the point of no return. Just the idea of having made the decision to get high again made him feel happy and at peace. Other times, he got better just by knowing he had the money or when he had already bought crack.

***

William Cope Moyers, in his book, Broken, perfectly describes the craving:

Drugs change the brain and alter its molecules and its chemistry. They even modify and change the basic structure and shape of the nervous cells. We know craving is not a mental desire but a physical necessity that emerges from the network of cells that have been changed permanently by drugs. The truly dangerous moments are when the addict's defenses are low and the world looks hopeless, and it is then when the addict's brain lights up these euphoric memories that whisper at night or during the day, when he is taking a shower or when the day is about to end. Do you remember how good you felt? If you get high again you are going to feel good again.

How can you explain this obsession to someone who has never experienced it? Researchers say that addictive drugs, when used in large amounts and for long periods of time, hijack the brain, like Trojan horses that sneak into the nerve cells and take control. That explains the biochemical process, but it doesn't get close to describing the desperate hunger, the consuming thirst, the unbearable craving, the furious yearning, the excruciating need that grabs you and shakes you and won't let you go. It reminds them of a howling, internal torment that overrides the need for food, for water, for sleep, for love. And then the calm that replaces the fury and the rapture that arises when the convulsions cease."[18]

Clarita...By this time, I remember I had told Gerardo we should talk with Alejandro again; I had seen him acting weird and anxious. The next day, he sent us an e-mail that left me at peace and made me think I was imagining scenarios.

E-mail from Alex: Tuesday, November 19, 2013

Dear Mr. and Mrs. Sierra,

How are you? I am just writing to tell you about how happy I am with all the things that are happening lately in our lives. It has been really gratifying to be able to share all these experiences with you. I think that, as always, thanks to your constant support, things are happening again that can enable me to get ahead. It is evident that I must be thankful to God every day because things are not only lining up, but surprisingly, they are making my life incredible. In addition to the thanks I must give to God, I also give them, once more, to you, because without you, none of these experiences could have been possible.

Regardless of EVERYTHING that you have given me, I adore you. I adore you for being the most special human beings! And yes, I have always liked to receive things from you, and I receive happily from life, but you can be assured that if this was not the case, the love that I have for you every day goes far beyond the material stuff. You have given me my life, and this has been a great privilege. You have given me your unconditional support, your time, your effort, your dedication, your tenderness, your compassion, your forgiveness, and every one of these things is worth millions, more than all the material belongings you have given me.

It is clear that the house goes beyond what I could or should have received. I know it is a novel opportunity to be able to start my life with Mar in that house after all the history we have experienced. I feel really lucky and thankful, and I hope to be able to live in it and keep it in as beautiful of a condition as you are giving it to me.

I thank you beyond what words can say. I am really excited and again, excited for the luck I have had to live.

Thanks for EVERYTHING!

I love you so much!

***

That Friday, Alex relapsed...

Marimar...I remember on Thursday, the twenty-first of that month. We went shopping for a lamp for the house, but he was already very nervous. Then Clarita mentioned to me that maybe by that time Alex had already bought crack and had it in his bag, and that's why he looked like that; he was anxious to get home and get high.

He had agreed to meet the next day at his house with some friends to go to a golf tournament. On Friday at about 11:00 a.m., Gerardo called me at work and asked me if I had heard from Alex because he got a call from the club telling him that neither Alex nor his other two friends had shown up. The first thing we thought was that he had been in a car accident, so I went to his house as quickly as possible. At that moment, we did not think it was a relapse because he was with his two friends.

We started searching for them everywhere—on the road, in all the hospitals. We were very concerned, and we decided not to tell Clarita anything for the time being. I do not know if it was part of our defense mechanism, but Gerardo and I were denying the fact that he had disappeared due to a relapse. Alex's cell phone was turned off, and we still had not reached his friends' cell phones. At that moment, the club called again to tell us that they had been mistaken and his two friends were at the tournament. Once again, our excellent defense mechanism was triggered, and we thought he had been kidnapped. I called a friend who helped us try to locate him. He explained to us how the kidnapping procedure worked, and we were told to go to Toluca with the security people. We were so afraid to think about a relapse that we almost preferred that he had been kidnapped. We went back home around 2:00 p.m. and that was when we told Clarita what was happening.

Clarita...My cell phone rang, and it was Liz, my daughter-in-law, who told me, "I am so sorry about what happened with Alex." I did not understand what she was saying. I felt as if I had been hit with a bucket of ice water. What could have happened if Alex was in a golf tournament? Very nervously, I asked her what was happening, but she, without knowing what to say to me when she realized I did not know anything, told me, "You should hear it from Gerardo." But I needed an answer, and that's when she replied, "Oh, Claire! I think he was kidnapped because he is nowhere to be found." At that instant, I knew Alex had relapsed.

Marimar...That night, I spent the night at Alex's house. We were awake the whole time, waiting until the phone rang at 3:00 a.m. It was Alex, who told his parents that the police had found him. "I am fine. I am in such and such a place, but tell all these policemen and patrols to leave." They asked the police to leave, and Alex told his parents he would be back at the house at eight in the morning. At that moment, we rested, knowing he was alive. He had gone to a hotel to get high, and in fact, he arrived at the promised hour. When we asked him what had happened, he only told us that he had no idea. All the while, he did not stop crying. He could not even look us in the eye. For him, it was too much. From Dr. Amen's hope to this, it was terrible to feel that he had failed. Also, when you have been clean for so long and your brain starts to recover and is much more oxygenated, relapse is much stronger. For him, it was terrible because there were many people involved in his life. The pressure was awful.

***

While Marimar was awake, she started sending desperate messages to Alex on his cell phone, all of them without a reply.

Marimar...

- I have been praying for you for hours. I hope you are fine.

- I do not understand what the trigger was for you to leave without telling us anything. We were doing well, you were happy, you had just told me that you NEVER wanted to lose me.

- If you get to see this message, I ask you to visualize what you have made me dream of all these months: the future, our home, a family, traveling, laughter, having fun, to grow old together, your job, your parents, your brothers, and your goddaughter.

- Think of all that you have received in your life, and if you do not want to get off drugs for yourself, do it for your family, for all the love they have given you, the time, experiences, trips, laughter, cries, and they have never left you to fend for yourself. Today it is your turn to not leave them. It is time for you to accompany them and go back to them.

Clarita...Alex came back home that next morning very sad. We talked a lot. He cried. He promised. He slept all day long, only getting up to eat something like always, and went back to sleep. We were really worried because his wedding was coming up. I even sat down with him and asked him if he wanted to put all the plans on hold, thinking maybe that's what was stressing him out. We really did not understand what was going through Alejandro's mind during this relapse when everything seemed so good.

His dad and I reminded him that he had a wedding that week in Acapulco, and he had committed to finding a house to stay at with a group of friends. Once more, he changed his mind and focused on getting through it, on being fine again.

That weekend, they went to Acapulco. They were very happy, and when he came back, I ran a drug test on him, which came out clean. He had gone eight days without using. The following day, he went to work, and then I learned that all that week he had been using drugs during the night in his room. Gerardo offered for Marimar and Alex to go with him to Ixtapa that weekend to get Alex away from his surroundings, but Alex did not accept that Gerardo would go with. He said he'd rather go with Marimar to make up for the damage he'd done.

That Friday morning, we kissed good-bye. Alex told me he was going to pick up Marimar at her house, and ten minutes later, he came back. He came into my bedroom and said, "Ma, I cannot leave. I got high during the night. I cannot drive. I have been using since Tuesday." He sat next to my bed and started crying. Gerardo woke up, and we asked him what was happening, but Alex only cried.

When Marimar arrived, we started to talk about what to do and where to take him. He could not stay in our house like that, and he obviously did not want to go to any treatment facility. We had promised that never again would he use at home. He put us in danger. We were very confused by this situation, and at the same time, we did not want to leave him out on the street. Still, there was that hope that when he felt alone in some apartment, he would think twice about all that he was losing. We felt like we were in a surrealistic film; while the three of us were deciding what to do, Alejandro was looking at us from his room with an empty look in his eyes and totally hunched over. In the face of this relapse, it was very difficult to ignore our anger and frustration. It was very difficult for us to remain empathetic when that is exactly what we needed to do, not organizing or solving his recovery, which we continued doing anyway.

Marimar...When I arrived at his house that morning, Alex told me, "I couldn't. I was using all night long, and I can't go like that." Since the last time, I had given him an ultimatum. I had told him that I was not going to put up with even one more relapse. So, I was torn and told him I could not go anywhere with him. I could not stay in that cycle, and I left his house. It was then that his parents took him to a furnished rental suite near their home

That night, on December 6, 2013, Clarita writes to Alex.

Dear Alex,

Once more, here we are, writing words filled with sadness and more hopelessness every time. Every time this process is more painful. Like we told you a few weeks ago, we thought we had "made it," that now you were going to be fine and your life was going to be everything that we had always wished for. We were filled with the promise of a great life for you next to Marimar, and in the future, a beautiful family. And because of that, it hurts more every time. Maybe your mind deceives you into thinking that you have nothing to do with what happens to you, that it is your disease, your addiction, but the truth is we believe that you do have a moment where you can decide, where crack does not make decisions for you. For some reason, you are not determined to make the necessary changes so that this does not happen to you over and over again. If we read all of the letters we have written to each other, it is always the same: a lack of follow-up in what you propose to do. You always start off so well, with enthusiasm for all of your activities, your self-care and achieving many important things both at work and in your recovery. In the end, you neglect all of this, and you start to forget how to use all of the tools at your disposal, like learning to ask for help, having a support system for the difficult times, your pride in thinking that you can do it all by yourself, leaving the therapists after a few sessions, not knowing how to listen, not finding something beyond yourself, not giving more of yourself to others, and overall, lying to yourself over and over again.

The reality is that you are again experiencing a period of use, and the only thing you must do now is ask yourself where it comes from.

What happens in you that you feel helpless, without control, without power? Do you feel trapped in your decisions? What powers your addiction? Is it anger or stress? Or just other emotions that only you can know? These different emotions that feed your addiction, those are what prevent you from paying attention to the consequences that you know well. When people do not direct their emotions appropriately to wherever they need to go, they channel them towards their drug use. What does this tell you? That maybe you have to analyze where these emotions are directed and learn to channel them in another way.

How sad that once more you do not know how to utilize all the tools you have learned over the years.

Clarita

***

There are many factors that cause stress for the addict. Among these are not sleeping well, poor nutrition, not finding a job, having a job, starting or ending a relationship, having a disagreement, being criticized, or something as mundane as missing the bus or losing one's keys. All of these have the potential to trigger a relapse since the brain has been conditioned to associate chemicals with stress release. Ironically, feelings of happiness can also trigger a relapse because the brain also associates the feelings of euphoria and happiness with substance use. The brain tells the addict, "Do you feel fine now? You will feel much better when you use."[19]

Chat Between Clarita and Alex: December 7 (10:16 a.m.)

A: Good morning, thanks for the letter. Like you say, except for how beautiful they are and filled with love, from both parts, it is like a sad repetition.

C: How are you?

A: I took a sleeping pill and slept from 2:00 AM to 9:00 AM. Today I took a shower.

C: Oh good, and did you eat?

A: A croissant that I bought at the store, a pastry and a chocolate roll, and half a Gatorade and apple juice.

C: You've got to eat food!

E-mail from Alex to His Parents: December 10

Last night, I got high again. It is clear that this situation I am in, the only one who can make the decision to get through it is me. Like we have said, I have said many things and made promises, and I think that in this moment the only thing I must say is that once again I will do my best stop this relapse. I will call the office to ask for a leave of absence. As always, this is not the best moment to talk. I have asked a lot of you, and I know I should not ask for anything. But I ask you that Marimar does not learn about this last episode. More than for protecting me, it is for her so she does not suffer anymore. Later, and hoping to be better, I will get in touch with you. I know that even these words hurt because they seem to be written with such coldness, but I promise you will soon find the true Alex.

Letter from Gerardo to Alex: December 10

My Dear Alex,

Again the nightmare continues and you, burning your life, your money...and your future becomes more uncertain every day. It seems to me like playing Russian roulette, and as always, you get ahead. It is the trick your mind uses to convince you that nothing ever happens.

Of course, the only one who can make the decision to get out is you, but where you keep lying to yourself is thinking that you will get out overnight, like magic, and it is not like that. Deep inside you know that in the end it is your decision. If you want to go somewhere to detox, you just have to ask, but the way you are going, you are right; every time it is going to be harder.

A kiss, and may God want you to go out for the last time and straighten out your life that has not only had, but will continue to have, incredible moments of happiness, not moments of destruction and desolation like the ones you are going through in this relapse.

Dad

Chat Between Alex and Clarita: December 10 (12:15 p.m.)

A: Hi, aside from asking you for an apology, I truly accept my responsibility. This process has been very difficult.

C: Alex, like you say, we are repeating ourselves. We all know the story and we know that the physical need and the need to end the emotional pain lasts 72 hours, then obviously another process comes, which is no less difficult, but if you do not stop at some point and get stronger, this process will be never-ending, and sadly, you are going to ruin everything that you have worked so hard to obtain.

A: Yes, I know, and several times when the difficult moments have started, I have taken the easy way out that in the end only makes it more horrible! And of course I do not want to lose everything. I just need to find the strength again to get through the difficult moments and trust that everything can be fixed. And I'm worried that I have already caused some damage that cannot be undone. I do not want to lie to Mar about my use, but neither do I want to hurt her, despite my actions to the contrary. Did you tell her? Or does she not know yet?

C: No, she does not know, and if you do not stop, what will happen tomorrow or the day after that? I truly do not want to stress you out with this, but Marimar is at her breaking point. Right now her parents support her, but if you keep using, they are going to do all they can so that you two do not get married. Christmas is coming. Ixtapa is coming. It's already the tenth. Your honeymoon has been paid for, and you worked so hard to buy the furniture you anticipated having.

A: I am going to do all that I can to stop. It is truly what I wish the most.

C: The truth is, this is the last time I am going to repeat it. If you cannot do this by yourself, do not lie to yourself, and learn to ask for help.

A: I have to do this no matter what.

C: Okay. We all are here to help you. Do not let your addiction beat you. Who knows? If you get in too deeply, maybe later nobody will be able to help you.

A: I know you are there, and it is clear that I need lots of support. I just need to sleep longer and let the craving pass. By then I will be able to start everything that has to be done.

C: Okay, go to sleep, and do not leave the room. You can do this. You have done it thousands of times.

A: I am not going to go out. And I hope to find my way. I read Dad's letter. I agree that I will not just magically stop. I know it is a very complicated fight and that I cannot do it alone. And yes, I know every time it is more difficult and the damage is greater.

C: I think that you can make it, now more than ever because you have so many dreams. Do not let your mind trick you.

A: Yes, my mind plays tricks on me. It is scary to stop using and take responsibility for all the damage.

C: Tell your mind that the damage right now in your relationship with Marimar can be repaired; your job and your future wedding are still there. Tell your mind to stop working against you, that right now there are still solutions, though painful, that are doable. Tomorrow, who knows? Tell your mind that you are stronger than it is, and you have always overcome the pain of seeing reality. Tell it that we all want you healthy and with us. Tell it not to take you to the point of no return. If you cannot be alone because your mind does not let you, speak up and ask for help.

A: I know it can be done. I just want to rest a little and really start 100% convinced that I am not going to fail again.

***

While Alex dealt with his drug use and tried every day, he lasted only a few hours, and in his loneliness, got high again. Marimar decided to go away for a while to think things over.

Marimar...I decided to go away for a few days to get away from the situation and be able to see things more clearly. It helped me a lot. After coming back, the only thing clear to me was that I was not getting married in May. I was very determined. I had the perfect proposal for Alex. I told him, "You have been using for more than two weeks. You are deep into your disease, and you cannot think clearly. Let's go to a hospital together for three days so that they can help you detox, and if after that, when you are thinking clearly, you tell me you want to continue in the drug world, I will respect you." But he did not want to do this. I left his house extremely sad.

***

While Alex was in the suite, not knowing how to ask for help and thinking he could do it on his own, Marimar was in Cancun. From there, they communicated occasionally. The messages with his parents also continued.

Chat Between Alex and Clarita: December 12 (10:22 a.m.)

A: Ma, How are you? I just woke up after what I hope is the last night of using. I think there is not a lot to say. Only time will tell.

C: I hope this is the last time you get high. I am glad you are going with Monica. It is a great sign for Marimar that you want to keep fighting for your relationship.

A: Ma, you ask me a lot what I think or feel. The most honest truth is very sad, but I do not feel anything, absolutely anything. I think it is the harm that drugs do to the body. It takes away everything I feel. And that is why it is very difficult to stop in these moments, because I feel nothing. It is just emptiness.

C: That is why I hope you can leave that drug behind and be able to feel again and be yourself again. I know right now you feel like this, but it is crack that wants to possess you and own all that is yours. Do not let it. Sleep and rest.

Chat from Alex: December 17 (9:41 a.m.)

Hello Ma. How are you? I am here, still struggling with my illness and my problems. I am sure that all of us are having a bad time. And we all want this to end. It is a process that has been very difficult, and I hope to find the way out. I love you so much, but I have to do this by myself.

Chat Between Alex and Clarita: December 19 (4:02 p.m.)

A: I have to tell the truth. Everything I said this morning was true. To be honest, I endured, and it took a lot out of me. I woke up, and I "felt it," and this is completely foreign to you, but I got this feeling that because I was not going to use anymore, all the difficulties would start again. I couldn't stand it. So, that's how I am, and I know it is horrible.

C: I am very sad for you. Don't you want to do the Ibogaine treatment?

A: Even though all the trust is lost, let's talk tonight. At 9 o'clock I will call you and we can make a decision.

C: (9:05 p.m.) Hello.

A: I will keep my promise, and we'll talk tomorrow.

Clarita...On December 22, Marimar was coming back from her trip, which meant a lot of stress for Alex because he would have to keep his promise of not using. I had gone to see him at the suite, and he was very paranoid, I sat with him on the bed and hug him, I told him that everything was fine, that nothing was happening and that he should come back with us to our house. Suddenly, he started saying that the police were downstairs. He thought they were coming for him. He had even torn out the television cables because he felt he was being watched from there and from his cell phone.

***

One day before Marimar's return, Alex wrote again asking for help, and later he sent a letter.

Chat Between Alex and Clarita: December 21 (7:47 p.m.)

C: How are you doing, Alex?

A: So-so, not well at all, but here I am. I will sleep later. And let's see how it goes with Marimar tomorrow.

C: I hope you have a good night and that you stop using so you can claim your life back.

A: I hope so. I love you, and I hope all of this ends soon and that tomorrow is a good day.

C: Alex, understanding your frightful craving, it is all in your mind. I hope your addiction allows you to ask for help. Remember, you are not alone.

A: I know, thank you.

C: Try the Ibogaine for 15 days, and maybe that will save you.

A: It could be. Let's see what Mar says tomorrow.

Letter from Alex: December 22 (8:35 p.m.)

One more letter! One more of the many that I have written over the years. It is not a matter of writing to talk about what I did and all that I will have to make up for. It is obvious the steps that have been taken, from your point of view and probably in the future, from my point of view, too, and I hope the end result is the one we are all looking for. In part, I write because of the fear that I am feeling in this moment, I also write from the good person inside me, you know is there. Perhaps now it is much more hidden and with more fear than ever. Like you, I am tired, confused, removed from reality, but I know that underneath all of this, there I am, and I know that this is what you see.

At some point, I entered this sort of madness. I know if I make the right decisions, this unreal world will end, and I will go back to the point where it all began. I apologize. I think that I did this without having freedom of thought, and I know that regardless of my condition, I've hurt you and me a lot.

I hope that even though we are still living more of this hell, I know that after some sleep is when I can wake up ready to start repairing the damage. I have repeated this countless times, but you know and I know that one of these times is all it takes, and with this truth I will start my path. I hope tomorrow, with lots of work and perseverance, I can keep what I can recover. Mom, thank you for always being there. Dad, thanks for all your support. Eddie and Mau, forgive me because I could never accept your help.

Mar, thanks for continuing to try to get back the life we had, life that right now is hard for me to feel and see, but I know it's there.

I will see you tomorrow, and I hope God gives all of us strength to forgive each other and start again.

Alex

***

Alex kept having hallucinations, and in his messages, his family could not understand what he was saying. During his calls, he told his parents that they were betraying him because he overheard policemen, and he told them that surely they had sent the patrols to go get him.

Chat Between Alex and Clarita: December 22 (1:00 a.m.)

A: Help me, Mom, please, please.

C: How can I help you?

A: I think that what you did will mark me forever.

C: What did we do?

A: Nothing.

C: Tell me, what did we do to you??

A: Nothing. When you tell me we will be in the same place. Meanwhile, we keep lying to ourselves.

C: Alex, I really do not know what you are talking about.

Hours after having slept and rested, at night he wrote again to his parents.

A: Really, forgive me. There is no need to say it. See you tomorrow at 11.

E-mail from Gerardo to Alex: December 23 (8:56 a.m.)

I hope you have been able to sleep some and that today you can be better. Pray to God, we love you so much, and we are really sad and desperate.

***

Everybody expected Alex to arrive home on the twenty-third so that Gerardo could take him to the airport to go for the Ibogaine treatment.

Chat Between Alex and His Friend, Maria: December 23 (12:42 a.m.)

A: and yes, I swore to everyone that I would be fine tomorrow

-and I am doing that in this precise moment

-looking for something that perhaps I will never find in my drug use

-more paranoia, more sadness, more pain

-but here I have it and the only idiot who understands himself is me

-I am speeding up so this ends

-whatever

-and tomorrow I will stop breaking promises

-and hopes

-I have hurt enough

-Already money badly spent, so many people who need it

-and yes, inside me there is a good person who will give back everything that life has given to me even though I didn't deserve it

-again and again

-the reason, someday I will understand it...

-but wow!

-what I have received

-and if in me I have "the illness"?

-that will always be there, present

-but I have the people who will always be there by my side

-And what if I find in the next few days the way to ask for help?

-Wow! The life I will have

-truly

-no more being foolish

-Looking everywhere, for a happiness that is only in front of me

-No matter what I do

-disappointment after disappointment

-They quickly run to be by my side

-and more love and happiness than that?

-NEVER

-I am going to find it in this shit

-curiously

-I will finish it

-because tomorrow I really do not want to have even the slightest doubt of doing what I have to do

-without any reservations

-I do not want it to be "I missed one more"

-it will be over

-and BOOM!

-a new life

-if God allows me

-that has always been there

At 12:49, Alex continued writing...

-and the people that life send to me, they deserve all my respect

-and beware

-because they are priceless

M: you know you are a great person!

A: I can be

-not yet

-I know I have a good heart

-but I am missing

-many things

-value what I have

-enjoy life

-so many beautiful things

M: You will find them soon, very soon

A: I know! They have always been there

-I just have to open my eyes

-and enjoy

-I am in love

-with the best woman in the world

-and I am not going to lose it

-nor her

-nor the best family of all

-well, now, to this shit for the last time…

-good night

Marimar…In the end, we convinced him to go to a clinic where they give you Ibogaine, an African plant "anti-drug cure." On the twenty-third, he went to sleep at his parents' house because Gerardo was going to take him to the airport in the morning. They left the house, and halfway there, Alex got out of the car and said he was not leaving. Gerardo brought him back to the car, and they went back to the house. He slept all day, and they could not celebrate Christmas at Mau's house because they had to stay with him, and on the twenty-fifth they tried again to take him to the airport. In reality, there were many failed attempts.

Clarita…Of course, on the twenty-fifth, after he was unwilling to go, he asked us to bring him back to the suite. On December 26, Marimar called us from Acapulco, telling us that Alejandro had called her asking for help, saying that now he wanted to leave and go to the clinic, but he did not want to tell us because he didn't want to fail us again. So, he asked her to buy the plane ticket for him. Before all this started, we had planned to go to Ixtapa on the twenty-seventh to spend New Year's. We had arranged everything, including taking Alex to the airport so he could go to his treatment, and from there go to our terminal to catch our flight.

When we came to get him, he was asleep. He had not packed, and he said he was not going, that he had told Marimar not until the twenty-eighth. We were trying to convince him to go with us because the next day it was going to be harder to go alone. We already had a van downstairs that would take everyone. It was pointless. He stayed in the suite and we left, feeling very sad. Since Alex had destroyed his phone before leaving—because he said he was being watched from there—I bought him a basic phone to be able to stay in touch.

Marimar...After Christmas, Alex stayed alone in Mexico City. There was a lot of emotional distress, and by then, he was already having very strong hallucinations. When he talked over the phone with me, he said, "Marimar, your parents are outside my apartment. Please tell them to leave," or "I do not know who you are, but please get me my girlfriend on the phone." He received other messages through the television, like the one from a little angel and a little devil who talked to him like his conscience. There were times that the hallucinations were positive; other times, he saw horrible things. One of those days, he destroyed his cell phone because he told me that through it they could also hear and follow him.

Alex told me that in one of his hallucinations, there was a group of about fifteen people who were considered, like, the best of the world—"the chosen." But for the group to admit a new member, someone who was already there had to die. "Look, Mar, I now know it is not real, but in the moment that I am having the hallucination, I believe it completely. I hallucinate that they want to get me into this group, and they tell me that the race car driver, Schumacher, is already very sick and that now I can get in."

The truth is that with all that, the greatest pain and helplessness for me was that no matter what I did, I could not help him. He suddenly had moments of lucidity and he'd call me crying to say that he could not do it anymore. "I do not know what I am doing," he told me. His pain was such that he had to go back to getting high because he could not tolerate reality anymore. It was the worst New Year's Eve of my life. In his last messages, we could not understand anything anymore.

Clarita...I went to Ixtapa with a terrible feeling of leaving him alone in Mexico City. The next day, he left the suite and started staying in different hotels. He called us every day to ask why we had left him alone. His emotional state was very bad. On January 1, he called me crying, asking me to please come get him at the hotel where he was and take him to a hospital. My ticket was for January 4, and because of the holidays, there was no way to get an earlier return. I called one of my brothers-in-law, so he went to get him. He picked Alex up at the hotel and took him to the ABC Hospital. When my brother-in-law arrived, Alex cried, very thankful, and very obediently went with him.

After a few hours at the hospital, the cravings started again, so he removed the IV, and he left. My brother-in-law's driver took him to another suite, where we agreed he would wait for us so that as soon as we got back, we could take him back home. The plan was that on January 6 he would go to some clinic. I was supposed to go back on the fourth, but the flight was delayed, so I called him to tell him that we would meet the following day.

He arrived the next morning very angry. He left all his clothes to be washed, and he told me that since he was going to a clinic, he had decided to use all day and would be back in time for the trip. On the sixth, he arrived punctually and went to bed. While he slept, everybody came to say good-bye. Every time the doorbell rang, Mau's dog barked like crazy, so I asked them to take him outside. Then, out of the blue, Alex came out of the bedroom and told me, "Quit watching my sleep. Why are you all here? And besides, I am telling you I am not going to the clinic anymore."

We sat down to eat in dead silence. At that moment, I did not have the courage to tell him anything, to tell him that we were all there for him, to see him and to say good-bye. I felt that I had to walk on eggshells to not upset him more. When he said he was not going to the clinic, Mau asked him, "Then what do you want to do?"

"Here, I am never going to stop," he said, to which Gerardo answered, "Go wherever you want." Then Alex added, "Since I already have the ticket to Tijuana, I am going to cross over to San Diego. I know people there, and the meetings are going to help me get out."

Marimar...After more than a month of him getting high, I was desperate. I saw him one day at his house and he told me, "Mar, this time you have no idea how horrible it was." On January 6, we were all at Clarita's house to say good-bye. He was skinny, broken, and yellow.

I could not leave him, but I was an endless cycle on the inside, on the verge of madness, helplessness, and desperation. Then I went up with him to his room, but he kept saying the same thing about not going to a clinic. I remember how I told him, "Look, Alex, think about it. Go ten days to detox someplace."

He had a ticket for Tijuana, and in the end he decided to go detox alone in San Diego, which everyone knew was a double-edged sword. As soon as he made the decision, it was as if a switch had been flipped; it was an impressive change of attitude. He was as sane as two months earlier. Even his mood changed for the better, as if nothing had happened. It was like a very intense fight between good and evil. I felt strongly how that duality existed inside of him. I had never seen in him such a radical change, as if he were bipolar. I was in shock.

I told him I would accompany him to the airport, but I was not going to go with him. We still went for tacos, where he—as if nothing had happened—kept making me laugh. When we were on our way to the airport, he told me, "Let's go to our house to say good-bye."

He had told me that he was going to be fine for the wedding, but I told him that we were definitely not getting married in May. I think that even though he was sad with my decision, somehow his addictive side relaxed. Finally, I took him to the airport where he bought me a lottery ticket. We said good-bye, like four times. I wanted to give him all my motivation to help him pull through.

Clarita...By now, we had already let Alex experience the consequences of his addiction so many times. It was the moment to step back and let whatever had to happen, happen. Let him take responsibility for his recovery, and that way we were giving him the opportunity to grow up and learn for himself. For that reason, we decided to let him go by himself to San Diego, to give him the opportunity that he had asked for: "I can do it by myself." Although we all knew that he needed help, we hoped that he would be the one to ask for it. We hoped in the near future Alex would feel the true pain of his illness, which would open a small window for his recovery.

San Diego

Clarita...When Alex came into my room to say good-bye, I was sitting in front of my computer, and he said, "I am leaving. Aren't you going to give me a hug?" I got up and gave him a very strong hug. If I had known this was the last hug I would give him, I would have not let go.

He left for the airport, and he called me from the road to ask me to make a reservation for a night in a hotel. Because he was going to arrive at dawn, he wanted to make sure that he had a place to stay.

We had two weeks of very harmonious and positive conversations. He sounded very good. We even sent him his credit card via DHL because it was becoming very hard to pay for his meals and hotel in cash. He rented a car. He told us he was very happy, that he was reading and pushing hard to get better. But in as much as I asked him whether he had contacted some of the people who could help him or if he had attended any of the meetings, he always evaded my questions or gave me some excuse. A few days later, Marimar told me he had kept using.

Marimar...Throughout our entire relationship, we spoke a lot via messages and cell phone. But being there, we only made one call per day because he told me he was going to work on being introspective. I understood perfectly what he was saying, but it was strange because with his personality he liked to stay close and connected. Mau was the only one who told us that he definitely had kept using. His parents had agreed that he would only go for two weeks to get clean there and that would be it. In reality, it was wishful thinking on all our parts, because within the month he was using already, and it would be very difficult to accomplish by himself.

Finally, the day came that he was supposed to come back to Mexico, but he made a mistake by sending me a message that in fact was for his dealer. Very sadly, I showed the message to Clarita.

Eduardo...Alex was a very nice guy, but when he got high, I did not pay any attention to him. I imagine that there are a thousand strategies so that an addict gets better, but for me, the key is in never leaving them alone. You think that whatever happens to them, it's better that it happens when you are around rather than when they are all alone. We never abandoned Alex. When he asked to go alone to San Diego, he told us that this way he could get better, and my parents wanted to respect his decision. Perhaps there he had had two good weeks, but finally anxiety took over, and he got high again.

On January 17, it was my daughter, Ana's, birthday, and since Alex was her godfather, I called him on the phone and told him, "Alex, call me in two hours so that you can say happy birthday to Ana." He called, and we spent two hours on the phone. It was weird because I hate talking on the phone, and that never happens to me with anyone. We talked about everything. He told me that he already wanted to come back, to which I replied, "Come back, Alex. We have a lot of things to do."

"Yes," he told me. "I already want to come back. Besides, I do not want Mom and Dad to keep calling me on the phone." Not even he knew what he wanted, because even though he said that, he never stopped communicating with them by phone. It was he who was keeping his distance. After that day, I never talked with him again.

Clarita...Eduardo called me that night to tell me what Alex had told him. Respecting this, I stopped calling him for a while. A few days later, he called me again to ask me for help. His voice sounded very desperate. I called the man at the Ibogaine clinic to ask him to pick up Alex in San Diego and take him there. The next day, they picked him up, and his detox started with the idea that as soon as he was clean, they could start with the treatment.

Six hours after being there, Alex asked to be brought back to San Diego, arguing that that was not for him. A few days later, I got a call from the hotel where he was staying to tell me he was roaming the halls, very disoriented. They asked for an ambulance and took him to a hospital.

After several hours of looking for the hospital where he was, I managed to speak to him. I begged him to stay and detox. He told me, "No way." I asked the nurse to stop him, but there was no way to do so. Unfortunately, together as a family and with Marimar, we decided not to go to San Diego and rescue him once more but to leave him alone with the singular hope that the moment would come that he would say, "I do not want this anymore." And even though that was also what *he* wanted, he did not know how to do it.

A few days later, I decided to call his sponsor from AA, David, to tell him: "David, Alex is in trouble. He needs you. Please call him."

I gave him the phone number of the hotel where he was staying, and indeed Alex did ask for help. Once more, he was picked up at the hotel and was taken to a ranch far from San Diego where the only therapies were AA meetings and reading the Bible every day. He spent the night there and the next day, he left again.

E-mail from Alex to Clarita

Mom,

The only reason why I called American Express was to talk to them and have them get in touch with you and connect our call. Please, for goodness' sake, get in touch with me. I do not have a single penny. I am on a reservation away from everything. I am hungry, I am sleepy. Please, please, please, please, please do not do this to me.

PLEASE, PLEASE, PLEASE, PLEASE.

I am not using. I am calm. But I do not want to sleep on the street, frozen on an Indian reservation.

Alex

Marimar...On January 22, which is my birthday, I asked him as a present to try going to the clinic. He called me that day, and it was very sad because he was hallucinating a lot. I remember clearly that he told me, "Everybody is lying that today is your birthday. For sure you are lying to me to force me to go to the clinic." I was crying like crazy.

***

Because of his hallucinations, Alex started wandering from hotel to hotel. He thought he was being chased everywhere. Since Helen lived in San Diego, Clarita also contacted her to help him.

Marimar...By that time, I had gone to an addictions specialist to learn what more I could do. The specialist was brutally honest, telling me some things that were very difficult to swallow, but that made me see the addict. Then he added, "God loves you, but walk away. You have to put a stop to this. Besides, if Alex is catered to, it is much easier for him to relapse, and if you are still there for him, you are going to push him towards suicide." I obviously did not want that for Alex. The hardest thing I heard was when he said, "Get out of there."

Then I went to speak with Clarita to tell her that I could not do it anymore. I did not see Alex improving, nor did I know when he was going to come back. Alex told me, "Mar, please, if I am clean for two days, come to see me." But I was scared to death of going, that he would escape or something, and I needed to put my life in order. So I told Clarita, "I cannot talk with him about anything, and I want you to know that I have decided to break up with him." I received an e-mail from him on January 27, and then I sent Alex one last e-mail.

E-mail from Alex to Marimar: January 27, 2014

Mar,

You have no idea how sorry I am for the suffering that I have caused you and your family. I know perfectly well that making it up to you is going to take lots and lots of effort and time, and even so, there are things that might be irreparable. I apologize for everything that has happened. I am telling you, I do not promise because I do not want to give you false hope, but I guarantee you that today will be the last day I will have gotten high. I hope to God that I am still in time to get my life back and get you back, because the truth is you and my family are the only wonderful things I have today.

I hope and I know that it is nothing short of impossible that you can one day understand why I have acted the way I have, and I hope you give me the opportunity to fall in love with you again and the life we had together. I will call you in two days, and it would be incredible if you could come and get me. I know you see it like the easy way out, but I see it this way: because I want to start my life over again with you by my side. I need a push by having you near me. I hope after all you have done for me—I have not given anything back—you can grant me this request. For me, it would be the best gift of all.

Alex

Marimar...On the twenty-ninth, I spoke with the specialist again, and I sent Alex the following e-mail:

Alex,

I do not know when you will see this. I have to write this now because I cannot do this anymore, and I have to move on. I have not heard from you since you said you were going to be clean for two days to be able to come back. What I know is you have not been able to keep your word AGAIN. All that I say here is because I am sorry and I love you, but I cannot go on living this nightmare anymore.

It has been two months since I've been able to talk with you, and I have not been able to have a normal conversation because you have not been clean enough to talk. I cannot even start to explain to you what I have felt. Having a future that I already felt was complete, a life with the person I loved the most, a planned wedding, a honeymoon, dreams of having children with that man in whom I had faith and with whom I knew I could be happy for the rest of my life. All those dreams were broken the day you decided to go and use. And that moment came because you stopped doing things that helped you stay strong. You could not be humble and accept that you could not do this alone, that you needed therapies,

NA meetings, and exercise. Otherwise, the moment comes when you explode, and you do not have anything to hold on to. That moment came. You could not take care of yourself. You did not take your future seriously, and this time, it was not only your future. It included mine, and you decided to ruin that, too.

In the beginning, because of the love and faith that I have in you, I decided to wait a little to think things through. It has been two months, and I have cried every day. I have had to go around canceling the things we had arranged. I know that you are sick, that it is VERY difficult to get out, but we have given you the opportunities to help you, and very cynically, you have declined them. I do not know if it is pride to think that you can do this alone, and I do not know if you simply want to continue using until you end up dead.

I cannot put up with all this pain, and I know the pain is going to continue until I know you are clean, that you are all right. Because you know what? In spite of everything, I care about you very much. I love you! Like everything else in this life, we have to set boundaries, and I have done it. And it hurts my soul because since the day I met you I knew I wanted a future with you, and I decided to opt for that, despite how difficult it was to go against everyone. But I opted for that because I was sure I wanted to be with you. Nowadays, even though I am clear about what I want, if you do not want it, there is nothing I can do.

I truly hope in my heart that you will be okay, that you will manage to get out of this mess. Every day I pray for you. I go to mass. I am praying to God so that He grants you grace and that you can make it, but I cannot be trapped inside that life and that dynamic. I wish you ALL the best, and I truly hope you can ask for help and that you can and want to have the life that we were about to have and you let go.

I do not want any more broken promises like the ones you have been making these past several months. The only way I could think of going back to you someday is if you go to meetings, if you are humble and accept that someone else has to help you, and you do a complete 180 degree turn in your life.

Obviously, anything can happen, but I hope you opt for fighting for yourself so that you can heal and make it through. I do not lose hope that you can do it, that you can get out and free yourself 100% from this illness, but you have to prove it. You decide what you want for your life, just like I decide TODAY that I do not want this life that I am living. Please, for now I just need to know that you are fine, that you read this e-mail and know what you plan to do with your life so that I can also move on with mine.

I love you so, so, so, so much, and it is because of that that I make this decision so that hopefully you can get out from under this. You have no idea how much I want to hug you, give you kisses, hold your hand, walk with you, sleep with you, and for you to tell me that everything is going to be fine. I miss you so much. I am sending you hugs and kisses, and may God bless you always, always!

***

On January 30, Alejandro replied to Marimar's e-mail, followed by a series of e-mails filled with suffering.

Mar,

I have gone one day without getting high, and the only reason I haven't been in touch is because it was only yesterday that I received my money from my parents. I just woke up. I did not use yesterday, and I have not used today. I do not have the words to reply to your e-mail. I cannot stop crying. Of all the nightmares this has caused, this was the worst that could have happened. With this, the pain I have inside, I just hit bottom, and the truth is that I have got nothing else to offer.

Like they say, this was the straw that broke the camel's back, the straw of suffering. I understand everything, but right now my heart and soul are broken. I also love you. I love you, I love you, I love you, and a life without you does not have any meaning anymore.

February 1, 2014

Mar,

I need you. I am going mad. I cannot deal with what my mind is seeing. Please tell me you are all right. Please tell me all I am seeing is a delusion, that it is not real. I need you, my love. I need you with me. Again they left me without any money. I cannot even pay for the hotel. As soon as they deposit some money, I will move from this hotel, and I will let you know where I am. I tried calling you like ten times, but I was never able to get through. Mar, truly, I cannot do this anymore…

I do not want to live without you, Mar! The truth is, I do not want...I need to see you and hug you. This is almost over!

Clarita...During that whole time, we had been seeing different specialists because we were worried about the fact that Alex had made a lot of money in his job, and he asked for it every week with the excuse of paying for his hotels and meals. The specialist from the Ibogaine clinic recommended that we should not give him the money, even though it was his. On the other hand, we consulted with David, and he told us, "No way. If it is his money, give it with the condition that he takes responsibility. It doesn't matter if he runs out of it."

Given the history of the *anexo* and Dallas, as a family we had decided that never again would Alex end up on the streets and that he could always count on a clean place to sleep and a warm meal. That was reason enough to continue giving him money. In the end, Alex only called us to deposit money. He continuously changed hotels.

On Monday, February 3, he called me to tell me he wanted to come back to Mexico. His dad and I offered to get him and take him somewhere, and he replied, "No, this nightmare is going to be over soon." We told him we were going to deposit the last of the money he had in his account and to use it to come back to Mexico. I added that he should call the person in the Ibogaine clinic to detox before coming back. Alex said yes to everything. We told him many times how much we loved him and that he could make it, to which he replied, "Marimar left me."

I tried to calm him down, telling him that when he cleaned up his life, she was going to go back to him, that she was only concerned, hurt. It wasn't easy for anyone to understand what was happening. We told him again that we loved him and then we hung up. I remember Gerardo told me, "He sounds very bad."

The next day, I told Gerardo, "Something happened to Alex." He reassured me. We no longer knew anything about what he was doing, and we even expected he would come back to Mexico on Wednesday like he had told us he would. We waited for him all day. On Thursday morning, February 6, Gerardo said, "Calm down. Nothing happened to him. He just withdrew the money we sent him."

At two in the afternoon—I was cooking because my children and brother were coming over—the phone rang. Juanita answered, and she told me, "Someone is calling from the United States." My first thought was, "What trouble is Alex in now?" I answered, and a person who spoke terrible Spanish was speaking to me slowly, asking me very strange questions: *Do you know your son is in San Diego? Do you know the reason he is here? Did he come here for business?* And so on and so on, a series of more questions. And suddenly, she says, "Do you know that your son, Alejandro, died?"

Everybody was talking in the kitchen. I did not know if I was hearing her correctly or what it was that this person wanted to tell me. Then I repeated, "How did Alejandro die? How? Where? What happened to him?" I did not understand a thing. I started saying, "No, of course not!"

Juanita cried and screamed desperately as she said, "Not my child! Not my child!" I could not hear any of what the woman was telling me. I asked her again, "Where is he? What happened?" And Juanita continued screaming. Desperate, I asked her to please leave the room so that I could hear.

Little by little, in her bad Spanish, she started to explain to me what had happened. She told me that Alejandro had arrived approximately at one in the afternoon at a Holiday Inn. He asked for a room, washed his clothes in the tub, and he asked for a pizza that he never ate. Two hours later, he came out of the room, screaming that there was a fire in his room and triggered the fire alarm that was in the hallway, which made tremendous noise throughout the hotel. Alex kept running up and down the hallway, asking where his mom was, insisting she was in room 220. The firefighters arrived quickly with the police. The hotel manager went upstairs with them to verify if in fact there was a fire in his room. I can imagine that because of his paranoia, Alex got very scared when he saw the firefighters and the policemen, perhaps thinking they were coming for him—his eternal fear. He ran toward the emergency exit where there was a balcony. He kept running and the balcony, which had very low fencing, could not contain him. He fell to the ground and died instantly. Sometimes I think that Alex, in his mind, only wanted to fly and escape.

While I listened to her story, Mauricio came into the kitchen and saw what was happening. He started asking me what happened, but the only thing I managed to say was that Alex was dead. "But how?" he asked. Gerardo, who was upstairs, heard and came down immediately. We all cried desperately. I do not understand from where I got strength, but I asked them to let me continue with the call. Then I asked this person what we should do. She gave me the information and phone numbers of the funeral home where we should call to get directions and go get Alex.

I hung up the phone. Eduardo arrived at the house to eat, and we all screamed and cried like crazy. We could not and did not want to believe it. We never thought this is how it would end.

We all went to San Diego to get him; we had to wait several days because of the paperwork we needed to bring him back home. We cried and cried. Nobody understood what was happening. We were in shock. We wandered aimlessly, as if powered by inertia, without a destination. And since Alex had lived in San Diego for such a long time, we had dinner and we ate at all his favorite places, remembering all the times we had been there with him, and we even ordered all his favorite dishes. It fills me with peace to think that God gave him two and a half years more of life after the shooting so that he could repair things and manage to fulfill his dreams.

When we came back to Mexico, we decided to take him to Ixtapa—his place. We could not dream of leaving him in an urn in some church. Alex had lived a life trapped in his addiction, and we wanted him to finally be free.

We had a beautiful ceremony, like he would have liked it—everyone in the boat, dressed in white. We put on his favorite music. Neither Gerardo nor I could, so we asked Eduardo to spread his ashes in the sea while everyone said good-bye in their own way. We let go some photos, a rosary, white flowers, and I read some words to him. We had five candles in the shape of lotus flowers, each one representing a member of our family. One at a time, Gerardo, Eduardo, Mauricio, and I let one go. Representing Alex, Marimar let go of the fifth one. The sea, that takes everything, as if it knew, put the lilies together once more.

In the end, Mau screamed heartbreakingly, "THANKS, ALEX!" At that moment, from the horizon and with an extraordinary sunset, a sparrow came to us as if to join Alex on his journey.

CHAPTER X

The Strength of a Family

We had an angel among us, but we did not see his wings.

—*Mauricio Sierra*

Ana Paula Rivas...Through these pages of moving narration, we witness not only Alejandro's story and his struggle, but we also bear witness to the strength of a family, the ability that Clarita, Gerardo, Eduardo, and Mauricio had to remain nearby. They always tried to stay united, no matter how heartbreaking the pain and helplessness. They decided to live Alex's process with him, without remorse and without reproach, in spite of the difficulty they faced due to the unimaginable scope of behaviors and actions of an addict.

Not that there were not disagreements or differences, and obviously there were many moments of desperation where wrong decisions were possibly made, but they learned to love the addict, even when his behavior was intolerable, and overall, they did not let the healthy parts of the family dynamic become destroyed. They understood there was a terrible illness, but they also had the capacity to keep seeing Alex without forgetting his true self.

They learned to communicate in the most complicated moments, to build a common front, and to respect different points of view. They also learned to negotiate, to listen, to not judge, to exchange opinions, and to yield without destroying each other. They also learned through trial and error that the true recovery always belongs to the addict; it is a personal job. Above all, they learned to stay together, to always be present, and to love unconditionally.

Reconstructing Alex

Sierra Family...Where to start? Faced with Alex's addiction and recognizing its essence, everyone in the family used the resources they had at their disposal, whatever little that we had on hand if not more, to be there when Alex needed us. Thousands of jumbled words start coming out of our mouths when we think and talk about him. In these words, the duality that inhabited him always comes to the surface:

- Generous
- Evasive
- Dreamer
- Fantasizer
- Empathic
- Survivor
- Aggressive
- Loving
- Expressive of his love
- Intense
- Sensitive
- Passionate
- Sweet
- Fearful
- Tender
- Positive
- Prosaic
- Deep
- Joyful
- Proud
- Childish
- Impetuous
- Spiritual
- Daredevil
- Playful
- Compassionate

- Fun
- Superman
- Romantic
- Insecure
- Dependent
- Manipulative
- Stubborn
- Guilty
- Brave

Concerned about his image, he never wanted to be seen as an addict. That is why it is so important to rebuild his essence, to speak about him like the character that he was, the one that did enjoy life, who loved it with intensity and took advantage of it, who milked it for all it was worth the years he was with us. He loved life deeply. We want to remember that Alex who, with his smile, lit up the whole room.

Without a doubt, we also have to speak about our deep pain and sorrow in seeing our loved one destroy himself, and with his death came a profound, persuasive lesson: Live day by day, and appreciate life as it comes.

Clarita: My Vision

> *Seeing my son destroy himself to death was one of the hardest things in my life. Part of me died with him.*

As Mauricio expresses in his farewell letter to Alex, we can now understand that Alex's illness was his costume, a mask that he wore to hide his true essence, and it put us through the necessary tests to get to know the magic and gift that is living. Alex taught us all, from the simplest idea of always having the heart and attitude of a child; he always gave us that present. He admired it all and got excited about everything. Despite being so mature in other situations, he always reflected his inner child. Every day he woke up with the hope of bringing us happiness and sharing it with everybody. He always had a beautiful and generous smile. He lived aspiring to reach his goals. He dreamed, and he knew that everything was possible.

With his relapses, he taught us that we can make mistakes, that we are not perfect, and most importantly, to accept and learn from our mistakes. He valued time and was thankful to life for all it gave him. He had a great heart—tender and loving—always caring and looking for ways to help others, like a tree that grows and finds its abundance and does not ask or judge who receive its fruit, but knows that to renew itself, to transform itself and keep growing, you have to give the best of yourself.

He always wanted to become a dad, and he showed the capacity to be a good one. He always won over the affection of children. He found ways for them to see him like one of their own, and they felt safe having him close. He had a great capacity to love, always reminding us of his immense love for life.

He taught us to support each other and be the shoulder to cry on that we all need in difficult times. He taught us to listen with an open heart without judgment or guilt. Alex gave of himself without condition and saw his neighbor as an opportunity to learn how important it is to celebrate differences. This acceptance and tolerance showed his human and empathic side.

He loved without limits and tried to give the best of himself. He made mistakes, but he always tried to remedy them and compensate for his failures. He always fought and made an effort to move forward, and he had the humility of giving his heart to show the others that those failures can become the product of a limitless love.

Now, it is also fair to say on the topic of addiction that it always leaves profound wounds. The happy endings seem so far away. Our story did not have a happy ending. After sleepless nights and feelings of helplessness, fear, sadness, and anxiety, we as a family—apart from the emotional fatigue—will always have the feeling that somehow we caused the addiction or that we could have done much more to avoid it.

In our case, we lived for years with sadness, desperation, fear, and anger, but always with much hope. We never stopped thinking, desiring, and looking out for Alejandro's well-being. We could see in the last two years a very strong light at the end of the tunnel. Unfortunately, the ending was much more devastating than the addiction itself.

We will never know the reason for Alejandro's addiction, whether he was born with a predisposition toward it, if it was latent in his genetic code, or if he caused it with his behaviors. To me, as his mom, it is very difficult to understand this, and I will always wonder. Having three children—whom we educated in the same way, to whom we gave the same values, and to all of whom we gave the same attention and love—why was one of them was afflicted by this horrible illness? What I do know is that addiction (or any chronic illness) not only affected my son, but our entire family, and over time, all who were close to him. For me, writing this book is not only a part of my journey, but it also gives us the opportunity to heal as a family after long years of pain and suffering, and at the same time we can try to fulfill Alex's mission: helping others.

Many people might say, "But Alex never recovered. How can his story help another person?" I think it is exactly for this reason that this mission becomes important. For the young people who are already consuming alcohol and drugs, they will be able to see in Alex's life the necessity to find resources and tools to succeed and not relapse over and over again like Alex. And for the young people who are flirting with the idea of experimenting, to educate them about this horrible illness that has the capacity to take them to the darkest places they can imagine.

To us as a family, this book has been like getting emotionally naked before the entire world. It means speaking about the pain, hopelessness, shame, and guilt that we experienced during all these years. It means talking about our mistakes, our successes, and the great love that has always united our family. The most important objective of this book is to be able to help other families, to help other parents to not live this horror story, and if they are already living it, to not feel so alone.

We are uncovering Alex's life and ours, with the only goal being to put it in the service of others. We want to show along these lines how this illness manipulates and lies to both the addict and his family, how Alex lived this experience, how this same experience was lived by his brothers, friends, girlfriends, and us—his parents—and how addiction trapped us in a world of lies, deception, and loss of trust, and as long as this deception existed, Alex continued being ill even without getting high.

We did all that we could however we could, but I will always wonder if it was enough, if we could have done more. I believe that both Gerardo and I used all the resources we had. We learned, listened, and took action according to what the experts said, and at other times, we only listened to what our hearts told us. We walked away, came close, protected him, threatened him, begged him, let him face his consequences, rescued him, and helped him try to repair his self-esteem. We paid for clinics, treatments, halfway houses, gyms, therapies and therapists, and hospitals for detox, always with the goal that Alex could recover.

I am completely sure that because of my great love, while I helped him on some occasions, on others I did him a disservice, all in my desire to rescue him in what I thought was a normal response and is what any mother would do. The bond between mother and son is so strong that I always wanted to trust Alex, and I became very confused and angry when I felt manipulated, betrayed, and involved in all of his lies. What matters to me is to know that we did the best we could, and that Alejandro also did what he could.

Alex faced all the consequences of his actions; he felt defeated and lived with loneliness, cold, hunger, and the fear of living on the streets. He found himself totally hopeless, broken, and many times he lost everything, even hope. Today, I can say with much conviction that all these experiences are useful to some people, but not to others. Many manage to get out and make important changes in their lives. Alex did not make it.

I can also say with conviction that gratification was not useful for overcoming addiction. Alex had it all: a family who loved and supported him, a pair of brothers who adored him, parents who loved him unconditionally, friends who loved and appreciated him, an education, generosity, a good job that helped him establish economic independence, and a girlfriend whom he adored who loved him back endlessly. Together they shared a life project filled with a myriad of dreams.

What a horrible illness!

What a horrible drug!

Alex lived a tormented life. He lived a life full of guilt and regret, and he hated himself for everything he did, for the destruction and damage he caused, and even despite this pain, he could not imagine his life without drugs. However, often I think he also had a fulfilling and happy life, and when we were able to learn that we did not have control over his illness—when we could stop judging him and creating expectations that caused us all so much pain—we could finally exist in a state of peace.

In medical family therapy, it is common to talk about how not to let illness occupy a place in the family. Addiction became a part of my family. It was able to get all our attention, and today it has left us with so much suffering that sometimes I feel it still sits at the table with us. It is a part of our consciousness and our thoughts. How could it not be? It took our beloved Alex's life with it.

Addiction took part of our lives. It changed them. It taught us to appreciate all moments of life, the good and the bad. It made us better people—more compassionate, more thankful, more tolerant, and more humble. It taught us to never take anything for granted, to celebrate and live every day to the fullest like Alex did. It taught us to forgive, to live in the present. It taught us fortitude and unconditional love. It gave us the opportunity to learn about ourselves. And most importantly, it taught us to see Alex's essence beyond his illness.

Alex leaves in all the people he touched an immense emptiness that nothing can fill; he has taken with him a part of us all. Thank you, Alex, for giving us so much, for showing the duality of human nature, and for making us all better people. We will eternally have you in our hearts, and you shall live forever in our memories.

CHAPTER XI

A Small Journey into the World of Addiction

I simply convinced myself that I was not vulnerable and I would not get hooked. But addiction does not make deals with you, and little by little, it expanded inside me like fog.

—*Eric Clapton*

What exactly is an addiction? There are many definitions, many statistics, and too many stereotypes around this illness. Why does a person become an addict? Is there a personality that is prone to addiction? Is it hereditary, a genetic disease? Is one born an addict, or does he become one through his behaviors? What are the circumstances that push an individual to use a substance that he knows hurts him severely? These are just a few of the questions that surround the world of addiction. Psychologists, specialists, and doctors have worked for years to answer this grave problem that afflicts society and that seems to be more serious as time goes by.

But, when in the heart of our families we discover with horror the guts of this phenomenon, fear and pain mixed with the deep love we feel for our loved one—be it our child, spouse, parent, or sibling—it takes over and leaves us with a desperate feeling of helplessness. We are faced with a confusing and discomforting picture. How can we help him? What is in my hands? What can I control? How can I prevent this person that I love so much from hurting himself and others? How does unconditional love work in ill-fated times?

From Alex's experience and the brave battle of his family, we will try to give some medical and psychological data in this chapter that are meant to help with understanding this disease. The data were taken from several texts whose information can be found at the end of the book. Nevertheless, this is not an in-depth study of addiction. It is simply a discussion of the general concepts that shed light on the problems generated for the individual and his family as a result of addiction.

What is an addiction?

Addiction is defined as a chronic, relapsing brain disease characterized by compulsive drug seeking and use despite harmful consequences. It is considered a brain disease because drugs change the brain; they change its structure and how it works. These brain changes can be long-lasting and can lead to the harmful behaviors seen in people who abuse drugs.[20]

Addiction is a neurobiological disease, not a lifestyle choice, and it is about time we start treating it that way. After changing the way we speak about addiction, we need to change the way people think about addiction. Both are crucial steps in overcoming the social stigma frequently associated with this disease. This books endeavors to be a small but important step toward the elimination of the stigma that surrounds the treatment of addictions.

Causes of Addiction

The etiology of addiction is complex. The origin of addiction is multifactorial, involving biological, genetic, psychological, and social factors. Studies show there are neurochemical changes in people with addictive disorders in addition to a biogenetic predisposition to developing this disease.

As well as with any other disease, vulnerability to addiction varies from person to person, and there is not a single factor that determines if a person will become addicted to drugs. In general, the more risk factors a person has, the greater the probability that drug use will result in abuse and addiction. On the other hand, protective factors reduce the risk that a person will abuse drugs and become addicted. Risk and protective factors can be environmental (e.g., home life, school, and neighborhood) or biological (e.g., genes, developmental state, gender, and ethnic origin).[21]

Biological and Genetic Factors

Scientists estimate that genetic factors account for between forty and sixty percent of a person's vulnerability to addiction. This includes the effects of environmental factors on the function and expression of a person's genes. A person's stage of development and other medical conditions are also factors. Adolescents and people with mental disorders are at greater risk of drug abuse and addiction than the general population. Although taking drugs at any age can lead to addiction, research shows that the earlier a person begins to use drugs, the more likely he or she is to develop serious problems. This may reflect the harmful effects that drugs can have on the developing brain. It also may result from a mix of early social and biological vulnerability factors, including unstable family relationships, exposure to physical or sexual abuse, genetic susceptibility, or mental illness. Still, the fact remains that early use is a strong indicator of future problems, including addiction.[22]

Drugs and the Brain

Addiction is a defect in the hedonic system, the system where we perceive pleasure. It is located in the deepest part of the brain (i.e., in the limbic or reptilian brain), and more specifically, in the area of the nucleus accumbens that takes care of our survival.

Limbic System

The limbic system contains the brain's reward circuit, or hedonic system. It connects various brain structures that control and regulate our ability to feel pleasure. The fact is that feeling pleasure motivates us to repeat behaviors like eating, having sex, and sleeping, in other words, essential actions for our existence. The limbic system is activated when we perform these activities, but also with drug abuse. That is why we start feeling that a drug is as essential as sleeping, eating, or drinking water. Moreover, the limbic system is responsible for the perception of our emotions, both positive and negative, which explains the ability of many drugs to alter our mood.

All drugs of abuse directly or indirectly attack the reward system of the brain, flooding the reward circuit with dopamine. Dopamine is a neurotransmitter located in regions of the brain that regulate movement, emotions, cognition, motivation, and feelings of pleasure. Overstimulation of this system that rewards our natural behaviors produces the effects of euphoria that people who abuse drugs seek out, and it teaches them to repeat this behavior.

Our brains are designed to ascertain that we repeat the basic activities that sustain life, associating them with pleasure, reward, or gratification. Every time this reward circuit is activated, the brain notices that something important is happening that must be remembered, and the brain teaches us that we must repeat it over and over without thinking about it. Due to the fact that drugs of abuse stimulate the same circuit, people learn to abuse drugs in the same manner.[23]

Frontal Cortex

The frontal lobe, known as frontal cortex or anterior brain, is the center of thought in the brain. The frontal cortex, specifically the prefrontal cortex, is the last zone in the brain to reach full maturity. Its development lasts until the age of twenty or older. This is a period of great opportunity but also danger. The fact that this critical part of an adolescent's brain is still a work in progress puts them at increased risk for making poor decisions, such as trying drugs or continuing to take them. Also, introducing drugs during this period of development may cause brain changes that have profound and long-lasting consequences.

Our daily behaviors and daily habits can hurt our brains or make us more vulnerable to addiction, or these very same behaviors can help and protect our brain from addiction.[24]

The frontal cortex controls emotions and cognitive abilities, such as memory, concentration, self-reflection, problem solving, and the ability to choose appropriate behaviors. Therefore, throughout development, you can see a progressive improvement in the capacity to inhibit responses in terms of attention and behavioral self-regulation.

The frontal lobe gives us empathy to not hurt other people, direction to understand outcomes, and whether you take this path or the other, it helps us to learn from our mistakes. It is our conscience, our Jiminy Cricket, of what you must do or not do. It is like our compass.

The Prefrontal Cortex and the Regulation of Teenage Behavior[25]

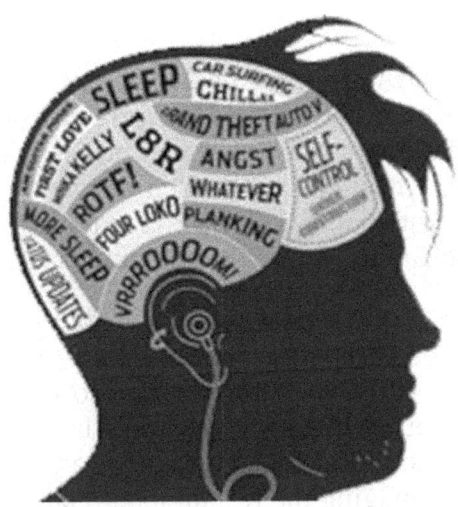

The mental faculties that depend on the frontal lobe are impulse control, decision making, planning and anticipation of the future, attention, the ability to perform several tasks at the same time, temporary organization of behavior, and the sense of responsibility toward oneself and others (i.e., the capacity for empathy).

The role that the prefrontal cortex performs in decision making is an indication of the greater impulsiveness and involvement of teenagers in risky behaviors related to sexuality, drug use, or antisocial behaviors. In adolescence, the lack of maturity of the prefrontal cortex, which is overall in its initial stage, and its associated impulsiveness, help explain greater involvement in risky behaviors during that period.

Maturity of the prefrontal cortex is slower than other brain changes. It is not accelerated by the hormonal changes of puberty, and it depends on age and learning. It does not reach its maturity until the third decade of life. This leads us to think that in the early stage of puberty is when there is greater imbalance, with a motivational circuit prone to participating in situations that can offer an immediate reward and a self-regulatory circuit that has not yet reached its full potential, which will therefore encounter difficulty in imposing inhibitory control over impulsive behavior.

Alcohol abuse during adolescence can negatively influence the memory center of brain called the hippocampus. The use of drugs and alcohol can also alter teenage brain development, resulting in a lack of ability to appropriately deal with social situations and the stressful events of daily life.[26]

Since Alex started drinking alcohol at an early age, it is probable that his frontal lobe never reached the proper maturity to make the right decisions, and that is why he sometimes exhibited the impulsive behaviors of an eighteen-year-old when he was twenty-six years old or older. His maturity came with his life experiences and the terrible circumstances he had to endure throughout his process of addiction.

Genetically, Alex presented a predisposition to addiction, and the other damage he caused to the frontal lobe is an indication of drug abuse that started early on. "Introduction to drugs at this stage of development can cause changes in the brain that have deep and lasting consequences."[27] All these elements become a vicious circle, wherein the addict keeps damaging the frontal lobe. That is, since I cannot be conscious of the danger of taking a particular path, the addict goes back to using. Alex would say, "My brain lies to me."

Reward Circuit of the Brain

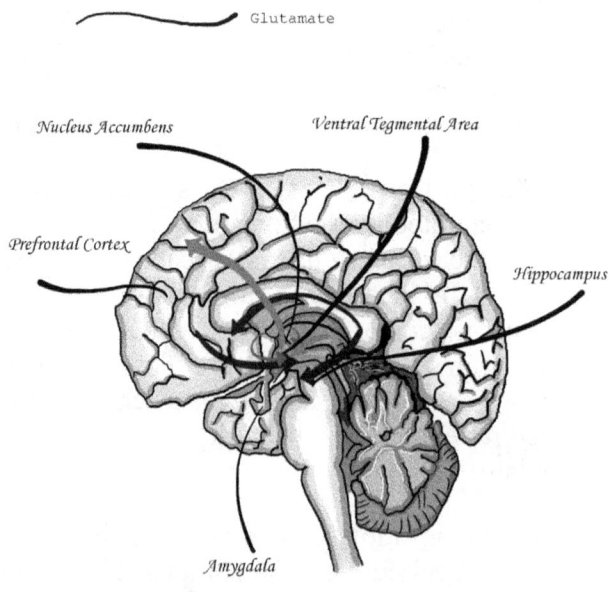

Social and Family Factors

The growth, development, and constitution of a person inside their family nucleus turn out to be some of life's most complex phenomena. Every factor in the environment—the relationship between parents as a couple and with their children, beliefs, styles, forms of education, and conflicts—can interact in multiple ways, which results in the formation of a particular style of interpreting reality and defining who we are and how we relate to others.

Some studies (Coombs and Landsver, 1988; Jurich, Polson, and Bates, 1985; Melby, Conger, Conger, and Lorenz, 1993; Volk, Edwards, Lewis, and Sprinkle, 1989), have managed to establish the relationship between family factors and drug abuse. The outstanding factors are those related to family union (e.g., isolation of the teenager from the family, lack of close relationships with his parents, unfulfilled need for acknowledgement, trust and love, parental rejection, links of dependency, absentee parents); conflict (e.g., marriage, lack of responsibility, unhappy home life, unhappy spouse, family discord, involvement in marriage conflict, high degree of stress, trauma); divorce and family fracture (e.g., broken home, absentee parents, one-parent home); discipline (e.g., autocratic or "laissez-faire," lack of clear rules or limits, excessive use of punishment); hypocritical morality (e.g., double standards, denial of the parents' personal problems); and empty communication (e.g., lack of communication skills of the teenager, little communication between the parents and the teenager).

In addition, the influence of the home environment, especially during childhood, is a very important factor. Parents or older members of the family who abuse alcohol or drugs or participate in criminal activity can increase the risk that they also develop problems with drugs.

On the other hand, the development of addiction is also facilitated by social factors that modify appearance. For example, there exist social aspects of specific groups that affect use and addiction. Some authors point out that our culture contains beliefs and social rules that are dysfunctional and that constitute the psychosocial nucleus of addiction. Consumerism and cult of the image are some of our societal characteristics that directly influence people's predisposition to addiction. This impacts the life of the addict in such a way that his system of values changes to create a whole different culture with its own beliefs and rituals.[28]

Friends, classmates from school, and acquaintances can have an even greater influence during adolescence. If peers consume drugs, they can convince even those who may not be at high risk to try them for the first time. School failure or lack of social skills can put a child at greater risk of using or becoming addicted to drugs.

Why is addiction a disease?

For the purposes of this book, it is vital to present addiction as a disease due to the great stigma that exists around addiction. It is rather important for society to see addiction as a mental illness if we want to have better results in its treatment and monitoring: "Only by understanding the humanity within those who suffer from it—as buried as it may sometimes seem to be—can we as a society find the courage and will to finally do what needs to be done to end suffering."[29]

Once a person develops an addiction, it must be treated as a mental illness, and therefore, the addict must not be punished, precisely because he is sick. Utilizing information from *Addiction* by Kevin McCauley, M.D. and Cory Reich, Ph.D., LMFT, I will present some concepts that, from our point of view and from the experiences we endured with Alejandro, have helped make sense of our situation.

We won't deny that addicts can do terrible things. So how can we call addiction a disease? Isn't calling addiction a disease just an excuse for bad behavior? Why should we send an addict to treatment when what we really want to do is kick them out of the house or fire them from their job or throw them in jail? Nothing else seems to work. Today it is very clear to me that there is something much more fundamental to addiction than bad behavior. And this is very true. Now we have an explanation as to why addicts seem like bad people, why they make bad decisions, and why they do not learn from their mistakes. They lose their sense of empathy.

Addicts can do terrible things. They can lie, cheat, and steal, and it turns out that it is not an inherent, personal characteristic, but there is a reason why they act like that, and this reason is an imbalance in brain chemistry. There is a disease process in all of those behaviors.

Something happens in the brain of these people when they consume alcohol and drugs that does not happen in other people.[30]

Badness? Or Symptoms?

If all we do is look at the addict's behavior, we are going to draw some quick conclusions about who they are. It is nearly impossible not to do this because the behavior of addicts is just so shocking. We might say that addicts are morally weak or that they do not have willpower. We even think that they have an addictive personality. We can judge their character, their friendship, how they were raised, or something bad their parents did. Often, the very same addict describes himself as a bad person of weak character who only knows how to hurt his loved ones.[31]

Dr. Kevin McCauley continues: "Therefore, the same ideas we have about addicts' behaviors are so powerful that these make us think they are in reality 'these behaviors.' Then, when we think about addiction, we must set aside all stereotypes and prejudices that during the history of medicine and psychology have characterized the behaviors of these people that we do not like or even understand."

The truth is that there is no such thing as an addictive personality. Five decades of clinical research have never been able to identify a particular personality behind addiction. Likewise, addiction occurs in people with strong moral values and regardless of their upbringing or social environment. While moral flaws, character defects, and family dysfunction can indeed affect addiction, they cannot, in fact, cause it.

In the last ten years, we have learned a lot about the brain. Now we know that the physical defect of addiction is localized in the deepest part of the brain that is responsible for survival. Because of this defect, the addict unconsciously thinks of his drug as an integral part of his own life. Beer is not a simple beer anymore; the addict needs the beer to navigate through life. He needs it to survive, and this is called "craving" or "obsession":

> When craving gets into my head, there is nothing that I can do to make it go away. I can use all my resources to let it pass, but it comes back. It owns me, and I cannot stop it anymore.
>
> — Alex

McCauley goes on: "What is true is that the person does have the choice of using drugs or not and does not have the choice of this necessity called 'craving.' If cravings (moments of obsession) become very strong, even the person with the strongest willpower, the most mature and the most responsible one, will go back to using drugs. Not a single brain can ignore the imperious necessity of survival. One of the reasons why it is so hard for us to call addiction a disease is our inability to understand this concept. "Craving" is an emotional and obsessive thought process that occurs in addicts. It is an overwhelming immediacy of thought, a survival level desperation to obtain and use drugs. It is a mental suffering so real that it takes the addict to the point of using drugs again, even though he does not want to and although the consequences are terrible: losing his family or his job, his economic stability, going to jail, even death."

This thought does not occur in people who are not addicted, even though they may abuse alcohol or other illegal substances. The craving is not a metaphor; is a neuronal activity that is visible in brain scans, and what is important for the addict is that craving equals suffering.

Also, it is important to understand that craving is involuntary. It is a disorder of volition in the brain's ability to make use of free will. In as much as it is difficult to understand this concept, there is concrete evidence that free will is broken or disconnected in the addict. This does not mean that we have to take away from the addict all the responsibility for his actions, but what we can say with certainty is that addiction is an illness, and the addict has to take responsibility for his recovery.[32]

Factors That Can Trigger an Addiction

In general, people start taking drugs for a variety of reasons:

- **To feel good.** Most abused drugs produce intense feelings of pleasure. This initial sensation of euphoria is followed by other effects, which differ depending on the type of drug. For example, with stimulants such as cocaine, the high is followed by feelings of power, self-confidence, and increased energy. In contrast, the euphoria caused by opiates, such as heroin, is followed by feelings of relaxation and satisfaction.

- **To feel better.** Some people who suffer from social anxiety, stress-related disorders, and depression begin abusing drugs in an attempt to lessen feelings of distress. Stress can play a major role in beginning drug use, continuing drug use, or relapse in patients recovering from addiction.

- **To do better.** Some people feel pressure to chemically enhance or improve their cognitive or athletic performance, which can play a role in initial experimentation and continued abuse of drugs, such as prescription stimulants or anabolic/androgenic steroids.

- **Curiosity and «because others are doing it.»** In this respect, adolescents are particularly vulnerable because of the strong influence of peer pressure. Teens are more likely than adults to engage in risky or daring behaviors to impress their friends and express their independence from parental and social rules.[33]

One of the most significant risk factors for addiction is tolerance. Tolerance to a substance is produced when, as a result of its administration (or self-administration) the subject presents less sensitivity to it. The habitual dose of the substance produces fewer effects.

Tolerance

- Tolerance implies a decrease in the effect obtained with a constant dose of the drug, which causes a progressive increase in the dose to obtain the degree of wanted satisfaction
- Deprivation implies The emergence of an abstinence syndrome due to the lack of drug.
- The emergence of an abstinence syndrome due to the lack of drug.
- Using a higher quantity or for a longer period of time than what is desired.

- Having a persistent desire to get high and failed attempts to decrease the quantity used.
- Spending considerable periods of time using or getting drugs.
- Rejecting or looking down on social and work opportunities in order to use.
- Continuing to get high even though one knows about the damage it can cause to health and all aspects of his life.[34]

Clarita...Why is it so difficult for our children to understand the damage that drugs cause? All drugs go through a honeymoon period; that is why it is so difficult to explain to a young person that even though in the beginning there are pleasant effects, later the continuous abuse will become a horror story, something out of their control because they do not have the proper perspective for the challenges they face that come with new experiences. They do not understand the intensity of the act. They only think that we are demonizing something that for them is mere amusement.

Types of Addictive Substances

The concept of addiction for all substances is the same; the only thing that changes is the substance used. However, there are certain factors that make a substance more addictive than others.

The first factor is the speed with which the drug produces pleasant effects. While it takes a person twenty minutes to feel the effects of alcohol, crack gets to the brain quickly, and its pleasant effects do not last very long—approximately seven minutes. Therefore, the action of lighting the pipe is constantly repeated, which makes it a habitual and compulsive behavior.

The second factor that makes a drug more addictive is the degree of pleasure that one experiences. Pleasure is an increase in enjoyable sensations or the masking of painful ones. A person with low self-esteem will find much greater pleasure in the abuse of drugs than a person who is sure of himself.

My dad had given me an American Express card that is given to only a few people. Just the fact that I had it gave me a certain status and prestige. For me, an insecure person who always looked for others' approval, this was a great gift. I felt important using this card wherever I needed it.

—Alex

Clarita...Whether he used the card is not very relevant because it was only for emergencies. However, in his insecurity, it empowered him in a special way (a behavior that was present throughout his addiction process). When Alejandro used, we took away that card, and when he was fine, the first thing he wanted was to get it back, as if this in and of itself gave him back his self-worth. Years later, it became some kind of symbol of his rehabilitation process: "When I get it back, I go back to feeling normal."

The third factor that makes a drug more addictive is the degree of pain or discomfort the person experiences when discontinuing it. With an alcohol addiction, the withdrawal syndrome can cause convulsions, tremors, and hallucinations, and this can be a motivation to not consume again. With a heroin addiction, the syndrome can occur a few hours after the last time the person used the drug. Its symptoms include restlessness, bone and muscle pain, insomnia, diarrhea, vomiting, chills, and restless leg syndrome. The acute symptoms of the withdrawal reach their peak between 24 to 48 hours after the last dose of heroin, and they settle down after approximately one week. The addict can die during withdrawal.

For the person that consumes crack, stopping can cause shakiness, depression, suicidal feelings, paranoia, and an overwhelming state of despair so great that just by knowing that in seven minutes the effects will disappear, the patient will use again.

To be honest, I endured, and it took a lot out of me. I woke up, and I "felt it," and this is completely foreign to you, but I got this feeling that because I was not going to use anymore, all the difficulties would start again. I couldn't stand it...so, I went back to using.

—Alex

The fourth factor is the duration of the psychoactive effects of the drug. For example, assume there are two different drugs. Drug A, for example, is methamphetamine (i.e., ice) that quickly creates a high degree of pleasure and leads to a high degree of displeasure when discontinued, but it maintains the pleasurable effect for approximately twelve hours. Drug B is crack. It has the same characteristics as Drug A, but the pleasurable effects last only seven minutes after each administration.

Obviously, Drug B will be much more addicting because the person will be more exposed to the drug in terms of buying, preparing, and administering the substance. We know that the more one repeats a behavior, the faster it becomes a habit.[35]

Use of Crack

Active addiction can involve auditory hallucinations, hypertension, and hyper vigilance. During use, a person may think they hear sirens, cars pulling up outside, music, and people talking, among other things. Some people will experience tactile hallucinations, such as skin crawling or seeing bugs on their skin. They will be extremely alert to the point of paranoia, perhaps suspicious of any movement around the area where they are using. It is common to hide out in the area where use is occurring and refuse to answer the door.

1) **Panic stage:** 1-3 hours after last use. During this phase, money for more is the prime concern. In this phase, a person may look for something around their house to sell or pawn or may consider where they may beg, borrow, or steal something to sell for cocaine. Looking for lint on the rug, hoping something has fallen, is common at this point. In this acute withdrawal period, people have been known to try to rob others in crowded public places (e.g., malls, stores, convenience stores, fast food restaurants) in order to obtain money or goods to sell for money for more crack. The withdrawal is so intense and the craving so overwhelming that the person has little ability to think or reason logically.

2) Crash Stage: 3-24 hours after last use. Characterized by depression, remorse, and suicidal behavior. The brain greatly needs rest. It has exhausted the neurotransmitters (serotonin) needed for sleep, so it is difficult at first to go to sleep. In this phase, the person feels guilt and remorse for having spent all of their wages, for having used funds that did not belong to them, and for having pawned valuable articles for less than their true value. They have stolen from the people they most love and care about. Often, under the influence of a cocaine-induced depression, they make promises to themselves that they will never use again and believe it. During this phase, there is a greater risk of suicide.

3) Honeymoon Phase: 1-5 days after last use. Characterized by feeling good. Cravings are not very noticeable and are manageable. The effects of the drug are disappearing, and the person begins to regain confidence in their ability to handle their addiction. During this phase, it is common to hear the addict say, "I do not think about it at all. I do not need it right now. I don't think I'll have any problem with my addiction." This is a form of self-deception, a deception that leads the person to forgetting their past cycles of relapse, which paves the way for their next use or relapse. At this stage, it is only small quantities of neurotransmitters in the brain (serotonin/dopamine) that need to enjoy the effects of crack; therefore, there is a lack of interest in the drug. This is a dangerous stage since it is easy to think that there is no problem and therefore, why bother to do anything about it? Addicts lower their guard during this phase and often use defense mechanisms, for example, rationalization and minimization of the problem to convince themselves that this time they have been cured and therefore do not need more support or treatment. There is a high risk of dropping out of treatment at this stage as they do not feel—or are not aware of—the physical and emotional effects of their crisis.

4) **Return of Craving:** 5-14 days after last use. Tremendous upsurge of acute drug hunger, depression, and anger. The body has produced enough serotonin/dopamine for the person to want to use more cocaine, but not enough to affect mood stability and emotions. During this phase, one may experience vivid dreams, fantasies, and acute drug hunger. Thoughts may cycle around using until a person feels like giving in to the obsession to use. Defense mechanisms (e.g., rationalization, intellectualization, denial, minimizing) begin to make a strong comeback after being knocked down by the original crisis.

5) **Emotional Augmentation:** 14-28 days up to 1-2 years. Over-response to the normal stress and events of everyday life. At the top of the mood swing, one is unusually happy and at the bottom, one is unusually sad. It is a state of making mountains out of molehills. This is related to biochemical responses induced by strong emotions that stimulate areas where mood- and mind- altering drugs act on the brain. The body is now seriously undertaking the repairs of areas damaged by drug use and is replacing important chemicals needed to regulate mood and emotions. As a result, one is slightly off balance chemically without being consciously aware of it. There is a strong need for accurate feedback on one's behavior from an objective support group (AA or NA or another type of recovery support group is recommended). This cannot be stressed too highly for long-term success in recovery. Also, low-impact exercise such as walking, jogging, bicycling, and low-impact aerobics, along with a well-balanced diet, will shorten this phase and reduce the severity of the symptoms. Irritability, depression, anxiety, mood swings, memory loss, difficulty concentrating, short attention span, nightmares, insomnia, fatigue, and headaches are some of the normal recovery symptoms of the emotional augmentation stage.

6) **Covert Cravings:** 28-35 days. Secrets and bad judgments characterize this phase. Craving is not as strong on a regular basis, but one may have periodic strong cravings

and not want to admit it for various reasons (e.g., thinking it is a sign of weakness, of poor moral character, that they are not working a good program, or that they simply should not be having cravings). Generally, the cravings are of a low level (e.g., euphoric recall or glorifying war stories, vivid dreams that trigger cravings upon awakening, or just general mild drug hunger). Without someone to talk with concerning these normal, protracted withdrawal symptoms, they can evolve into high-level cravings (e.g., acute drug hunger, drug-seeking behavior, obsession, and on to compulsion). Again, the need for a support system is strongly recommended.

7) **Cue Conditioning:** 35 days and upward. Cue conditioning, referred to as triggers, which could be money, anger, disappointment, music, a film, or extreme joy. Anything strongly associated with using could cue/trigger a craving. The strength of these cue cravings will diminish in time but continue on for years, though becoming fewer and farther between. They can catch a person off guard and evolve into higher-level cravings. Again, a long-term support plan for sobriety, such as AA/NA or a recovery support group is recommended to alleviate these natural manifestations.

It is a normal part of recovery to have strong cravings within three to seven days due to acute withdrawal and then continued cravings at a lower level well into protracted withdrawal between six months and two years. Time and severity of protracted withdrawal depend upon type, amount, and frequency of drug used. Again, a program of good nutrition and low-impact exercise can alleviate these normal recovery symptoms.

Please note that behavioral symptoms—compulsion, obsession, loss of control over time, place, amount used, and continued use despite adverse consequences—are secondary symptoms of the disease process. With continued treatment of

> the disease via abstinence and a good support system, these behavioral symptoms will diminish over time.[36]

What is codependency?

The family, as a system, directly receives the impact of an addiction in such a way that every family is affected and shows symptoms of dysfunction when one of their members gets sick with addiction. Paradoxically, the family affected by the addiction ends up producing a system of behaviors that support the development of addiction. This is called codependency.

Codependency is an illness in which concepts like obsession, lack of limits, and inappropriate and rescue behaviors are generated, as well as compulsion and control, wishes to change the addict, and ceasing to live one's own life in order to live the other person's life. It is also defined as the cycle of behavior patterns and dysfunctional thoughts that produce pain and that are repeated in a compulsive way as a response to a sick and alienating relationship with an active addict or in a situation of relational toxicity.

Family Dysfunction

Family relationships and communication become more dysfunctional each time due to the fact that the family system gets ill progressively. Communication becomes more confusing and indirect in such a way that it is easier to cover up and justify the addictive behavior. Family rules become confusing, rigid, and unfair to its members, and the roles of each family member start becoming distorted throughout the process of the addiction. All family members are affected in this system of dysfunctional rules.

Enabling

Codependent behavior is a sickness response to the addictive process, but it also becomes a key factor in the evolution of the addiction. We call this concept "enabling." Enabling takes different paths and oscillates between collaboration and aggression. Codependents cannot realize they are enabling the problem, in part from denial, and in part because they are convinced their behavior is justified due to the fact that they are "helping" the addict not to deteriorate more to prevent family disintegration.[37]

Family Roles

With all the impact that addiction generates over family dynamics, the members of this family develop the sickness of codependency progressively. Many times, this translates into an investment of a great amount of time and energy into the performance of familial dysfunctional roles whose only purpose is to provide the family with a defense mechanism to diminish anxiety and fear and give the sensation of "doing something" to solve the problem of addiction.

Unfortunately, the end result is that addiction is strengthened and the family gets even sicker. Little by little, a series of patterns of illness start emerging, like denial, anger, obsession, manipulation, dishonesty, and enablement. The family members, without realizing it, start acting out different roles to minimize or distract from the true root of the problem.

> **The Rescuer** This member of the family takes care of saving the addict from the problems that result from his addiction. Those are the ones who make up excuses, pay the bills, call the office to justify the absences, etc. In general, they self-designate the task of solving all the crises the addict produces. In this way, he promotes the addict's self-lying, keeping him blind to the consequences of his addiction and convincing him that there is no problem with his use.
>
> **The Caretaker** This person performs all the tasks and responsibilities they can, as long as the addict does not have responsibilities or that he has the least possible amount. The caretaker does that, convinced that at least "things are moving along." What they cannot see is that this burdens them with tasks that do not belong to them and with responsibilities that are not theirs, producing an overload that affects their health. This promotes, at the same time, a lack of consciousness in the addict regarding the damage that addiction produces.
>
> **The Rebel** The function of the rebel, or black sheep, is to distract the family and grab the attention for himself in a

way that everyone can turn their anger and frustration toward him. Many times, this is the little kid who continuously has discipline problems at school, or even the young man who experiments with illegal drugs.

The Hero He also insists in diverting the family's attention and distracting it towards him through positive achievements. In this way, he makes the family proud and helps distract the family's attention from the addict. He can be the impeccable academic student, the athlete that is outstanding in tournaments, or the one that is always achieving more than what is expected of him.

The Recriminator This person takes care of blaming the addict for all the problems of the family. He takes care of having tremendously bitter recrimination sessions that are exaggerated and only work to offend the addict, giving him a perfect excuse to keep using.

The Lost Child Usually, this role is taken up by a minor that stays on the periphery of discussions and family dynamics. In fact, this is a mask that covers up a great sadness and disappointment that he is unable to express.

The Disciplinarian This relative introduces the idea that what is missing is a little discipline, and he attacks the addict, physically or verbally. That attitude is born out of the rage and frustration that accumulate in the addict's family and feelings of guilt that many parents feel due to the addiction of their children.

Everyone in the family performs these roles without any idea that they are promoting the development of addiction. To the contrary, they are more than convinced that they are helping. This is why it is necessary to be aware of the necessity of changes in the family to be able to achieve a greater quality of recovery.[38]

Symptoms of Codependency

Careful communication; manipulation; difficulty in establishing and keeping intimate, healthy relationships; relationships without limits; abuse; invasive behavior; emotional freeze (denial of feelings); perfectionism; victimization; obsessive necessity to control others' behaviors (possessiveness); power struggle; compulsive behaviors; feeling responsible for the behaviors of others; deep feelings of inability; idealistic relationship; toxic shame; negative self-image; low self-esteem; dependence on external approval; chronic headache and back pains; gastritis and chronic diarrhea; depression, jealousy and insecurity; inflexibility.

The codependent suffers from the above-mentioned characteristics in all relationships—with himself, with his family, with his partner, etc. The family system progressively gets sick. The family relations and communication become more and more dysfunctional.

Family Work Toward Recovery

Despite the fact that the family is affected by addiction and that the family dynamic enables its development, the organized family can be an excellent vehicle of intervention. The family is an important part of the clinical handling of addiction, so it is necessary that they get involved both in the treatment and in the recovery of the addict. In the majority of cases, it is first a family member who becomes cognizant of the problem and takes the first steps in searching for help. Individual therapy can be of great help in the first stages of treatment as a way to be able to express feelings, get emotional support, create an intervention strategy, and start the individual recovery of the codependent.

Family therapy is basic for recovery.

The family groups and the groups to which addicted patients belong are of high utility in treatment. They provide emotional support and structure in the recovery process. One of the first goals to work toward in the family's recovery is for the belief system of the family to be able to work out all the shame and guilt that may have been generated.

Addiction harms family relationships, making it very difficult to express healthy love. With treatment, people learn to exercise and provide the love that the codependent feels for the addict and allows him (the codependent) to set healthy limits in a clear and firm way. This is called "responsible love."

As relatives, sometimes the road of addiction can prevent us from setting adequate boundaries to protect ourselves or to avoid conflicts. Nevertheless, the family's love, combined and expressed in a balanced way with the necessary boundaries to establish healthy limits, is a vital tool in the process of living or sharing with an active addict. Limits have to do with healthy love and care, and the limits determine the territory, or place, of every member of the family.

The organized family, under the guidance of a specialized professional, can become an extremely valuable intervention tool to break the addict's denial. However, it is necessary to be able to start that process and that the members of the family are willing to start and keep their own personal recovery as codependents.[39]

CONCLUSION

The reality and complexity of the illness of addiction is that at the end of the day, the physical changes that have taken place in the brain are very real. Irrational thoughts have become ingrained. Dysfunctional behaviors and bad habits have taken root, and the addict's value system has become very distorted. He has lost his ability to function socially and at work, and the only thing that exists in his mind is, "How am I going to get my next fix?"[40]

Clarita...For these reasons, I think treating addiction is incredibly complex. The problem not only lies in detoxifying the addict. Treatment must be integrated; all aspects of the patient's life must be addressed—the physical, social, psychological, and spiritual—in order to increase his or her probability of success.

APPENDIX A

Farewell Letters to Alex

Eduardo Sierra

My dear Ale,

Even though time has passed, there is not a single day I do not find you in my thoughts. I see you every day—in my daughters, in Ana, in my parents, in Mau, in my friends, and at work. You will always hold a very important place in my heart.

I have a very clear memory of the last time we spoke. I miss you.

See you soon.

I love you,

Eddie

Mauricio Sierra

Dear Alex,

Your parents, your brothers, your girlfriend, Marimar, your sisters-in-law, your uncles, your cousins, nieces, nephews, your goddaughter Ana, and all your friends want to share with you our faith that today you are resting in peace, and we are confident that God—always merciful—gave you this gift of starting your new life with Him and to us the good fortune of having an angel who will always watch over us.

It is hard to understand how God works, always in mysterious ways that we cannot understand, but everything is and will always be the result of a perfect plan.

Now I understand Alex was an angel! Of course, we could not see his wings, which would have meant giving us the answer without having to work for it. Now I can understand that Alex's illness was his costume, a mask that he wore to hide his true essence and help put us through the necessary tests to get to know the magic and the gift that is living!

I understand now that as a godsend, Alex taught us everything, starting with the simplest idea of always having the heart and attitude of a child. He always gave us that gift—seeing him as a child who got excited about everything and admired it all. Despite his great maturity in other situations, he always reflected a great inner child. I wish we could all wake up every day with the hope of filling ourselves with happiness and sharing it with everyone day after day, just like he did with his enormous and generous smile.

The most important thing is to accept and learn from our mistakes, that stumbling again over the same obstacle is not a reflection of clumsiness, but on the contrary, it is a demonstration of constantly striving to improve the path traveled!

He taught us to be patient. Not everything comes overnight, but we have to value the time that it takes for things to take shape and give thanks for them, even though they do not come in the moment we want them.

He taught us that wanting to receive more is only a precursor to giving more. This is like a tree that ripens and finds its abundance, that does not ask or judge those who receive its fruit but knows that in order to renew itself—to transform and to keep growing—it has to give and let go of the best of its being.

As parents, he showed us the constant struggle for unconditional love that they have for a child. Alex always wanted to become a dad, and he always showed the capacity to do so. He won over all the little children. They saw him as one of their own and felt safe having him close by. This showed once more his capacity to love, tolerate, be patient, and overall, he always reminded us of his immense love for life.

As brothers, he taught us to always be there to support each other, to be the shoulder that we all sometimes need to cry on in difficult moments, and to learn to listen with an open heart without prejudice or guilt.

As a friend, he taught us to give unconditionally, to see our neighbor as an opportunity to see how important it is to have differences, accepting and tolerating those differences to become more human every time and once more know that the most important thing is the great love that we are all able to give.

As a boyfriend, to love without limits, to give the best of you forever, to know that if you make mistakes, fixing them is a matter of accepting them. Also, to know that we can fail, but having the humility to give your heart to the other so that those failures become the product of a love without limits.

Alex, you leave us in this dimension with much work to do. First of all, to accept that life comes and goes in the same way, so we have to live every day to the fullest, pouring out love to all and following God day after day. You leave us with the opportunity to grow like that tree and ripen to give our fruits. I am sure we will work on this from now on so that this is possible and you are proud that we continue following your steps.

You also leave us with the opportunity to see the light in the dark moments, learning from those moments, and letting them go when they have reached their purpose.

It will be hard to know you are not among us, but once we understand you ARE part of the LIGHT of day, just by opening our eyes we will see your radiance on everything and on everyone.

I thank God for letting us live 30 years beside you, for sending you to this world and being part of this great family that today is more united and stronger thanks to you!

Your example of life touched many people in different ways, and for that we will remember you and will be forever thankful to you.

Thank you for giving us so much, Alex, for being our angel and the light in our lives. We will keep you in our hearts eternally, and you shall live on in our memories for as long as we live!

Marimar

I think I will never understand why Alex left this life, but I can begin to understand why he crossed my path and all the teachings he left me. I will always be eternally thankful that he came into my life, and even though he physically left, I will always have him in my heart.

Alex taught me to love in a selfless and spontaneous way. He taught me we can love, but then we can love stronger every day like he did—with a simple smile, dancing in a store, giving to the one in need, being thoughtful, always looking for ways to help others, and all this is accomplished by going beyond ourselves. Thanks for your great heart!

He taught me to value family more. It is the most important thing we have, and we must not be careless about it. For him, it was always his priority.

He taught me the power of an embrace and how this can change the mood of the other person instantly. Thank you for your embraces, Alex!

He taught me that we have to enjoy life, that we cannot get stuck in ridiculous fights, and that we have to live every moment as if it were our last because we do not know when it will be the last. He taught me to forgive and start over and to learn how to overcome what others have done to hurt us in order to really forgive.

He taught me that God is everywhere—in the silence, in our heart, in our partner, in our parents. There is not too much science in finding God. We simply have to learn to feel him and decipher him in every action in our lives. Thank you for teaching me to feel God throughout my day!

He taught me the value of empathy, that virtue forgotten by so many and so necessary in this world. We will never manage to understand the illness of addiction without having empathy.

I learned to understand and feel Alex while he was pain and in his moments of happiness.

I came to understand that drug addiction is not what defines a person. We are used to classifying someone as a drug addict or alcoholic, and in that moment we see the person and reduce the totality of his being to a simple label. Before, if you had talked about a drug addict, in my mind I would picture a filthy person—evil, abandoned, selfish, with no way out. And certainly, when the addict is using, that is what he becomes, but the person does not leave his spirit behind. Drug addiction is a disease, a burden that the person carries, but it is not the person. We have to learn to discover the true spirit of the person without staying fixated on the superficiality of his illness. Thank you for letting me know your essence deeply—that great person, so strong, so smiling, so attentive, so thoughtful. To me, you will always be those things, and I will remember you like that, Alex.

He taught me to learn to endure pain up to the point of borderline madness. He taught me my capacity to love and endure pain and keep fighting for my loved ones, even when we believe we cannot anymore.

He strengthened my faith and my relationship with God when I learned to put ALL my security in HIM, knowing that nothing depends on us and that in the end all is in his hands. I had never had the experience in my life of really "letting go" and leaving it in God's and Our Lady's hands. And in spite of finding myself in so much pain, it was a beautiful freedom.

I spent some of the best moments of my life with him, and with his death, the most painful moment of all.

Not a single word of comfort, embrace, or word of advice diminishes the pain, because a part of my life—of my person—disappeared, too. And although I intellectually understand it, it is something my heart does not understand.

I learned that in spite of having made all our plans—a home, an engagement ring, a wedding, and thousands of dreams—God has other unknown plans for us. We have to plan less and trust more. Despite the fact that our plans won't get carried out, I cannot stop being thankful to God for having chosen me to make all these plans with Alex, for having lived out his dreams with him, and the way he expressed so much emotion for building something else was an incredible experience.

I learned to feel and let myself feel everything, to cry whenever I needed to, to scream whenever I needed to, to write everything I needed to, and not try to understand the "why" of things and start discovering their purpose.

To me, having met Alex was one of the greatest learning experiences I have had in my life. When I saw him for the first time, I never imagined I was going to get into this story filled with love and pain and at the same time so much learning that led me to nothing but growth.

Alex, I will never be able to thank you enough for all you left to me and how much you taught me during this journey together. Thank you for all the growing I've done.

I will carry you in my heart forever, and I will try to live to the fullest those teachings you gave me. You take care of us from there and guide us down the path we must follow.

Marimar

Daniela

What was Alex Sierra for me? At a certain moment, he was just the man I needed, somebody loving, cute, expressive, thoughtful, and cheerful, somebody who made you smile, even in the darkest moments (how he managed to do it, I don't know), and mostly for his very passionate view of life.

Alex was light and dark at the same time, and serendipitously, and thanks to the very intense and dedicated relationship we had, I got to see both sides. Nevertheless, his light was always much brighter before the eyes of those who knew and loved him.

Sadly, in different times of his life, Alex held on more to his dark side, but without a doubt, his moments of light are what remain in our memories and hearts. What for me started as a story of friendship between two people who needed to fill a void became a love story that stays with me, but at the same time, it was my biggest learning experience. Having a relationship with a person who suffered from this disease and where the other person was vulnerable from a recent divorce made it all the more passionate, but at the same time, all the more sick. That is why today I can say I met Alex at the height of his life...

...But the reason why I really fell in love with Alex was not the way he looked at me, but how he looked after my daughter. That meant a lot to me.

After my recent divorce, one of my main fears was not being accepted easily by a partner because of my baggage. And he, contrary to looking at the situation like that, always saw my daughter as one more blessing, as a plus, somebody to love, take care of, and for whom he could start taking responsibility for his actions. In fact, one of the things that still stays with me from Alex was him telling me constantly, "She is not yours. She is ours." For him, he was her dad.

As Alex's mom told me during the mass ceremony for him, "I thank you and your daughter for having entered Alex's life, because thanks to her, Alex knew what it meant to be a dad." For example, I will never forget when one night Daniela had a very high fever. I had to go out for her medicine, and when I came back, I found both of them in a tub filled with cold water until Daniela got better. And that is only one of the many times he showed his unconditional love for my daughter. Needless to say, he helped me down a road that seemed too difficult. He made it easy. He gave my daughter and me unconditional love filled with joy and generosity. It is not only me who remembers Alex as a joyful person full of light. My daughter, Daniela, always remembers him with lots of joy and love. In short, Alex was somebody who always made people feel both special and unique.

Unlike what you might think of Alex and his illness, he was a man who loved life and whose love and enthusiasm for living were contagious, and at the same time, he infused us with joy and strength in the worst moments, always with that unforgettable smile that characterized him. Not only did I feel protected through Alex in the moments that I needed somebody, but I felt the same support and love from his family since I had the opportunity to meet them. Both for Daniela and for me, Alex's family is the family I miss so much, and for that, I will always be thankful to him.

Like I mentioned in the beginning, Alex also had a rough side, which I experienced very intimately. It is not easy to say anything bad about a person who gave and left me so much. However, today I realize the struggle he had to survive day after day. Probably our relationship would have had more of a future if I had been able to understand or imagine what he was suffering. Codependence with a chemical substance is a more complicated issue than what you can see or imagine on the outside, and I lived that frustration firsthand. Alex tried to explain to me that his problem was something that belonged to him; it did not have anything to do with me, and even worse, it was something bigger than him and against which he had to fight every second of his day. And today it is clear to me that at that moment, what he wanted more than anything was to overcome his addiction, to have a fulfilled life next to Daniela and me.

Understanding it now does not mean that I would have changed my mind in certain stages of the relationship because my daughter was, and always will be, my priority, and I only wanted to protect her from a relationship that was getting out of hand. But of course I would have supported him differently…

…What Alex and his illness also left me with was the understanding that living dangerously made him a person who lived every day to the fullest, very involved and thoughtful. He always filled me with surprises, and for him it was never enough. What I admired about him and at the same time was jealous of was his capacity to forgive the unintentional hurt I caused him with my impulsive behavior and mistakes. I think that being aware of his imperfections made him more human and sympathetic to others.

Anyway, to me, my relationship with Alex and having had the opportunity to spend two years of our lives together was a watershed time in my life. As of today, I only have memories of a human being so filled with virtue, teachings, and the life lesson of always fighting to the end for what we want, and I will always be thankful with life for having put him in my path.

GOOD-BYES ARE NOT FOREVER. GOOD-BYES ARE NOT THE END. THEY SIMPLY MEAN, "I'LL MISS YOU, UNTIL WE MEET AGAIN."

We love and miss you much,

Daniela

Helen

My relationship and the mourning process I experienced with Alex have been some of the hardest struggles in my recovery. As someone who has been in recovery for a long time, death is a very sad part of addicts' histories. It is almost impossible to walk through the meeting halls of Alcoholics Anonymous and not meet someone that has not ended up dying because of this illness. In fact, it is even expected at times, but it is very different to lose someone who was very close to you and that you loved so deeply. All the pain I suffered alongside Alejandro during his illness does not compare with the pain of his death.

Before Alex passed away, I knew my path was to help other addicts and alcoholics in recovery. After such a painful day, it was clear I was going to dedicate my life to this. Alex transformed me in ways that I cannot explain in words. The decisions I made early on in my recovery were fundamental in achieving a lasting recovery. I learned to be close to my support system, to communicate my pain or my joys to others, to overcome myself before my illness, and the most important thing: I learned to leave my life in God's hands and trust in his strength every day.

Alex's teachings always went beyond recovery. He taught me that my weaknesses could one day become my strengths and that I deserved to be loved (something that is very hard to believe in early recovery). He taught me that life in sobriety is worth living. And through all this tragedy, he gave me one of the greatest gifts in life: showing me that life is a gift from God and that you can lose it at any time, no matter how old you are. For this reason, we must value, respect, and love those who surround us and do all that we can to support them, because when the day of our last breath arrives, the only thing we leave behind to others are the memories.

Susy

Over the years, Alex became my best friend, and we really had a deep, close communication between the two of us. He always had a lot to share about what he was learning and about how to be strong in a world where it is not easy to live. To tell you the truth, it was as if Alex wanted to heal everyone who surrounded him and give them part of his great light.

He showed unconditional love and compassion towards all people, friends or strangers, and he always wanted to share his huge heart. I have never known another person like him. He had a great understanding of life, of the deepest feelings of human beings. He had an exceptional perception about everyday things and a great wisdom.

The last time I saw him, after many years of not having seen him, I was very happy because I really saw him in good shape. He shared with me so many positive thoughts, and I realized that he always had the determination to be healthy and happy. He was very proud of himself, and he mostly felt thankful for all the opportunities he had to get better.

I have to confess and share that I had had a few very complicated years, and from the time I saw Alex, he shared his strength, his faith, and gave me a lot of advice so that I could feel happy. That day, he said something very important that I have internalized in my daily life: "Every difficult moment shall pass." After listening to those words, I realized his great philosophy and wisdom. He analyzed the difficult situations he had experienced in order to overcome other more difficult moments, and when he shared these words, they made a lot of sense to me and gave me peace. He told me that those difficult moments—when we feel we do not want to live and where anything feels impossible—are only temporary. That idea gave me strength. I know Alex wanted to share his strength and everything he had learned with everyone. I have to say that he has really been one of the people that has most impacted my life, and every piece of advice he gave me could not have been more accurate

It really was as if Alex could feel our hearts. He could feel my heart and read my thoughts. His sensibility towards other people is something

I have not seen in any other human being on this planet—vulnerable but filled with so much love—and at the same time, he was a soul that also needed so much love!

Every time he disappeared, I knew he was in some kind of treatment, but I did not know where. He had told me that when he did not communicate with me, he was in his darkest moments. I truly wish I could have found him in those dark moments to try and give him the same strength and love he gave us.

In 2013, I spent some of the best days of my life with him, and sadly, those were also some of my last days with him. I saw an Alex who came here with so much strength and who knew what he wanted for his present and his future. His goal was to be healthy, and he also wanted to do all he could to keep up his mental, emotional, and physical health. He told me he wanted to get married and have a beautiful family. He loved children so much. I know he wanted to be a great dad. When he spoke of all those incredible things he wanted to do and have, his eyes were filled with intense rays of light.

He also said there were moments in which he could not stop and that nothing or anyone could stop him, and the only thing that stopped him was when he thought about his concerned family waiting for his return. His family was always the force that helped him wake up from darkness and say "enough," his reason to get up and leave drugs again. I feel it is very important that I share this, because he mentioned that he was writing a book about all of his experiences and about how every time he relapsed and every time he recovered, he went back to the light. He also said to me he was not going to ever give up because God's great strength and angels were always helping him go back home and go back to himself. He wanted to share this with the world to demonstrate that it was possible, and he wanted to give hope to those that were in similar circumstances.

Alex told me that if it were not for the unconditional love and support that his parents gave him, he would not have been able to fight every battle he fought. In those moments, he looked me in the eye and told me how thankful he was for them and how loved he felt because they were his reason to keep on living. They had never failed him or let him feel unloved.

After talking with him about all the times he relapsed, he realized that many of those relapses happened because of some disappointment when it came to love. It happened to him with all his girlfriends. He had a very vulnerable heart and so much love to give. He felt he could not get out alone. He would feel such a deep sadness and defeat and felt that he could not get out of the hole by himself, and then he fell once more. And yes, he got into drugs to escape from pain.

Also, at that time, he told me that every time he got out, it was love that picked him up again and got him going—his family's love and his promise to himself of having a happy and healthy life. And then he started all over again. He always got up, over and over and over! I would say that made him an incredible fighter. Alex won because he fought and always got up! And getting up meant he won a battle. I feel that Alex not only won his battle, but much more, because on his path and in his struggle he went picking up all of us. After all the battles he had, he would fall and come back even stronger.

I cannot forget that last day I saw him in Laguna Beach. While we watched an unbelievable sunset, he told me I should never forget that God is love. So, when I can, I go running by the ocean to meet the sunsets, and especially when I feel sad, that is when I remember every word that Alex told me, and that strengthens me.

There are no words to describe how especial Alex *is*. And I insist on using the word "is" because I know he is still with us.

My heart broke into a thousand pieces the day I was told he had left this world. I could not find a reason for it and turned it over a thousand times in my mind to try and understand what it was that had happened, or rather, what had hurt him this time, what it was that destroyed him, and I wish I could have known what was happening to him, because I wish with all my soul to have been able to help him, save him, hug him. I think we all felt like that…really devastated.

I can say that Alex always struggled a lot, and his faith in God was so great that I feel his mission in this life was more that fulfilled. With all my heart, I can say that he lifted up so many people who were sunk down in deep sadness and gave them so much light and love that God wanted him back in his arms.

I have so many positive things to say about Alex. He was never selfish. On the contrary, he was a person with endless love. He never left me alone. I miss our conversations very much—his funny talks and his ease of happiness. I have those with me today and every day. Alex was an extraordinary human being.

One day he told me he regretted all the pain that he caused his family and friends every time he relapsed. And on the other hand, I feel Alex was making himself healthy and happy, and that is why he felt incredibly proud of himself. He wanted so badly to prove to the world that "Yes! It is possible!" What he did confess to me one day was that he felt anguish and was nervous thinking that sometimes he had to be perfect in everything he did. How I wish now he knew that he *did* excel in all respects!

Alex leaves me with a smile in my soul and with the great impact that he has had on my life. In every moment and every day that I live, he is more than present. His words are a constant, everyday echo when I wake up and when I go to sleep. If it is a good day or a difficult day, I just have to remember his smile and especially his eyes that shone with so much light.

Alex took the darkest side of his addiction and turned it into something incredibly positive. I feel everyone must know this. Alex took the hardest sides of his experiences and his pain and shared them with us, to give us light through his wisdom and the strength that he used to get ahead and demonstrate to us that darkness can be distinguished and that he could shine again with the light and love of God. He wanted to share his story so much and lift us up one by one.

The only thing that I miss tremendously and that I want so much is to be able to hug him physically!! Alex's hugs were always the best, and I will never forget him telling me that one hug could save our lives.

"I Saw You Coming"

(Song written by Susy to Alex after meeting him: May 2004)

I saw you come

I saw you come

That winter night

Your empty look said it all

I saw you come

And you came through the door

Your smile lied

You did not feel anymore.

You had decided it already

You wanted to be far from here

And the same way the wind brought you here

You left me here too soon.

Look at me

And tell me it is not true

Swear to me that what we have lived

Is not dead

And Feel me.

Let's see if I can open your heart

Let's see if I can open your heart.

You saw me arrive that night in May

Your eyes told me it all

I saw you fly

Your smile charmed me

Slowly you came close to my lips

And as soft as the ocean's breeze

I was captivated by your sweet eternal kisses.

You had decided

You wanted to get close to me

Your eyes hypnotized me

And suddenly love was born in me

And suddenly love was born in you.

Andrea

Alex,

For so long, you were, and will always be, the greatest love of my life. I met you when I was fourteen, and since then you remained a part of my life. Thanks for having painted it with emotions and experiences so wonderful for so many years. I can say you were my first love and also my great friend.

I will continue to talk with you always. I know that of course you will be laughing a lot when you see me trying to write this letter. Ha ha ha! I know you watch over me now, you accompany me, and you send me messages. I often get them in my dreams, in the sky, in the air, and in nature. I receive them, Skinny Boy!

I know you will always find a way to make yourself present. I ask you for this wherever you are. Always make yourself present. Even though I do not see you, I love you, I talk to you…I carry you with me always!

I admire my great first love, friend, and person who suffered and fought, and today I acknowledge him as one of the bravest people in my life. His life was not easy, and even so, his smile and enjoyment of life were infectious to the end. None of us knows the loneliness he could have felt, even in spite of the companionship and support that surrounded him. Today, Alex is someone who made a mark on my life. He made it magical and gave special meaning to it. There is no good or bad. Everything is part of his being, imperfectly whole as he was.

Andrea

Maria

We were always in touch, until one day he sent me a message at night asking me if we could talk. He wanted to tell me something very important. After several hours, he confessed that he had relapsed in a horrible way. I heard him. He sounded sad and confused. So, for almost a month, we talked over the phone. I think it was a way for him to unload, and for me, it meant the hope of being able to help him.

He told me he wanted to go back to a clinic. He had lots of motivation to move forward, and he felt he had control like a lot of other times. As always, he told me that today was going to be the day he was going to do it, that this was the last time, but later I would get the call telling me he had used again. He did not know how to fix all the damage he had caused to the people around him and how to get his life back on track. How would the people he had hurt going to forgive him?

He told me a thousand options for getting out of his addiction, his steps to follow that, according to him, had always worked. We talked about how thankful he was for his parents and siblings and how much he loved them, especially how he wanted to be the best person he could be to make Marimar happy, how he was in the perfect moment of his life, how suddenly he had all he ever wanted—everything he thought that, because of his addiction, he would never have. He told me about his addiction, his relapses, talked about all the good and bad things he experienced, of how he had enjoyed every second of life. He asked me to forgive him for having hurt me at the time we were a couple, and we realized it had all been because of his addiction.

He never stopped swearing he was going to make it—for himself, his parents, his brothers, Marimar, and for all that he had left to live for.

He had very good days and others that were bad. I was sure he was going to get out of this one. He had all possible motivation, and he was constantly struggling to get ahead. Finally, the time came when he said he was leaving the following day for a clinic to rehab. He said good-bye. He sounded very sick, tired, and desperate to get out of that state.

Alex was a great teacher in my life. He taught me to love and to give unconditionally, to not judge people by an illness, to be a partner, and to accept that sometimes people need only to be heard.

Maria

Rodrigo

Alex was the most thoughtful person I have ever met. He had the best ideas for the most original and best presents to give for every occasion. I got a trophy for "best boss" for my birthday and pizzas the day I moved to my new house. The last time he came to the office, during Christmas of 2013, it was to leave me some cornflakes with chocolate donuts. He knew I loved them, and in spite of already having problems, he took the time to bring us our Christmas presents.

At the office, we all thought that Alex's charisma and charming personality were his greatest qualities. We will always remember his great smile and cannot stop missing him. To me, he was a great friend, someone with whom I have inexplicably felt a deep connection, and I know he will always be present in my life. I will remember him and miss him eternally for his exquisite smile and his endless source of energy. I thank him for having given me the gift of spending together a few very happy years and having allowed me to be his boss for a while.

Rodrigo

APPENDIX B

Letters Between Alex, His Parents, and Marimar's Parents

Letter from Alex: February 2009 (arriving in Utah with Kevin McCauley)

I start this e-mail without much direction and without really having enough time (of sobriety) to write something that goes beyond pretty words that I can write on occasion but that are not backed up with much value.

What I cannot get out of my mind these days is the necessity to find some way to express my thankfulness for your unconditional love, support, tolerance, and patience. Unfortunately, I have not yet found the way or the necessary courage to do it.

The only thing I can do is take time to pray to God that little by little my actions speak louder than my words.

For now, I tell you that when you have doubts that all you have done for me has not made sense and has not been worth it, I can only say that you have—like I mentioned in a prior e-mail—made me want to get ahead.

You might wonder how a twenty-five-year-old man with such incredible opportunities and experiences has lost his sense of life and has gotten lost in a dark world, apparently without a way out. The truth? I do not have the answer yet. I can only tell you that you and your love have been the only rays of light that have entered that dark world and have shown me the way to get ahead.

I dug a hole for myself so big and deep that there was a moment I lost my path. You ignited a light in that darkness, and that light is what is guiding me now.

Love you so much,

Alex S.

P.S. "You alone can do it, but you cannot do it alone."

Together we will overcome this. You have already given your all, and now it is my turn.

Letter from Alex: August 31, 2009 (San Diego)

Dear Parents,

I write this letter with much pain in my heart and much uncertainty in my words, but overall, I write this letter worn down, sad, and really empty. What would be the reasons that I had to live an experience like this? I have not found them yet. Why it was you who had to join me on this journey, I do not understand either. The last thing I want in my life is to be a person who only causes pain to others, to my most beloved. Why I failed, why I was weak once more, it is still hard to understand. In the blink of an eye, I saw six months of effort, work, tears, and hope go down the drain. I am really in pain. I do not wish this on even my worst enemy. Thank God my body could not give any more. It is clear that my illness wants to kill me. But God protects me, I am "ALIVE".

I cannot face my illness, having the pain that I am making you go through. I need all my strength to get ahead. I do not want to ask for anything. I do not deserve anything. The only thing I deserve is to get ahead by myself. Try to fix my life. Ma, I am so sorry. It breaks my heart to tell you this. So many dreams! Pa, do not lose hope. It is the only thing I ask of you. I am going to make it. I know I can.

For now, my tears do not let me write anything else.

Alex

Birthday Letter from Clarita to Alex: July 11, 2012

Dear Alex,

This life is our choice. It is the one we chose to live, and how we live it is also our choice. Change can be difficult and scary, but it is part of our growth as living beings. You are a privileged being because you have in yourself thousands of possibilities, and if you fight for them, they will help you feel empowered. I think you are on a path of change. You are already feeling the satisfaction of giving yourself incredible things, and little by little, there will be more. Obviously, from an emotional standpoint it is harder, and the only advice I can give you is that you have given so much to your addiction, and it has taken so much away from you, that I would not give it one more minute of your time, nor of your life.

Choosing freely is the greatest gift that God has given us. What we have done does not belong to anyone else but to us, and everyone has to take responsibility for their actions. The time to choose has come, and God opens up the path once more so that you choose how you want to live your life.

THIS IS AN INVITATION TO LIVE. Today you are turning 30 years old, and the best way to celebrate is by celebrating your new life. I invite you to love your life, to be present in it, in you and in everyone else with LOVE. Take care of your power, take care of your health, take care of your life, and be HAPPY.

CONGRATULATIONS! May today be the beginning of a great life.

With much love as always,

Clarita

Letter from Clarita to Alex: Summer 2012 (after Alex's relapse that occurred a year after his friend's death)

My Dear Alex,

Even though before leaving for our trip you had a slip, I left thinking it was only that. Hope is the last thing you lose, and for that reason, I left feeling a little more peaceful. At the end of the trip, though, my heart told me something was wrong. The return was devastating.

Honestly, it has been very hard to digest, especially after Dallas, the shooting, and José. Yes, I thought you were never going to relapse again, that it was all behind us like a horrible nightmare. And once more, that horrible pain came back—that helplessness, hopelessness, and sadness.

It is clear that things have to change. I do not know what you have to do or how you are going to do it. You cannot keep living and repeating the same pattern every time your head and your emotions lie to you. You have to find a way to resist the macabre games of your compulsive and accelerated mind.

I, Clarita, cannot—nor do I ever want to—connect again with your addiction. It is not that I would leave you; I would never do that. I do not say this in a threatening tone, but simply, I cannot do it anymore, nor do I want to. My heart is completely tired, hurt, sad, and hopeless. And I hope in my heart that you understand.

Since we arrived, we have tried to be patient, tolerant, compassionate, and loving. We have tried to love you, be there for you, etc. But your addiction takes advantage and horribly manipulates our love for you. The fact that we create higher expectations every time turns into something very painful.

Today, once more, we are trying to help you and save you from yourself. This trip you and your dad are taking, it is not a reward. It is simply a trip with the intention of moving you away from your addiction so you can try to understand and make it click in your mind that everything has to change and that you have to try one more time. But the one that has to get out of that dark place is you!

Believe me, little by little our defenses are growing, and our limits are becoming stronger. This time, your dad was already determined to pay for a few nights in a hotel until we found a small apartment where you could decide how you were going to live your life. In reality, it was I who changed his mind, but for my part, it is the last time. You have to change, learn, grow, and modify your life.

You have in your dad a generous, tolerant, loving man who goes beyond unconditional love. I wish you would take advantage of this opportunity he is giving you once more, as a space for reflection and meditation and not as an easy way out. Think about your life. Take a look at all your experiences, both good and bad, and walk towards the future taking advantage of everything you have learned, working every day to forgive yourself for all that has caused harm to you and others.

I wish you would take advantage of this space to find God once more and the greatness of his love for you and that this is not just one more talk, but that you will find the purpose and the why's of your life, of your pain, and the path you've traveled.

Look for the way to give back to life all the love it has given you. I wish you could understand that God did give you FREE WILL, the ability and strength to choose and decide. If your addiction lies to you, it is simply that—a lie. You have the control and power over your thoughts and your decisions. You can choose between walking the path of darkness and destruction or walking the path of light and love.

My love for you will always be there to help you and be by your side.

Clarita

Letter from Alex: September 25, 2012 (after a trip with his father)

Hello Dad,

The trip really got me out of all the bad and dark of my addiction and my thoughts. It transported me to a place of peace, tranquility, and much beauty. I thank you for your effort in making it possible that we enjoyed some time together. It is a demonstration of what we can have in life if we dedicate ourselves to going down the right path and always making an effort to be better.

It is clear that you cannot do more for me that you have cleaned and straightened my path, and you have given me a precise roadmap with very clear instructions of how to navigate through this life. Now it is on me to follow it.

You and Mom are great people. Your character really impresses me, and I look forward to one day being able to handle myself like you in the face of adversity. It is clear that it will take time and years of reprogramming myself, but as they say, nothing is impossible.

Pa, again I thank you from the bottom of my heart for all the time you give me while I'm trying to recover and for all the things we've been through together during this difficult process.

Love you,

Alex S.

Letter from Gerardo to Alex: September 25, 2012

Thank you, Alito. I also had an incredible time. You do not have to fall into the stress game. Like you said, you already have many experiences that have become tools to help you out of any kind of situation or that can help you accept circumstances that cannot be changed. I have no doubt that with effort, dedication, humility, and the company of the people who love you day after day, you will succeed for many, many more years to come. These ten years have been a learning experience for the rest of your life, at least some 60 years more. For now, you have the unavoidable commitment of having short-, medium-, and long-term objectives that are better defined. This will help you focus and find your path more easily. A hug, and we will keep growing together.

Pa

Letter from Alex to Clarita: March 2013

Claris,

Now that you have seen the letter I sent to Marimar, I hope that when you see only a text in yours you do not get disappointed and think I did not put the same effort into your letter. Perhaps less time, yes, but the truth is, the message will be what matters the most in this letter.

I want you to know that being able to write a letter to Marimar like that is only and exclusively thanks to you, thanks to you teaching me to be creative and what it means to put our time and effort into some detail for our fellow man.

My capacity to love is thanks to the countless demonstrations of love that you have always shown me. There is not a single detail that goes unnoticed. These always make me a more sensitive person and a more loving one.

Ma, there are so many letters, so many words I have sent to you over the years, and what I like the most is what I feel when I write them. It is a sensation of joy, admiration, unconditional love, and gratitude. I do not know, but I would love to be a poet that could put in this letter the happiness there is in my heart when I try to find the words so that you know how much I love you.

What an interesting life we have had, with many difficult paths at times. But if anything—if there is something that I'm grateful for in my dark moments—it is that I always had a light along my path, and that light, although dull at times, always accompanied me. And although sometimes I did not follow it, it was always there, willing to wait for me in the distance and show me the path again. That light saved me. That light is *you*.

And today…today that we are together in peace and looking towards the future, you are still my light, not necessarily showing me the path, but rather accompanying me, lighting the way and always filling it with joy.

Mami, I really love you.

You are someone very special!

Letter from Alex: April 2013 (after the trip to see Dr. Daniel Amen)

Dad and Mom,

Thanks for the patience before the trip, because despite your desperation, you held on a little more each day. Yes, these are dark and very unpleasant times that should not have to be part of your life. It is clear that by you doing so, it is only to give me the opportunity to have the future that you have always wanted for us.

Count on my total presence in this new stage of my recovery. I am fully aware of all there is ahead, of the changes that have to happen and the daily effort I will have to make so that now, once and for all, I will leave this nightmare behind.

Truly, you have no idea how much I acknowledge and admire what you have done for me. There are days I forget it, and there are days that despite the fact that I remember it, I do the wrong things. That will be something I hope improves day after day and that I can fix with time, along with learning to control my impulses and my emotions. Then I will be able to treat you like you deserve—with total respect and love in any situation.

The tests and their results helped me understand a lot of my behavior. I feel good with the medication. I feel awake and motivated. As always, there are fears and many things that I have to do. I don't yet know what some of those things are, but I know they have to be done. I feel I have so much to do.

Anyway, I want to tell you a lot of things, but thanks to God and to you, we are still together and can talk every day. I hope that these are not merely words and that with my actions you can see my efforts, and I hope they can communicate my gratitude to you.

Love you,

Alex S.

Letter from Alex to Emilio and Lucrecia Planas (Marimar's Parents): September 2, 2013

My Dear In-Laws,

I write because in the midst of so many things and emotions, I have not been able to find a time to thank you for the love you have shown me by welcoming me into your home. I am really very excited about our engagement and the life that Mar and I are about to start. I think that, like everything in life, this will be an adventure filled with challenges and commitments. I am sure that with much love and dedication, Mar and I will have a relationship that you can be proud of.

To me, as I mentioned to Emilio over breakfast, it will always be important to have your blessing, and even more than that, to count on your companionship and love during this time.

Going down this road, I know we will have many opportunities to spend time together during which we will get to know each other much better, little by little, so that eventually having earned a place, I can be part of your great family. It would be a great honor for me.

I do not mean to sound so formal in this letter, but instead I want to approach you out of love, my sole intention being to express to you my happiness because of this wonderful engagement and what it means to me to start a life with Marimar.

With love,

Alex

Letter from Gerardo and Clarita: December 12, 2013 (Alejandro's last relapse)

Today, your dad and I want to address you with all the love we have in our hearts. It is very hard that you don't understand how your bad decisions cause damage to the people that love you. It is difficult to understand why you hide behind your illness to avoid responsibility for your actions, and if your disease and your cravings are so overpowering, why don't you do everything necessary to control them? The sad truth is that you do not listen. The truth is that you have to see your reality, which can be wonderful, but you are different. You have an illness that requires you to live life differently, to always be more careful than others, to understand that you can do nothing to alter the levels of your consciousness—alcohol, drugs, gambling. I am not saying you cannot have a job with its ups and downs, but you do have to get out your toolkit and find the tool that can serve you every time you feel pressured or even exited due to a great moment of happiness.

It is clear to us that you cannot go on like this, because at the end of the day, you will end up dead from cardiac arrest, respiratory failure, or somebody will end up killing you. You have to find the strength, first in you, then in Marimar's love, and then in ours. If we measure that strength by the great love we feel for you, then it has to be huge. We pray to God that you do not use, that as you say you are meditating, reflecting, praying, etc.

There are several options if what you want is to ask for help...go to rehab. We can find a doctor to help you with your anxiety and cravings. You can take a sleeping pill and try to sleep three days in a row to try to detox by yourself. You can ask that someone takes you to the supermarket, or you can order something to eat, drink a lot of water, go to some therapy, or walk to your meetings. Anyway, anything is better than to keep on using. Utilize this time to reflect, to try and get yourself back, and to fight for your relationship with Marimar.

Alex, I hope you choose love and light, that you make the right decisions, and that you do not allow the darkness to destroy you.

Always remember how much we love you.

Mom and Dad

E-mail from Alex: February 1, 2014 (days before dying, lying to himself, and perhaps trying to ask for help)

— If I have 1500 a week

— I've got an idea

— I just saw that there are cruises that depart from here, from San Diego…there are many…

— From 7,14,21, up to 30 days…with everything included…no drugs

— Why don't you think whether it would be a good idea to pay for one of these and I go for a few days…

— Maybe it is good to be away from it all, in the ocean, with all the food included…

APPENDIX C

Talk Given by Alejandro Sierra June 2011 for the Foundation "Convivencia sin Violencia"

Good evening everyone.

It is an incredible opportunity for me to be here. I think that in life we have to take advantage of any opportunity where our experience can serve others.

When Joaquin invited me to this project, I started thinking what would be the best way to share my experiences so they had the biggest possible impact.

I have to be realistic and realize that few are able to experience what is in someone else's mind, and therefore it is sometimes difficult to raise awareness. It is hard to make people see that nobody is safe from what happened to me.

Believe me, when I was fifteen years old and started drinking, I would have never imagined that twelve years later I would end up living on the streets.

Telling you all the details of my history is not necessary, but what I can more or less give you is an idea of how partying became such an important part of my life, so much so that I started leaving behind the things that really mattered.

In short, I started drinking like I mentioned, I think about fifteen years old. But let's just say that it was from sixteen to eighteen years old that alcohol gave a different meaning to my life. Alcohol made me feel more popular. It helped me to talk with girls, to feel more comfortable with my friends.

I remember how intoxicated I'd get, always competing with my friends to see who could drink the most. There was the danger of drunk driving, but as a good, innocent boy, I felt invincible. I felt that nothing would ever happen to me.

It was when I was nineteen that my "best friend" invited me to try cocaine. Of course, at the time I had already drunk a lot before, and of course when my friend put coke in front of me, it was as if he had offered me a new kind of Doritos. I was not conscious at all of what I was doing. It was simply one more adventure. My ability to make good decisions had disappeared because of the disinhibiting effects of alcohol.

And of course, what had to happen, happened. I liked it! I had acquired a new tool for partying, one that helped me drink and then simply diminish my drunkenness with one line. It made me feel invincible. And for a little insecure kid like me, having a tool like this was really tempting.

Here I think it is a good time to talk about addiction. I have many friends who use drugs and can do so without any greater consequence. To this day, they are functioning people that for some reason have never developed an addiction. I was not so lucky. Genetically, I was predisposed to react differently to drugs, and without realizing it, this illness began to develop inside my brain. It became a disease—progressive, chronic, and deadly.

If I had known this, my story could have been different. Now, whoever wants to take a risk, it's their own right, but what I experienced because of this illness I would not wish on my worst enemy.

I understand that for many, talking about drugs goes beyond their reality. But do not lie to yourselves: Alcohol is a drug!

Playing with alcohol and other substances is like playing Russian roulette. You never know if because of your drinking you will cause an accident. You do not know if the drugs that are being sold to you are good or will get you into an accident. Anyway, the combinations of things that can go wrong are countless. And then you run the risk of falling into the world of addiction or alcoholism, which sooner or later can cause an accident.

I understand that young people experiment. I understand that fun is a part of growing, and I understand that we live in a society where drinking is accepted. I do not expect that after listening to me you will stop drinking or experimenting, but I do hope that you understand there is a very fine line between fun and disaster. I crossed that line several times, and thank God I am still here to tell the story.

I can tell you some details of when I crossed that line and could have caused an accident.

It was a get together like those that we have all gone to. I started drinking, then the cute girl arrived, and I drank a little more. Of course, I had no inhibitions, and up to that point everything had worked out. Later, we continued the party at a restaurant. I think we drank all the sake from that place.

When it was time to leave, I asked for the car. My brother had also his car with him, and I agreed that we would follow each other. The valet drove my car up first, and I decided to go on ahead. My intoxication was such that I was not responsible enough to drive. Instead of going directly back home, I kept going without knowing where I was headed. I remember I was speeding. I had a car with a standard transmission, but I was driving as if I were in a Formula 1 car race, and when I realized this, a car pulled out in front of me into one of the roundabouts on Reforma Avenue. I was going so fast that I could not brake in time. I hit that car so hard that I left him spinning, and my car stopped some five hundred meters ahead of the place of impact. Luckily, both the other driver and I were unharmed.

Another time, I invited my friends to go on vacation with me to Ixtapa. After a long night of mixing alcohol and drugs, we went back to the house. We realized we had finished all the alcohol and drugs—it was about seven in the morning—and instead of going to bed, we made the bad decision to go buy more. Of course, we chose the most drunk guys to go get it. It is the kind of decision you make when you are under the influence of substances that alter the area in the brain that controls reason and sane judgment.

Some one hundred meters after leaving my house, I fell asleep, and when I woke up, I was upside down in a Suburban. I was left standing on top of my friend, who was thrown against the door. Luckily, we were unharmed once again.

I can tell you that before these accidents, I swore I was never going to crash, that I was immune to that kind of thing. But again, I have to insist that no one is safe, and sooner or later we can all have accidents.

I think it is necessary to send an honest message, to say as I stand in front of you that for quite some time I enjoyed alcohol and drugs. Yes, these gave me sensations that I think I will never feel again. I mean the physical sensations. Of course they did! You release a lot of dopamine and serotonin—substances that produce pleasure—in amounts that your body is not used to. And yes, the sensations can become very pleasurable. But pleasure like this does not come free; it has a very high price. And drugs will sooner or later send you their bill!

It was very costly for me. Seeing my parents, brothers, people who love me cry, losing their trust, changing my personality completely, losing many material possessions.

It was very peculiar. For a long time I looked for those material things because I thought they were going to make me feel better. People were going to love me more if I had the nicest clothes, the prettiest car, the nicest watch, and addiction is so strong that none of this mattered. The only thing that mattered was using!

One time, my need to get high was so strong that I sold my car—a brand new, very nice car—for about five hundred dollars in drugs.

I want to think that telling you tough stories, horror stories, will not do anything except reinforce the idea that you are never going to get to such extremes.

That is why I believe that it is easier to tell you that I am simply someone like you. I have a really beautiful family. We never lacked anything; we had it all and more. I went to a very good private school. I went out with many girls. I had fun for a long time, and when I least realized it, when I least thought it was going to happen, it did, and little by little I started losing everything. I lost the meaning of life. My dreams disappeared. My desire to live disappeared. And the only thing left was getting high.

But as long as we still have life, we are in time, in time to make good decisions and decide what it is we want to do with our lives.

I personally want to make my parents proud and see them smile, share this life with my brothers, form a family, develop as a human being, and help others. And I have learned that a life filled with alcohol and drugs does not get along with a life like the one I want.

Friends, in the beginning, I told you I think that no one can experience what's in somebody else's mind. Well, today I ask you to do it.

Trust me. I dare say it only because I have already lived it. It is not worth it! Nowadays, I leave at night, and you have no idea how much fun I have without drinking. When it is four in the morning and everyone is really drunk, I give thanks to God that I am not like that. I can talk with girls, and you have no idea what a positive response I get when they see me sober and coherent and not hammered trying to hook up with them.

I wake up the next day, and I do not have to call a friend to tell me what I did the night before.

Overall, I ask you to trust me when I say that you can save yourself many years of suffering. You have no idea how many times I have knelt and prayed to God to go back in time. I did not want to suffer anymore. I did not want to make my loved ones suffer, but it was too late. I had crossed that fine line. Do not take chances. I promise you that drugs promise something that they will never give you, and little by little, they will take more and more away from you.

APPENDIX D

"Those Things Are So Far Removed from My Family"

Moises Kleinberg N. Consejo, Editorial Council for the Pact of Non-Violence

This article was published at www.convivenciasinviolencia.com after Alejandro Sierra's talk.

Those things are so ugly, they will not happen to us. A "good" family. A father of high status in an important company, able to perform difficult operations and skilled in negotiations both in Mexico and abroad. A professional mother, with graduate degrees from a renowned university, recognized widely in her field. Well-behaved children, sports lovers with the best grades, earning awards in their schools and warmly welcomed in their social circles. Family stories of success, love, sharing, and mutual help. In a warm home, filled with culture. With members, all of them highly functioning with healthy habits. No! It is impossible that those things could happen in a family like mine.

We are so far removed from those bad influences. Things like that only happen to dysfunctional families. In which there are unwanted children. In which fighting is common. In which children are abandoned by parents who are only focused on their own well-being. In those where tending to the needs of the children is a nuisance. Where lack of love is the common denominator among every family member. Families with ancestors that have fallen victim to their vices. In which the father is violent with his wife and children. Families of failed people, lazy people, disconnected from religion and good manners.

We are completely protected against those evils. We are continuously watching after our children. We know what happens both in their schools and outside of them. We know where they are, who they are with, what they do. We take them to their parties, we analyze their environment, and we pick them up.

We have academic and extracurricular programs that do not let them think about anything else. They do not have the free time to get their hands dirty with this kind of rubbish.

Is it true that there is a shield to avoid falling into some kind of addiction? Is it true that a proper education keeps children away from addictive substances? Are our children really so removed from these substances that we can ignore this problem?

Last Tuesday, June 28, it was demonstrated once again that the problem of addiction is much closer to all of us than we would like to think.

A bright young man who fell into the hell of addiction up to the point where nothing, not even his own life, had any value. His mother, who lived through the nightmare of seeing her son self-destruct, experiencing guilt, helplessness, frustration, and a series of failures for several years, finally, almost miraculously, seeing him reemerge.

They both offered lectures where they testified that addictive substances—all of them—are within anyone's reach, and contrary to this myth that we all believe, do not belong to some defined social group. That in reality there is not a definitive shield to prevent children from falling prey to addiction, but there are some behaviors that can minimize the possibility of this happening.

On one hand, Alex told us that entering the world of addiction is something that happens very slowly and subtly. It is not that one day life changes and a person becomes addicted to every drug. You start with smoking, and little by little, you have the opportunity to try some other substance. In his case, alcohol. He had lost control over his drinking, and within the unconsciousness of intoxication, he easily tried other drugs.

Slowly but surely, relationships with family, school, and work start deteriorating because drugs are what take control over your life. It is not that we do not realize what is happening. It is just that at this point, you cannot change. The avalanche has trapped you, and getting out seems impossible.

In addition to the physical hardships that you experience when using drugs and alcohol with abandon, besides the danger that you are exposed to and the exposure to others who have nothing to do but see what happens as they live a life filled with excess, you experience immense suffering when you know you are guilty of the destruction of your family nucleus and the loss of lifelong friendships.

At the point where it is no longer possible to look your loved ones in the eye, when all the guilt emerges for being responsible for the agony of the people closest to you, you look to escape into loneliness. That monster that little by little takes over, worsening your dependence on addictive substances, accelerating the fall into that vicious circle in which greater dependence leads to a greater estrangement from society, and this withdrawal, in turn, multiplies dependence.

I want to get out…but I cannot!

In this case, having abandoned all hope of being saved, having resigned himself to complete abandonment, there were glimpses of human kindness from strangers who offered a helping hand and made him see that the world is not as cruel as one might expect. This was the divine sign that his self-destruction was a waste. That somebody else needed him. That in the same way that he had been helped, so too could he help others in need. This was the thread that kept him tied to life, the thread by which he now offers to everyone who needs it the possibility of clinging to that seemingly weak but undoubtedly potent thread of life, strong enough to prevent certain death. A hope for life.

This is a singular case, and without a doubt is quite rare. But unfortunately, it is not the only one. It is another story that shows that the battle is not lost. That despite all the pain that an addiction can cause, there can be hope, and yes, there might be a way out.

It is this message that makes us understand that even when the problem of addiction seems irreparable, tormenting, unending, overwhelming, and heartbreaking, we should not give up. However, as we see from the testimonies of families that have been able to escape this hell, it requires a superlative degree of patience, a tireless search for information, an unbreakable faith, and overall, a huge…and when I say huge, I do not think that that word can really convey the true size of the tolerance to the frustration that is required to be able to overcome the family crisis that a family member's addiction causes.

In short, the true message here, without a doubt, is that there is a light at the end of the tunnel. Even with all the pain that it represents, we have to look for it.

REFERENCES

Bibliography

Amen, Daniel G., and David Smith. *Unchain Your Brain: 10 Steps to Breaking the Addictions That Steal Your Life.* California: MindWorks Press, 2010.

Beattie, Melody. *Codependents› Guide to the Twelve Steps.* ISBN: 97806717622278.

Boletín del Instituto Nacional Sobre el Abuso de Drogas (NIDA) Cocaina. "Cocaina, Abuso y Adicción." Serie de Reportes de Investigación: January 2001.

Clegg, Bill. *Portrait of an Addict as a Young Man: A Memoir.* New York: Little, Brown and Company, 2010.

Conyers, Beverly. *Addict in the Family: Stories of Loss, Hope, and Recovery.* Minnesota: Hazelden Foundation, 2003.

Conyers, Beverly. *Everything Changes: Help for Families of Newly Recovering Addicts.* Minnesota: Hazelden Foundation, 2009.

Cope Moyers, William, with Katherine Ketcham. *Broken: My Story of Addiction and Redemption.* London: Viking, 2006.

De Granda Orive, J.I., Solano Reina, S., Jareño Esteban, J., Pérez Trullén, A., Barrueco Ferrero, M., and C.A. Jiménez Ruiz. "De la neurobiología de la adicción a la nicotina al tratamiento del tabaquismo." *Progresos Terapéuticos*, Madrid, Servicio de Neumología, Hospital Central de la Defensa Gómez Ulla.

Fantín, Beatriz, and García Horacio Daniel. "Family factors, its influence on substance abuse." *Ajayu,* 9 (2), August 2011, pp. 193-214 (Factores familiares, su influencia en el consumo de sustancias adictivas).

Gopnik, Alison. (2012). "What's Wrong With the Teenage Mind?" *The Wall Street Journal.* Retrieved from https://www.wsj.com/articles/SB10001424052970203806504577181351486558984.

Grof, Christina. *The Thirst for Wholeness: Attachment, Addiction and the Spiritual Path.* San Francisco: Harper, 1994.

HBO Documentary Films. *Addiction: New Knowledge, New Treatments, New Hope.* 2007 [DVD].

HBO Documentary Films. *Thin—If It Takes Dying to Get There, So Be It.* 2006 [DVD] (John Hoffman and Susan Froemke, producers).

Kennedy Lawford, Christopher. *Recover to Live: Kick Any Habit, Manage Any Addiction.* Dallas: BenBella Books, 2013.

May, Gerald G. *Addiction and Grace: Love and Spirituality in the Healing of Addictions.* New York: Harper Collins, 1988.

McCauley, Kevin, M.D. and Dr. Cory Reich. *Addiction.* Utah: The Institute of Addiction Study, 2008.

McCauley, Kevin. *Memo to Self: Protecting Sobriety with the Science of Safety.* 2015 [DVD] (Lauren Greenfield, producer).

McCauley, Kevin. *Pleasure Unwoven: A Personal Journey About Addiction.* 2006 [DVD] (en español: *El Placer Destejido: Un Explicación de la Enfermedad de la Adicción*: 2011).

Medzerian, George. *Crack: Treating Cocaine Addiction.* Florida: Tab Books, 1991.

Meyers, Robert J., and Brenda L. Wolfe. *Get Your Loved One Sober.* Minnesota:

Hazelden, 2004.

NIDA. (2010, February 22). Why are some drugs more addictive than others? Retrieved from http://www.drugaddictiontreatment.com/addiction-in-the-news/addiction-news/why-are-some-drugs-more-addictive-than-others/.

Parent, Jake D. (ed). *Hearts and Scars: 10 Human Stories of Addiction.* Modern Minimalist Press: 2015.

Schultz, Sherry. *Coming Back From a Relapse.* EUA: Hazelden, 1991.

Sheff, David. *Beautiful Boy.* Mariner Books, January 6, 2009

Swenson, Sandra A. *The Joey Song*: *A Mother's Story of Her Son's Addiction.* Central Recovery Press, 2014.

Web Pages

- https://7stagesofcrack.wordpress.com
- ww.aa.com (Alcoholics Anonymous)
- www.adicciones.org
- www.adicciones.org/familia/codependencia
- www.al-anon.alateen.org (Al-Anon)
- www.drugabuse.gov
- www.familiesanonymous.org (Families Anonymous)
- www.instituteforaddictionstudy.com (Ten Tips for the First Year of Recovery by Kevin T. McCauley)
- www.manantiales.org
- www.na.org (Narcotics Anonymous)
- www.salud.nih.gov
- www.samhsa.gov/www.csat.samhsa.gov (Substance Abuse and Mental Health Services Administration)

Citations

1. Conyers, Beverly. *Addict in the Family: Stories of Loss, Hope and Recovery.* Minnesota: Hazelden Foundation, 2003, p. 17.

2. Conyers, Beverly. *Everything Changes: Help for Families of Newly Recovering Addicts.* Minnesota: Hazelden Foundation, 2009, pp. XV, XVI.

3. McCauley, Kevin, and Cory Reich. *Addiction.* Utah: The Institute of Addiction Study, 2008, p. 1.

4. Cope Moyers, William, with Katherine Ketcham. *Broken: My Story of Addiction and Redemption.* London: Viking, 2006, p. 72.

5. McCauley, op. cit., pp. 36-37.

6. McCauley, op. cit., p. 35.

7. Conyers, Beverly. *Addict in the Family.* op. cit., p. 21.

8. Conyers, Beverly. *Addict in the Family.* op. cit., p. 23.

9. Boletín del Instituto Nacional Sobre el Abuso de Drogas, Cocaina. "Cocaina, Abuso y Adicción." Serie de Reportes de Investigación: January 2001.

10. Cope Moyers, William. op. cit., pp. 112, 113.

11. Kennedy Lawford, Christopher. *Recover to Live: Kick Any Habit, Manage Any Addiction.* Dallas: BenBella Books, 2013, position 686 of 8325.

12. www.drugabuse.gov

13. Roffe de Sierra, Clarita. "The Importance of Spirituality in the Recovery of Substance Abuse and Addiction." Institute for Transpersonal Psychology: Introduction to Transpersonal Theory, January 12, 2008.

14. Grof, Christina, *The Thirst for Wholeness: Attachment, Addiction and the Spiritual Path.* San Francisco: Harper, 1994, p. 191.

15. Grof, Christina, op. cit., pp. 193-210.

16. Grof, Christina, op. cit., pp. 193-210.

17. Schultz, Sherry. *Coming Back From a Relapse*. EUA: Hazelden, 1991, p. 1.

18. Cope Moyers, William. op. cit., p. 278.

19. Conyers, Beverly. *Everything Changes: Help for Families of Newly Recovering Addicts*. op. cit., p. 97.

20. www.adicciones.org

21. www.adicciones.org

22. www.salud.nih.gov

23. www.salud.nih.gov

24. Amen, Daniel G., and David Smith. *Unchain Your Brain: 10 Steps to Breaking the Addictions That Steal Your Life*. California: MindWorks Press, 2010, p. 110.

25. Gopnik, Alison. (2012). "What's Wrong With the Teenage Mind?" *The Wall Street Journal*. Retrieved from https://www.wsj.com/articles/SB10001424052970203806504577181351486558984.

26. National Institutes of Health (www.salud.nih.gov) and National Institute of Drug Abuse (www.drugabuse.gov)

27. www.drugabuse.gov

28. Fantín, Beatriz, and García Horacio Daniel. "Family factors, its influence on substance abuse." *Ajayu*, 9 (2), August 2011, pp. 193-214 (Factores familiares, su influencia en el consumo de sustancias adictivas).

29. Parent Jake D. (ed). *Hearts and Scars: 10 Human Stories of Addiction*. Modern Minimalist Press: 2015, position 43 of 1497.

30. McCauley, op. cit., pp. 1,2.

31. McCauley, op. cit., p. 2.

32. McCauley, op. cit., pp. 6,7.

33. www.drugabuse.gov

34. De Granda Orive, J.I., Solano Reina, S., Jareño Esteban, J., Pérez Trullén, A., Barrueco Ferrero, M., and C.A. Jiménez Ruiz. "De la neurobiología de la adicción a la nicotina al tratamiento del tabaquismo." *Progresos Terapéuticos*, Madrid, Servicio de Neumología, Hospital Central de la Defensa Gómez Ulla.

35. Medzerian, George. *Crack: Treating Cocaine Addiction.* Florida: Tab Books, 1991, pp. 29-33.

36. 2007, 7stagesofc, blog chosenFast.com

37. www.adiciones.org/familia/codependencia, Dr. Salvador Alvarado, Médico en adicciones.

38. www.manantiales.org/ Fundación Manantiales

39. www.adiciones.org/familia/codependencia, Dr. Salvador Alvarado, Médico en adicciones.

40. Conyers, Beverly. *Everything Changes: Help for Families of Newly Recovering Addicts.* op. cit., p. 10.

Acknowledgments

I want to thank all the people who, in the beginning, read the essays from this manuscript and shared with me their invaluable suggestions and corrections:

My publisher and friend, Lisa Umina, who motivated and guided me in the production of this book.

My son, Mauricio, who worked with great dedication and imagination in creating the book cover.

My son, Eduardo, for always being there.

My parents, for their love and the strength they instilled in me.

My brothers and sisters—Sergio, Paulette, Tony, Talo, and Rocio—for your unconditional love and support.

My daughters-in-law—Ana Torre and Elizabeth Lerch—for always being present and sharing our path with so much love.

My granddaughters—Ana and Elena—for the joy and light they bring to my life.

My family and friends—thank you with my deepest gratitude for always being present.

Helen, Daniela, Danielita, Susy, Andrea, Maria, and all those who touched Alex's life in a special way—my gratitude for having been part of his history, and to each one of you, my thanks for having accompanied him on his journey, for having accepted and loved him as he was.

I want to thank in a very special way my medical family therapy team that always took time for me and listened to me for ten years.

A very special thanks to Juanita for all the love she has given us through the years and for loving my children as if they were her own.

My gratitude to all those dedicated to helping people who suffer from this disease and their families, especially Dr. Kevin McCauley, who was always present during Alex's process, listening to us patiently and guiding us with empathy and compassion.

To our friend and award-winning author, Francisco Martin Moreno—thanks for listening, for helping undertake this project, and for writing the wonderful foreword for this book with so much love and compassion.

I can hardly find words to express my gratitude to Ana Paula Rivas for having structured my story and Alex's legacy, for helping me put forth all my emotions and feelings with great sensitivity, and for always listening with her heart.

And finally, very especially, to Marimar Planas, who has my love, admiration, and respect forever. I really do not have enough words to thank you for the happiness and love you gave Alex and the strength and dedication you put into helping us create this project.

About the Authors

Alejandro Sierra

Alejandro studied business administration at Universidad Anahuac and worked for Vidalta Parque Residencial. He was a loving, sensitive, generous, and impulsive individual, and was more than anything a lover of life. He believed that he was invincible, and little by little, he got involved in an unknown world, thinking he could leave it at any time and fix his life.

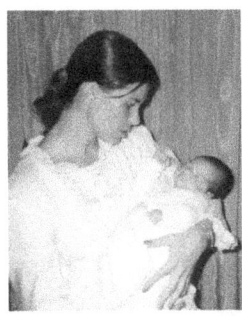

Clarita Sierra

Clarita holds a bachelor's degree in behavioral science from the University of Texas. She specializes in transpersonal psychology and medical family therapy. She currently works as a medical family therapist with cancer patients. She loves to cook, and she enjoyed giving others cooking lessons when her children were young. Clarita lives in Mexico City with her husband, near her sons and granddaughters.

www.ingramcontent.com/pod-product-compliance
Lightning Source LLC
Chambersburg PA
CBHW071110160426
43196CB00013B/2521